Ballone Castle

THE CASTLES OF WESTERN AND NORTHERN SCOTLAND

A guide to castles and country houses
from the 12th century to the mid 17th century
in the counties of Argyll, Bute, Caithness, Inverness,
Nairn, Orkney, Ross & Cromarty, Shetland and Sutherland

Mike Salter

ACKNOWLEDGEMENTS

The illustrations in this book are mostly the product of the author's own site surveys since 1970. Plans mostly redrawn from his field notes are reproduced to scales of 1:400, 1:800, 1:1250, and 1:2000. The author also drew the sketches and maps, took many of the photographs, and designed the layout of the book. The old prints and and most of the old postcards are reproduced from originals owned by the author.

Particular thanks are due to Max Barfield of Hyde without whose support none of the Scottish volumes in the series (see list inside back cover) would ever have been produced. Max provided word processor facilities, checked the text, did the driving on the 1994 expedition, and took the two photographs of the east side of Cawdor.

Charles Henderson of Auchtermuchty took the photographs of Ardvreck, Breachacha, Brimms, Cadboll (two views), Dunivaig, Innis Chonnel, Kisimul (back view), Newmore, and Tulloch. He sent a copy of the photograph of Dounreay which is reproduced with permission from the U.K. Atomic Energy Authority, and he sent photographs of Birsay, Langskaill & Noltland by David Eaton of Meigle. Charles also made available originals of the prints of Dalcross, Dunivaig, Erchless, and Finlaggan, provided accommodation, and gave much help and advice.

Alan Sorenson of Glasgow took the photographs of Achadun (two views), Camus, Coeffin, and Gylen (two views) and provided useful information. Adam Byrne of Glasgow took the photographs of Asgog, Nan Conn, Caisteal Na Nighlin Ruiadhe, Carrick (page 8), Castle Sween (page 36), Fincharn, Rothesay (two views), Skipness (page 68), Tarbert, and Toward. Phil Plevey of Aberdeen took all the photographs of buildings in Shetland. Charles Walton of Marple Bridge took the photograph of Castle Stalker. Thanks are also due to Rob Faulkner and Geoff Leet for help and advice.

The old postcards of Duntulm and Dunvegan on pages 154 and 157 respectively are reproduced by kind permission of Christopher J. Uncles of Haywards Heath.

AUTHOR'S NOTES

This is the last of a series of five volumes aiming to include all the castles and related buildings in Scotland from c1100 to the 1660s. They are intended as portable field guides giving as much information and illustrative material as possible in volumes of modest size and weight. The books should be used in conjunction with O.S. 1:50,000 scale maps. Grid references are given in the gazetteers together with a coding system indicating which buildings can visited or viewed by the public which is explained on page 16. Nearly every building in this book can be observed by the public even if only from a distance. Remember to close gates behind you, keep dogs on leads, and always leave the buildings and their environs in the condition in which you find them.

Several of the plans show buildings as they were when first visited by the author in 1970-82, and which have collapsed or been restored since. In some cases (eg Little Tarrel), the photograph shows the building in a different condition from the plan.

The old county names and boundaries have been mostly used, but three castles in Wester Ross have been more conveniently grouped with Skye and the Western Isles.

Each level of a building is called a storey in this book, the basement being the first storey and at ground level (i.e. level with the courtyard if there was one) unless specifically mentioned as otherwise. Attics wholly within roof spaces are mentioned separately, a building thus being described as of so many storeys plus an attic.

The aim in these books is to mention, where the information is known to the author, all those owners or custodians of castles and houses who erected or altered parts of the buildings, who were the first or last to hold an estate or be honoured with a title, or who were the owners or custodians when the buildings were the scene of historic events such as sieges, royal visits, or the signing of important charters. Other owners are not normally mentioned, nor are ghost stories, myths and legends.

Girnigoe Castle

CONTENTS

Maps and notes on other sites occur at the ends of the gazetteers.

INTRODUCTION

The word castle came into use in Britain during the 11th century. It was recognised that the many privately owned residences with which the followers of Duke William of Normandy filled England after the invasion of 1066 represented something new in both function and appearance. Strategically positioned castles allowed the new Norman landowning class to establish their rule over the native populace. With them the Normans brought their system of feudalism in which the King granted groups of manors to tenants-in-chief in return for specified periods of military service. The tenants then in turn gave land to their knights on the same basis. Castles were not only residences and strongholds, they were symbols of status and power. Most of the early castles in Britain were quickly constructed of earth and timber. Only later, under more settled conditions, were lords able to go to the much greater expense and trouble of constructing buildings of mortared stone. Such works often took many years and required the services of skilled and expensive craftsmen who were in short supply.

After he came to the throne in 1124 David I brought to Scotland some of the Norman knights who had served him in England under the rule of Henry I. King David himself built a number of earth and timber castles and many more were built by his Norman followers on lands that the King gave them. Before long some of the native chiefs began to imitate their Norman neighbours, building castles and adopting the French language and Norman customs such as primogeniture in which the succession passed to the eldest son instead of any capable adult male close relative, a system which frequently led to violent squabbles. Earthwork castles are not numerous in Western and Northern Scotland, most of which only later came under the control of the Scottish Crown and where the Gaelic language and customs still partly survive to the present day. There are half a dozen mounds of various shapes and sizes and mostly uncertain date in Argyll, and others are grouped around Inverness. There is a quadrangular enclosure at Roybridge, and at Ardersier, Boath, and Proncy are ring-works, or embanked enclosures. By 1180 David's grandson King William (The Lion) had castles at Inverness, Dingwall, Dunskaith (on the Nigg peninsular) and Eddirdovir (Redcastle). Nothing remains from this period at any of these (except possibly some walling at Redcastle) so little can be said of their design or the materials employed. The minimal amount of walling remaining at Ormond on the Black Isle, another of King William's new castles, may be as early as c1200-10, whilst there is said to have been an early castle of mortared stone at Contilluch.

Some of William the Lion's castles were built as part of his campaign against a kinsman called Donald Bane MacWilliam who under the old Scottish system of inheritance had a claim to the throne. Donald was killed near Inverness in 1187 by Roland of Galloway, and his son Guthred was later defeated by Fearchar O'Beolan of Applecross, created Earl of Ross in 1226 for services to the Scottish crown. Orkney, Shetland, Caithness, Sutherland, Argyll and the Western Isles were still under Norse rule, although by the time of King William's death in 1214 he had established suzerainty over Caithness and Sutherland. The latter was given to Hugh Freskin, a member of the Pictish ruling family of Moray, ancestor of the Sutherland family. Alexander II succeeded in imposing his rule over Argyll in 1221-2 but he died at Kerrara in 1249 before subjugating the Isles. In 1262 his successor, Alexander III, forced the elderly Haakon IV of Norway to a show of strength by invading Skye. In the following year Haakon's invasion fleet was battered by storms and then repulsed when it tried to land at Largs in Ayrshire. The Norwegian King died in Orkney on his way home and in 1266 his successor ceded the Western Isles and Man to Scotland for 4,000 merks and an annual tribute of 100 merks. In practice, however, the western chiefs retained much of their independence until the claims of the MacDonald Lords of the Isles to the Earldom of Ross and their general hostility to the Scottish Crown prompted their defeat and forfeiture by James IV in the late 15th century. Not until the early 17th century was the Crown fully able to control the western chiefs.

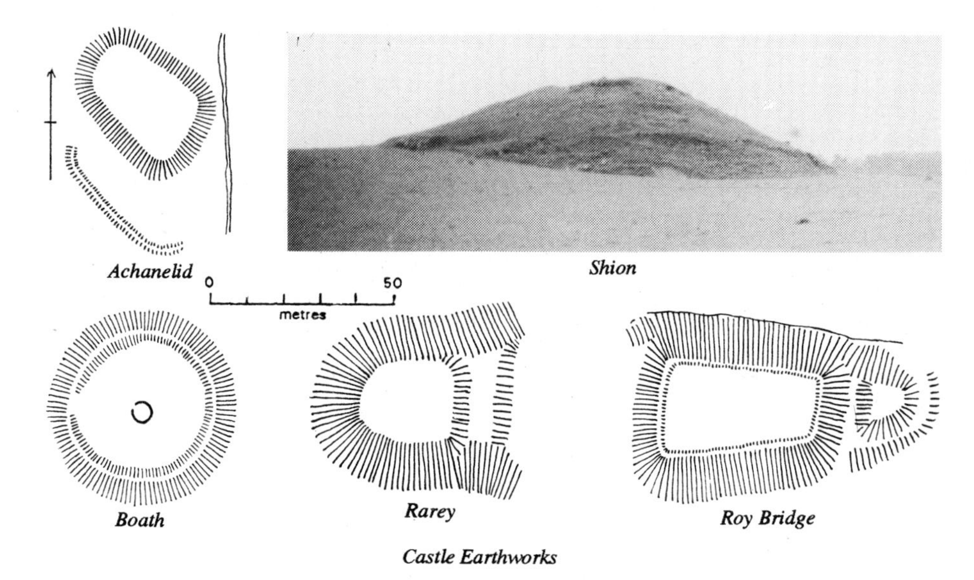

Castle Earthworks

The former Norse-ruled territories all lack good building timber, so constructions have long tended to be of stone, either with or without mortar. As a consequence these areas contain many of Scotland's oldest stone castles. There are good reasons for assuming that the square tower built of slabs set in mortar at Cobbie Row's in Orkney was built in the 1140s. Only the storage basement remains but it is assumed that there was a hall above, at which level was the entrance, reached by a ladder or steps, and one or two levels of private rooms above. The minimal remains of a D-shaped tower and a small court containing an hour-glass shaped hall and bath-house, probably of c1130, were excavated at Gernaness on the Orkney Mainland in the 1920s. In Caithness and Sutherland there are remains of primitive early towers at Dun Creich, Forse and Old Wick. They could be of any date from c1150 to c1350.

Tioram Castle

The small quadrangular court at Sween which is entered through a round arched gateway and has pilaster buttresses at the corners is thought to be of c1200. The similar court at Roy has evidence of pointed arched openings and may be of the 1230s or 40s, the likely period of the irregularly shaped citadel at Urquhart and the one remaining wall of what appears to have been a rectangular court at Redcastle. The wall of the circular court at Rothesay was probably fairly new in 1230 when it was breached during a siege by Norsemen. There were presumably originally wooden buildings within these courts and a 13th or 14th century chapel raised over a basement remains at Rothesay. The rectangular court with stone lean-to buildings on all four sides at Tarbert, of which only traces remain, was probably built by Alexander II in the 1220s. A hall-block occupied the whole of one side of the square court at Achadun. Duart and Innis Chonnel have small rectangular courts, Tioram and Mingary have tiny polygonal courts and Dunvegan has fragments of a larger polygonal court, but all these are probably of the late 13th century. The thickly walled court at Dunivaig may be of the same period. There was a more ambitious castle at Eilean Donan, having a D-shaped court rather bigger than those just mentioned with at least one large and massive tower, possibly two, and several other quadrangular towers. The castle existed in this form by c1300 but what was built when and whether there was an inner court, possibly built first, on the site of the existing modest court on the highest part of the island has not been established. Inverlochy is one of a series of stone courtyard castles built by the Comyns, Earls of Buchan and Lords of Lochaber in the 1270s and 80s. It has four boldly projecting round corner towers, one of which is larger and served as a keep. A similar series of four corner towers was added at this period at Rothesay. Dunstaffnage also had corner towers but the constricted site of the top a small knob of rock means that they hardly project beyond the curtain walls. Here one of the towers contained the gateway and adjacent to it was a block containing an upper hall.

Achadun Castle

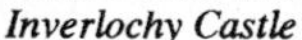

Inverlochy Castle

Dunstaffnage Castle

Ardtornish, Aros, Caisteal Na Nighinn Ruaidhe, Castle Camus (Knock), Coeffin, Fincharn, Fraoch Eilean, Loch Ranza, and Skipness, all on the western coast, are hall-houses. None can be closely dated but they are probably all of c1240 to 1310 like several comparable buildings in Ireland and Northumberland, plus two examples in Ayrshire, at Craigie and Terringzean. All were long rectangular buildings of two storeys (although some may have had attic rooms within the battlements). Each had external steps up to a hall set over lower rooms divided by wooden partitions and having their own entrances at ground level. Several have evidence of one end of the upper storey being divided off to provide a private room for the lord, this part usually having a latrine either in the wall thickness or a projection. Another hall-house at Rait, near Nairne has the unique feature of a round corner tower which contains a vaulted chamber opening off the private room. There is much variation in size among the hall-houses, Aros and Ardtornish being huge, massive buildings comparable in size and massiveness to 12th century Norman keeps in England, Fraoch Eilean is large but less massive, whilst Fincharn is much more modest overall. Skipness had a detached chapel parallel to it but some years later both buildings there were incorporated into a walled court with a two flanking towers and a gateway closed by a portcullis. The new works have cross-shaped loops similar to those in additions of c1270-1300 at Rothesay. The fragmentary courts with the hall-houses at Aros and Caisteal Na Nighinn Ruaidhe may be of later date. Loch Ranza was remodelled in the late 16th century and a house later built within one end of a large hall house at Fraoch Eilean.

Loch Ranza Castle

As in the rest of Scotland, there is little work in the castles of Argyll and the Far North that can be safely attributed to the troubled years of the early and mid 14th century. The castles there were, except for Urquhart, little affected by the English invasions and the subsequent demolition of most castles by the Bruce faction to deny the English and their supporters any strongholds. None of the castles show evidence of slighting in this period. Bruce himself authorised the addition of a large outer court at Tarbert, a place of great strategic importance. Parts of the spacious domestic ranges in the lower bailey at Urquhart are probably also of this period. Some time during the 14th century a square tower, later remodelled, was added there. The block with an adjoining round latrine turret added at Sween is probably of c1290-1310.

Self contained towers having a dark basement, a hall above, and a private room for the lord on top came into fashion during the last third of the 14th century. Probably of that period, although none can be closely dated because all records of their construction have been long since lost, are the towers at Braal, Cawdor, Kames, Kildonan, and Tor, plus towers added to older courts at Duart, Dunvegan, Eilean Donan, Redcastle and Tioram, and perhaps also the tower at Dunrobin. Little remains of towers probably of this period at Eilean Dearg and Proncy. The almost complete and unaltered building at Carrick is a hybrid between the two storey hall houses and three or four storey towers. It is a long structure of three storeys, all of them originally subdivided. Probably also of this period are the curtain walls and keep at Skelbo. The keep may have had two rooms side by side on each of just two storeys.

Plans of Carrick Castle

The fashion for lordly residences in the form of massively walled towers continued throughout the 15th century. Craignish probably dates from c1400-20, whilst the towers with courts at Breachacha, Dunollie, Kiesimul, Kilchurn, plus Moy (where the court has vanished) are likely to be of c1445-65, and Ackergill, Armaddy, Asgog, Claig, Kilravock, Kinlochaline, Loch an Eilean, Maol, and Toward, plus Glensanda and Uisdean (which both seem to have only had two storeys instead of three or more) are of c1470-1500. Also of this period are small courts containing later buildings at Duntrune and Lachlan, a tower-like block at Sween, footings of towers at Halberry and Island Muller, a tower and court at Duntulm, and parts of the buildings at Girnigoe, Nothing remains of a tower at Inverary. Towers of this era usually have vaulted basements and are entered at the level of the hall, although sometimes there is an entrance at ground level as well. Pit prisons only entered from above are common and the upper walls contain latrines and mural rooms for servants to sleep in.

The first half of the 16th century has left us less relics in the area under discussion. There are much altered towers at Brodick and Tulloch, restored towers at Stalker and Saddell (the latter with part of its court), a gatehouse large enough to contain a hall at Rothesay, footings of a possibly never completed tower and outbuildings at Knockkinnan, two ranges of apartments at Lachlan, and a ruined tower at Tarbert. Much of the outer walls at Urquhart, including the gatehouse with twin-U-shaped towers is of this period, and probably also parts of the extensive but very ruined domestic ranges there. A notable L-plan tower at Cromarty with a wing projecting diagonally from the outermost angle (a unique piece of planning in Scotland) has unfortunately gone but is known to us from old drawings.

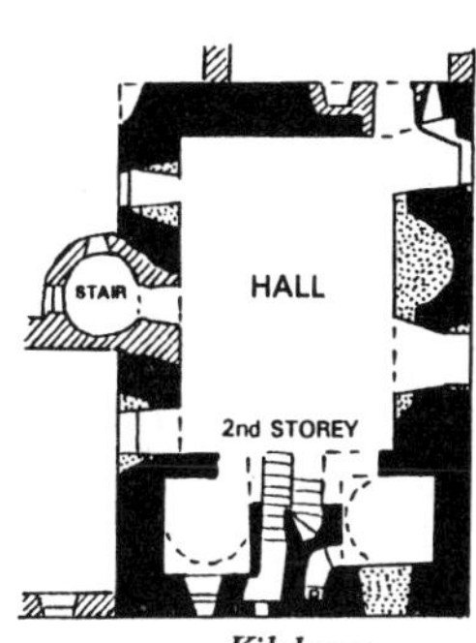

Kilchurn

0 10
metres

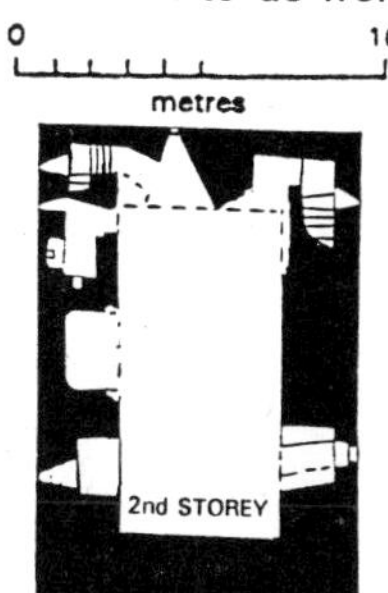

Glensanda

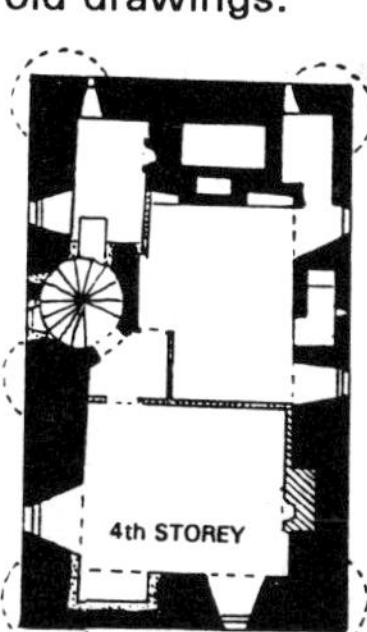

Saddell

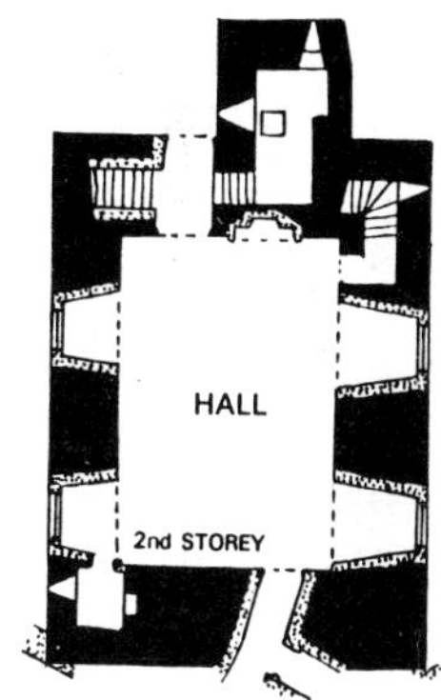

Dunvegan

Tower House Plans

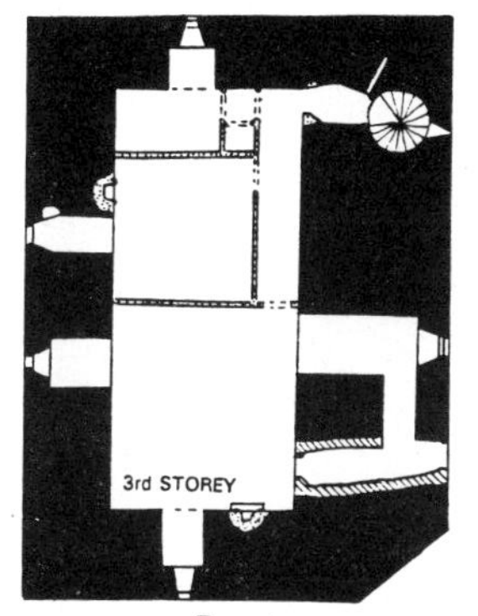

Duart

Kilchurn Castle

Buildings of the late 16th and early 17th centuries form the most numerous group of castles and houses, although by a smaller margin than in other parts of Scotland. They were not generally intended to withstand cannon-fire but the walls were stout enough to keep out small parties of raiders only able to mount short-lived attacks. There was normally just one entrance at ground level which was secured by a yett (a hinged gate of interwoven iron bars) with a strong wooden door secured by a drawbar behind it. Storage and food preparation spaces at ground level are generally vaulted and lighted only by narrow vertical slits and gunloops splayed out horizontally from round openings halfway through the walls. Noltland in Orkney is particulary well provided with such openings but on the whole they were for show as much as defence and it is rare for them to be provided in such a way as allow an attacker at any range or angle to be fired upon. Larger windows higher up were secured with iron stanchions or projecting grilles. Usually these have been removed later as they made it difficult to escape from buildings which either maliciously or accidentally caught fire. By the 1580s the continuous open wall-walks and embattled parapets of earlier towers were out of fashion and roofs were brought down directly onto the outer edge of the wall, from which often rose dormer windows with pedimental heads. The angle roundels fashionable earlier were retained in the form of "pepperpot" turrets or bartizans with conical roofs containing closets opening off the topmost storey. These bartizans were carried on finely moulded corbelled courses which are a feature of buildings of this period. Frequently they were added to older towers, as at Cawdor and Kilchurn. Sometimes they contain small round shot-holes either for ventilation or discharging firearms, and those at Ballone have machicolation slots ingeniously worked into the corbelling, but generally they were for show so as to make houses look like castles. Indeed many of the buildings of this period were not called castles when they were built and were only labelled as such by 18th and 19th century romantics.

Old postcard of Dunstaffnage Castle

Dunvegan Castle

Datestone at Muckrack

From the mid 16th century onwards stones carved with dates, initials, and heraldic arms commonly appear in niches over entrance doorways, on dormer window pediments, and occasionally on other features such as fireplaces and the brackets or skewputs supporting the stepped gables then fashionable. Original furnishings and panelling where they survive may also have these features. The dates usually refer to new construction or additions, or remodelling, although in some instances they may refer to an inheritance, a marriage, or a coming-of-age. These date-stones are useful since building accounts and other reliable contemporary documents indicating periods of construction rarely survive for buildings earlier than the 18th century.

Fairburn, Gylen, Ardvreck, Muckrack and Wester Kames are all square towers containing at least four rooms stacked one upon another. A square staircase wing was later added at Fairburn, and a similar wing was provided from the start at Gylen, where the lowest level contains a passage which connected two courts. The other three have at one corner a round staircase turret. Higher up these turrets are corbelled out square and contain small rooms and a narrower stair is provided in a tiny turret perched on corbelling over the entrance in one of the re-entrant angles. Newmore and Kinkell are similar to these three but are rectangular rather than square, thus allowing enough space for both a cellar and a kitchen with a connecting passage under the hall and the rooms above the hall to be subdivided. The stairs are similarly arranged at Erchless, an L-plan building with a wing on one side. The wing also projects slightly from an end wall too, a layout originally repeated at Castle Leod and also found at Dalcross, where the two parts just touch by one corner. At Achallader the staircase was contained in a corner of the main block without the need for a wing or turret, whilst at Shuna the round staircase turret against one side is an addition. At Brimms the stair only starts at hall level and the wing is solid below unless it contains a long-forgotten prison. No original stairs survive at Little Tarrel which has only two storeys with a private room over a kitchen in the wing. Barcaldine, Dundarave and Invergarry are more ambitious buildings with a stair turret rising from ground level within the re-entrant angle of an L-plan. At Barcaldine the turret is round; at the others it is square and there is an additional round turret which at Dundarave lies on the outermost corner of the L, whilst at Invergarry it contains a stair at the corner furthest from the wing. The very peculiar building at Cadboll was also an L-plan with a round tower on the outermost corner. Craig had an L-plan building within one corner of a slightly earlier court. There the wing is large enough to contain a tier of vaulted rooms in addition to a stair.

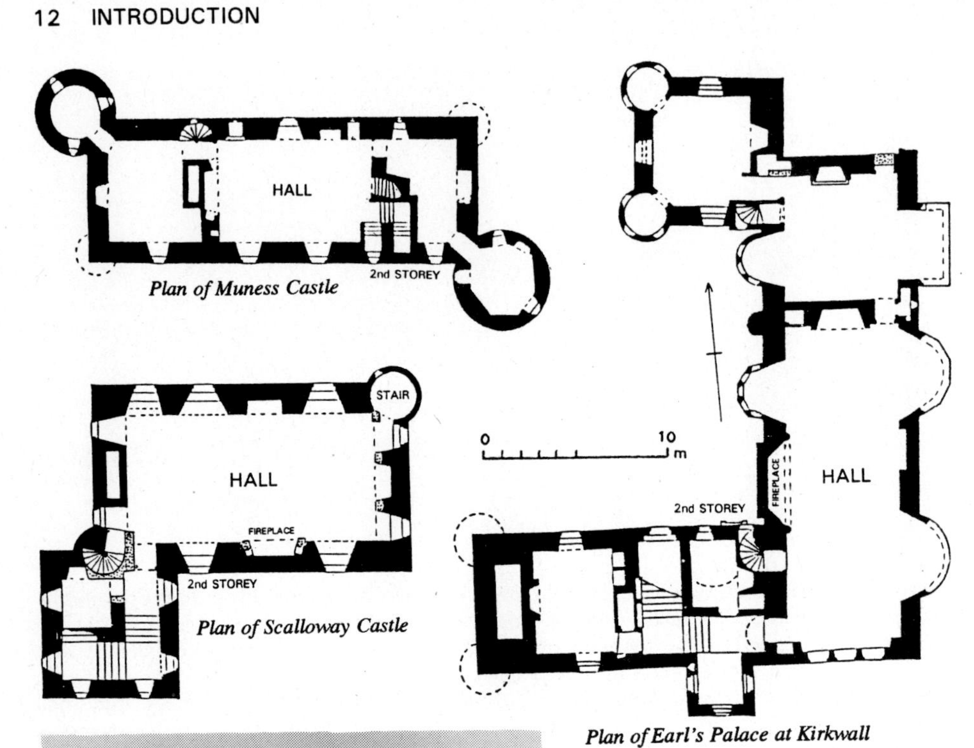

Plan of Muness Castle

Plan of Scalloway Castle

Plan of Earl's Palace at Kirkwall

Barcaldine Castle

Gylen Castle

Carnassarie has a long main block comprising a hall over a kitchen and cellars plus a suite of private chambers over another cellar in a tower-like block at one end. A stair turret containing the entrance projects from a side wall at the other end. An older hall-house at Loch Ranza has been altered into a similar plan, although the wing does not contain a stair or entrance and the hall part of the main block adjoining may have been left open to the sky at this period as a small court. The episcopal palace at Dornoch also has a wing at one end and a stair turret at the other end of the same side. Another episcopal palace at Kirkwall has a lofty and imposing round corner tower which contained the Bishop's rooms. At Inshoch and Kilcoy a round tower projecting from one corner contained a private suite with its own corbelled-out staircase turret for the laird, whilst at the diagonally opposite corner is a smaller round turret containing the main staircase. Ballone has a similar plan but with the main staircase in a square wing as big as the other tower. This so-called Z-plan also occurs at Mey (or Barrogill) and Noltland, which both have rectangular wings. Other Z-plans with round turrets are Keiss, where the main block is square, Kilmartin, where the block is long enough to contain a hall and chamber end-to-end, and Muness, which is long enough to have a chamber at each end of the hall. Kilmartin has an additional turret containing a staircase projecting from a sidewall. It would appear that Ardfad was also Z-planned. A tower at Girnigoe and the mansion of Castle Stuart both have two square wings both on the same side, one containing a suite of chambers and the other the main stair. At Castle Stuart, where the wings are both square, the staircase is of the scale-and-platt type and rises only to the hall. Such staircases became fashionable in the 1580s and also occur in L-planned buildings at Dounreay and Scalloway, in a domestic-looking palace with notable oriel windows at Kirkwall, in buildings mostly of the 1640s at Invergarry and Redcastle (where there is also older work), in an extension to Castle Leod, and in ranges added to the towers at Cawdor and Kilravock.

Interior of Carnassarie Castle

The Bishop's Palace at Dornoch

Dunderave Castle

Invergarry Castle

A few additions and alterations of the period 1550-1625 to older buildings need to be noted. At Breachacha, Cawdor, Inverary, Kilchurn, Urquhart and elsewhere the upper parts of older towers were remodelled, bartizans usually being added. A block added at Tioram has a stair wing facing the court and is continued up at one end as a tower with bartizans at the corners. A wing was added at Castle Camus, hall blocks at Dunvegan, Girnigoe, Kilchurn and Skelbo, a court and single storey house at Toward, and an L-planned block and a polygonal barbican at Eilean Donan. An L-plan mansion was erected within a probably older court at Dunrobin. The outer wall was given thin round corner turrets and vaults were introduced in the old tower house.

External walls of castles were usually weather-proofed with harling. Roofs were sometimes covered with stone slabs but on the west coast heather thatch held down by ropes and stones (and requiring almost annual maintenance) was common. Internal walls at all periods were plastered and painted with biblical or heroic scenes or covered with woven hangings with similar themes. Carpets only became common at the end of the 16th century. The floors of halls set over vaults might be of polished stone slabs but other floors were usually of planks laid on heavy beams and were sometimes covered with straw or rushes. Both ceiling beams and the plaster or wooden boards between them might be painted, again with biblical or heroic scenes, simple patterns, or heraldry and other allusions to family history. Windows in the medieval period were also closed with wooden shutters sometimes secured with draw-bars in the same way as doors. Glass only became common in the 16th century and even then was normally only used in the upper half of a window, with a pair of wooden shutters below. The sash windows found in the largest openings of still inhabited towers and mansions are 18th and 19th century insertions. Latrines with shoots descending to a pit or outlet at the foot of the walls were less common in the late 16th and 17th centuries, when chamber pots were normally in use. Fireplaces sometimes have impressive hoods supported on moulded jambs. Others have lintels formed of many stones which are joggled (cut to a dog-leg shape). The inventory of the furnishings at Barcaldine in 1621 given on page 24 indicates the usual sparsity of permanent fittings and furnishings.

There was often a lack of personal privacy in castles, especially in the medieval period. Only the laird and his immediate adult relations and any honoured guests would have individual rooms allocated to them. Servants would sleep in attic dormitories. The curtains of four-poster 16th and 17th century beds gave their occupants some privacy. Less than a dozen people might normally reside in some tower houses although others would live within hailing distance either in outbuildings or nearby hovels.

By the 16th century even the most modest tower would have beside it a walled garden, a dovecot, an orchard, and various outbuildings providing storage and workshops. In Western and Northern Scotland such outbuildings were sometimes of drystone construction with thatched or earth roofs. These adjuncts are sometimes mentioned in 16th and 17th century documents. Occasionally some relics of the outbuildings or gardens have survived the destruction of the main house.

A number of strongly-positioned castles on rocky headlands or vertical sided islands in Argyll such as Cairnburgh have remains of thin breastworks. These are mostly 17th century in their present form as such lightly built walls exposed to violent storms must have needed frequent renewal and repair until final abandonment. Loch Gorm and Lan An Sgoltaire are small drystone rectangular forts with round corner bastions thought to have been built by Sir James MacDonald during his rebellion of 1615.

A mansion with round turrets built at Thurso in 1660 has gone. Duart has a range of the 1670s and Kilchurn has from the 1690s three flanking turrets and two ranges intended as barrack rooms for a peace-keeping force. With the same purpose what remained of the castle at Ruthven was replaced by a barracks in 1718. However, castle-like features gradually went out of fashion after the mid 17th century, and Jarlshof has a house as early as c1590 without any such features. Mock-castles of the 18th and 19th centuries such as that at Inveraray lie outside the scope of this book.

Many castles on the west coast saw action during the conflicts of the 1670s and 80s and there is evidence of sentries being posted and other defensive measures being taken at some castles until the 1715 rebellion. Eilean Donan was blown up during the abortive Jacobite rising of 1719, and others were slighted after the 1745 rising. Few secular buildings erected before the 1670s were still in use by the end of the 18th century. Cromarty and Inveraray became dangerous as a result of subsidence and were replaced by new mansions. Only Ackergill, Ardmaddy, Ascog, Balnagown, Brodick, Buncrew, Castle Leod, Castle Stuart, Cawdor, Craignish, Dornoch, Dunbeath, Dunrobin, Duntrune, Dunvegan, Erchless, Kames, Kinkell, Langskaill, Mey, Moniack, Saddell and Tulloch have remained habitable. Kilcoy and Kinlochaline were restored in the late 19th century, and Barcaldine, Dalcross, Duart, Dundarave, Eilean Donan, and Wester Kames were re-roofed in the early 20th century. Kisimul was restored and re-occupied in the 1950s, and since then Breachacha, Castle Stalker, Kinkell, Little Tarrel and Muckrack have been restored (Kinkell never actually became roofless), whilst Ballone, Carrick and Kilmartin are expected to be habitable within a few years.

Datestone at Carnassarie

Restored datestone at Kilchurn

FURTHER READING

A Highland History, The Earl of Cromartie, Gavin Press, 1979.
Castle in The Sea, The Macneil of Barra, Collins, 1964.
Highland & Islands volume of Buildings of Scotland series, Penguin, 1993.
Kinkell, A reconstruction of a Scottish Castle, Gerald Laing, Latimer, 1974
Medieval Archeology (published annually).
Portrait of The Highlands, W.Douglas Simpson, Robert Hale, 1969.
Proceedings of the Society of Antiquaries of Scotland (published annually).
Romantic Lochaber, Arisaig and Morar, Donald MacCulloch, 1939.
Royal Commission on Ancient and Historical Monuments inventories for Argyll (6 vols 1970s-80s). Caithness (1911), Sutherland (1911), and The Western Isles (1927).
The Castellated and Domestic Architecture of Scotland, 5 vols, David MacGibbon & Thomas Ross, David Douglas, 1883-92. Facsimile reprint by James Thin 1977.
The Fortified House in Scotland, Vol 5, Nigel Tranter, Oliver & Boyd, 1976.
The Queen's Scotland series: The North East, Nigel Tranter, Hodder & Stoughton,1974
The Royal Incorporation of Architects in Scotland (Rutland Press) has recently produced architectural guides to Orkney, Ross & Cromarty and Shetland.
The Scottish Castle, Stewart Cruden, Nelson, 1960
The Statistical Account of Scotland, 1st, 2nd, 3rd editions, each in several volumes.

PUBLIC ACCESS TO THE CASTLES

In the gazetteers the names of the buildings are followed by Ordnance Survey grid references and codes as below indicating availability of access. The vast majority of the buildings in this book are ruins and can be visited although permission should be obtained from owners where there is no obvious means or right of access.

A	Buildings now in use as hotels, restaurants, etc.
G	Grounds or gardens only open to the public (A fee may be payable).
F	Ruins freely accessible at any reasonable time.
HS	Maintained by Historic Scotland (Fee payable at some sites).
NTS	Administered by The National Trust for Scotland (Fee usually payable).
OP	Buildings opened to the public by private owners, local councils, etc.
V	Visible at very close range from a public open space or right of way.

Erchless Castle

Kilchurn Castle

A GLOSSARY OF TERMS

Ashlar - Masonry of blocks with even faces and square edges.
Attic - A top storey used for servants or storage within a gabled roof.
Aumbry - A recess or cupboard for storage.
Bailey - A defensible space enclosed by a wall or palisade and a ditch.
Barbican - A building or enclosure defending a castle entrance.
Bartizan - A turret corbelled out from a wall, usually at the summit.
Bastion - A squat projecting tower rising no higher than the curtain wall.
Caphouse - Small square gabled space over a staircase or round projection.
Corbel - A projecting bracket supporting other stonework or timbers.
Crannog - A small artificial island occupied as a dwelling.
Crow Steps - Squared stones forming steps upon a gable.
Curtain Wall - A high enclosing stone wall around a bailey.
Dormer Window - A window standing up vertically from the slope of a roof.
Entresol - A level intermediate between the main floors of a building.
Gargoyle - A projecting spout, often resembling a cannon barrel
Gunloop - An opening for firearms with an external splay. See also shot-hole.
Hall House - A building containing a hall on the uppermost of two storeys.
Harling - Or Roughcast. Plaster with gravel or other coarse aggregate.
Jacobite - A supporter of the exiled James VII and his successors.
Jamb - The side of a doorway, window, or other opening.
Keep - A citadel or ultimate strongpoint. Originally called a donjon.
Light - A compartment of a window.
Loop - A small opening to admit light or for the discharge of missiles.
Machicolation - A slot for dropping stones or shooting missiles at assailants.
Moat - A ditch, water filled or dry, around an enclosure.
Motte - A steeply sided flat topped mound, usually mostly man-made.
Moulding - An ornament of continuous section.
Oriel - A bay window projecting out from a wall above ground level.
Quoin - A dressed or shaped stone at the corner of a building.
Palace - An old Scottish term for a two storey hall block.
Parapet - A wall for protection at any sudden drop.
Pediment - A small gable over a doorway or window, especially a dormer.
Pit Prison - A dark prison only reached by a hatch in a vault.
Plinth - The projecting base of a wall. It may be battered or stepped.
Portcullis - A wooden gate designed to rise and fall in vertical grooves.
Postern - A secondary gateway or doorway. A back entrance.
Quoin - Dressed (i.e. carefully shaped) stone at a corner of a building.
Rebate - Rectangular section cut out of a masonry edge usually for a door.
Redent - A step in an outer splay of a gunloop to reflect incoming bullets.
Roundel - An open bartizan forming a lookout post at a corner.
Scale-and-platt Staircase - Staircase with short straight flights and turns at landings.
Skewputt - Bottom bracket of a gable upstanding above a roof.
Shot-hole - A small round hole in an outer wall face for discharging firearms.
Solar - The lord's private living room, usually doubling as a bed-chamber.
Tower House - Self contained house with the main rooms stacked vertically.
Wall-walk - A walkway on top of a wall, protected by a parapet.
Ward - A stone walled defensive enclosure.
Yett - A strong hinged gate made of interwoven iron bars.

ARGYLL AND BUTE

ACHADUN NM 804392

This building formed the main seat of the Bishops of Argyll from the late 13th century until Bishop David Hamilton built a new castle at Saddell c1508-12. It is assumed to have been allowed to decay afterwards although there is an unconfirmed report of Sir James Livingstone occupying the site in the 1640s. Hector MacLean, the last Bishop before the Revolution of 1688 is said to have lived here, perhaps in a drystone cottage in the courtyard. A hall block 7.6m wide internally occupied the SE part of a courtyard 22m square enclosed by a curtain wall mostly about 1.5m thick. Most of the SW wall fell c1890 and the remainder is very ruinous. The hall block seems to have contained a hall with a chamber partitioned off at the NE end over a pair of lower rooms each having a doorway and a single loop towards the court. A latrine contained in a thick end wall served the private room. The court was entered through a doorway on the NE side from which a straight stair led to the wall-walk. Much of the NW wall is 2.4m thick and it contains a secondary entrance with a bridge pit in front and two latrines entered from the upper storey of a lost building, perhaps of timber, on this side.

ACHALLADER NN 322442

A house here is mentioned in 1567 but the existing building was begun c1597 by Sir Duncan Campbell of Glenorchy. It was burnt in 1603 by Alastair MacGregor of Glenstrae who was executed for this offence and many others in 1604. The "castle, tour and fortalice" were wadset (mortgaged) by the 1st Earl of Breadalbane in 1680 to John Stewart of Ballachulish. In 1683-4 Achallader was the scene of justice courts for pacifying the Highlands and it is assumed that the Commissioners stayed in the castle. Breadalbane opposed successfully a proposal for a garrison to be stationed in the castle in 1689 on the grounds it was too small to hold a worthwhile force, so he was particularly incensed when it was burnt in October that year by a party of Stewarts and MacNicols, although there was doubt as to whether the Jacobite leaders had authorised this action. The castle was never repaired, although temporary accommodation was put up for the conference between the Earl and the Jacobite leaders resulting in the Treaty of Achallader in 1691, and there was a proposal to station a garrison there in 1746. The tower measured just 8.7m by 6.7m over walls averaging 1m thick. Stairs in the NW corner, which is corbelled out higher up to contain them connected a hall over an unvaulted cellar, a bedroom above, and an attic on top with a pair of round bartizans on the NW and SE corners. Most of the south and west walls have fallen and only one jamb now remains of the entrance in the south wall at hall level. There are an assortment of shot-holes in the walls, one being a horizontal dumbbell-shaped loop and others round and square externally.

Achallader Castle

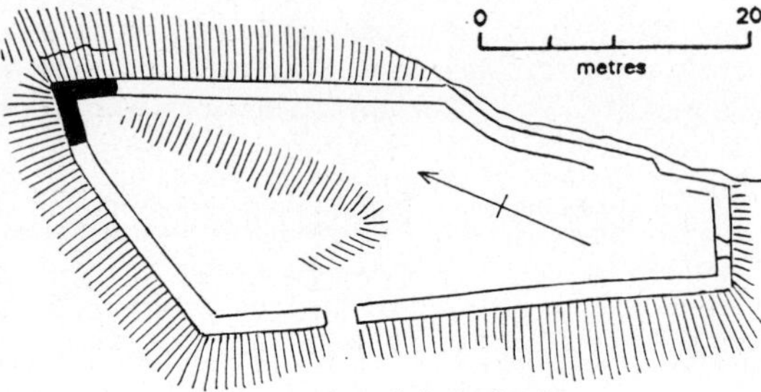

Plan of Airds Castle

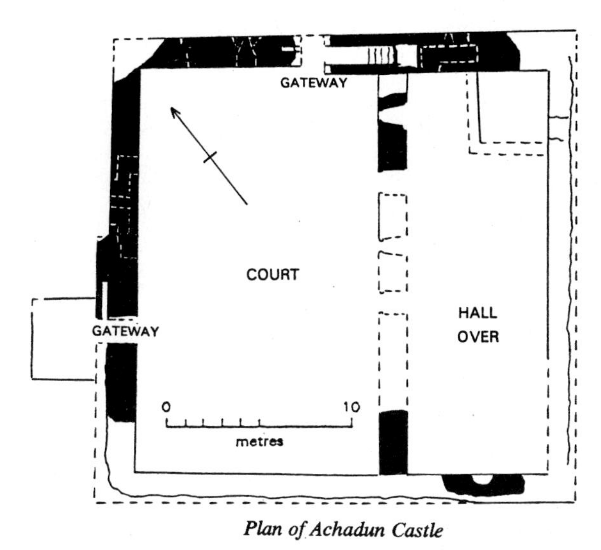

Plan of Achadun Castle

Plan of Ardfad Castle

AIRDS NR 820383

On a rock south of Carradale Harbour on the east side of Kintyre are footings of a wall up to 1.7m thick around a pentagonal court 67m from north to south long by 24m wide with an entrance on the west side. The only mention of the castle is when after the Lord of the Isles was forfeited in the 1490s James IV granted it to Sir Adam Reid.

ARDFAD NM 769194

This castle on a rock 7m high near the north shore of the island of Seil is thought to have been built by John MacDougall, who died c1614, and was a tenant of the Campbells of Glenlyon. A gully gives access onto the rock which has footings of a building 14m long by 6.7m wide over walls 0.9m thick built across its width and then an irregularly shaped court extending for 18m beyond. Footings remain of the court wall on the east and SE. The oblong building was probably just of two storeys with a hall and chamber on the uppermost and a passage through the lower level, although no signs of divisions or any other features remain except for the base of a round turret on the west corner, a probable latrine turret on the east, and another small wing on the north corner. A long corbel projects from the NW wall close to the round turret.

Achadun Castle

ARDKINGLAS NN 175102

Ardkinglas is thought to have been given by Colin Campbell of Lochawe to his son Colin about the time of his marriage in 1396 and was long held by his descendants. The castle ruins are shown on an estate map of 1790 and are described in the Statistical Account of 1792 but had been removed by 1798 despite an intention to retain them as a "Gardener's house and hovell for Cattle". It had a court about 30m square enclosed by a wall 4.5m high with round corner towers and a gate tower in the middle of one side with round turrets on the outer corners. There were lean-to ranges against the walls. The building is said to have been repaired or rebuilt in 1586 so there may once have been a datestone with that year. There was possibly an older residence on a glacial ridge 400m NNE where there is a square well but no other remains.

ARDRISHAIG NR 849866

One of the MacIvers or the MacVicars is thought to have occupied this site in the 16th or 17th century, and it is traditionally known as the "Robber's Den". A rock-cut ditch nearly isolates a promontory 60m long by up to 25m wide above the gorges of the Kilduskland Burn and a tributary. In the middle of the site, dividing it in two, are footings of a building 16.4m long by 6.3m wide over walls up to 1.2m thick, probably of one storey. The north end was divided off by a cross-wall.

ARDTORNISH NM 692426

Ardtornish is best known for an infamous treaty signed in the castle by John, 4th Lord of the Isles, under which he, Edward IV of England and the recently disinherited Black Douglases agreed to divide a defeated Scotland between them. John, 1st Lord of the Isles, died in the castle in 1387, and it is thought to have been built about a hundred years earlier than that by his MacDonald ancestors, although it is possible that the MacRuari lords of Garmoran then ruled here. After the 4th Lord of the Isles was forfeited in 1493 Ardtornish was acquired by the MacLeans. Ewen MacLean of Kingairloch held Ardtornish illegally in 1501 but his successor Roderick seems to have been the legal tenant in 1541. The castle was later held by the MacLeans of Ardtornish as Baillies of Morvern for the MacLeans of Duart, and was abandoned about the time of the acquisition of the estates by the Campbells in the 1690s. The castle seems to have been a two-storey hall-house but is much ruined and has been partly rebuilt in 1910-15, the east wall then being refaced and the south wall upper parts made anew. It measures 14.2m wide over walls 2.7m thick and the north side is 23m long, the south wall being shorter. The modern east doorway probably reproduces an original opening giving directly into the basement, now choked with debris, which has traces of former loops on the south side. A straight stair from the entrance to the SE corner led up to the hall, at which level there was a latrine in a projection at the NW corner. There are a number of outbuildings one of which was 22.6m long by 11m wide.

STAIR

Achallader: plan

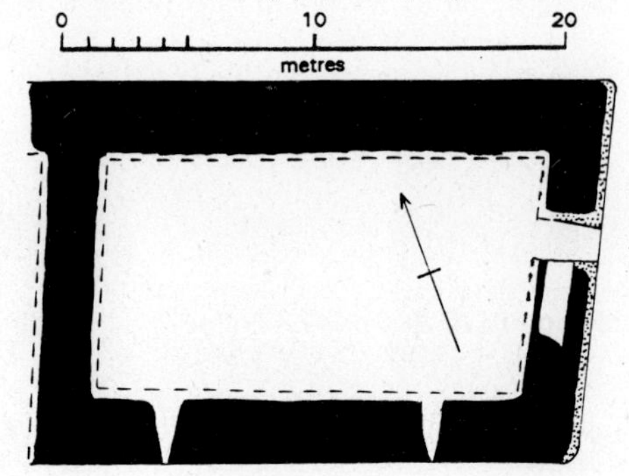

Plan of Ardtornish Castle

Ardtornish Castle

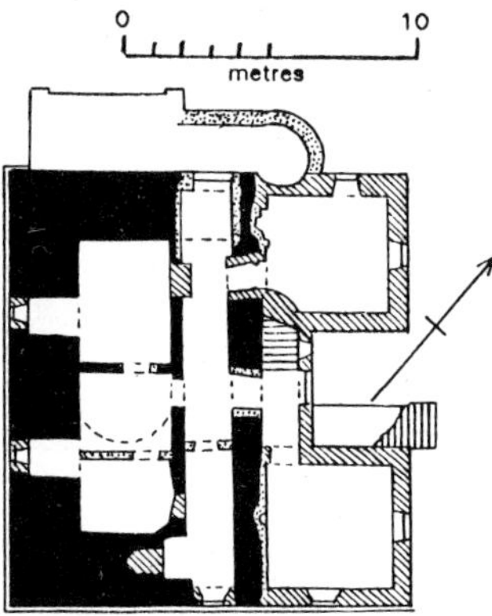

Plan of Armaddy Castle

Ardmaddy Castle

ARMADDY NM 785164

The basement of a late 15th or early 16th century tower, built by the MacDougalls to replace an earlier and more modest seat at Rarey, is incorporated in the main block of a house with two NE facing wings built in 1737 by Colin Campbell of Carwhin, Chamberlain of the Breadalbane estate in Argyll. The tower measures 14.5m by 8.7m and has a SW wall 2.3m thick in which each of the two cellars has a loop, whilst the NE wall is 3m thick but contains a passage the full length of the building. No original stair remains so there may have been a stair wing. The 1737 house has a portico in the re-entrant angle at second storey level which is reached by an external stair and which gives onto a central hall with a stair leading up. The range added to the NW end of the tower dates from 1862. In 1648 John MacDougall was imprisoned by the Marquis of Argyll and obliged to resign Armaddy, which in 1650 was given to Neil Campbell, a younger son of the Marquis. Charles II confirmed the transaction in 1666 and a surviving stone dated 1671 suggests Neil carried out some building work soon afterwards. After he died in 1692 his son sold the house to the Earl of Breadalbane.

AROS NM 563450

Although the rocky promontory on which it stands is only 15m high, this ruin forms a prominent landmark on the west side of the Sound of Mull. Fragments of walling 1.5m thick best preserved on the south side enclose an irregularly shaped court 70m long by 45m wide entered in the middle of the west side. On the east side are footings of an important building 20m long and at the north end, commanding the whole site, are ruins of a 13th century hall-house 25.3m long by 12.5m wide over side walls 3m thick (above a plinth on the west side facing the field) on the lower level, reduced by an internal offset to 2.4m thick on the upper level, the height to the wall-walk being about 10m. The lower level formed two rooms with separate entrances in the east wall. The south room was at a lower lever than the other and has two eastern loops, whilst the other room has one east loop and two loops in the north wall. Both rooms are now much choked with debris. The upper level probably had its own separate entrance reached by steps against the curtain wall at the east end of the south end wall. The only feature remaining of the hall itself is a much damaged two light window in the east wall. The northern third beyond the hall was divided off as a private room having remains of a two light north window, a narrow east loop, and a latrine in a turret added later against the west end of the north end wall. Above the hall and chamber was a space originally probably used for the roof but perhaps later utilised as sleeping space although it has no openings for light or heat.

The castle was probably built by the MacDougalls of Lorn and after their forfeiture by Robert Bruce passed to the MacDonalds. It later became one of the main seats of the Lords of the Isles. After they in turn were forfeited in the late 15th century, Aros went to the MacLeans of Duart. Here in 1608 Lord Ochiltree held a court in the name of James VI, many of the island chiefs being tricked into boarding a ship and imprisoned. Duart and Aros were returned to the MacLeans upon a promise to surrender when required, although Ochiltree reported to the Privy Council that Aros was not worth maintaining. It passed to the Marquis of Argyll in 1674 and was probably held against an attempt by the MacLeans to recover their estates in 1681. Aros also seems to have been garrisoned in 1690 but was in 1688 described as "ruinous, old, useless and never of any strength" and was not used again.

Asgog Castle

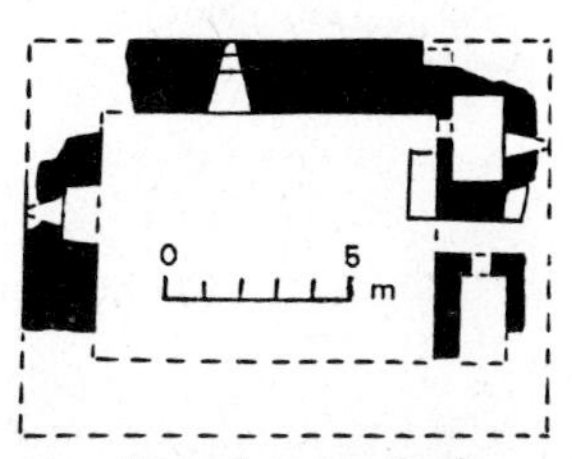

Plan of Asgog Castle

Aros Castle

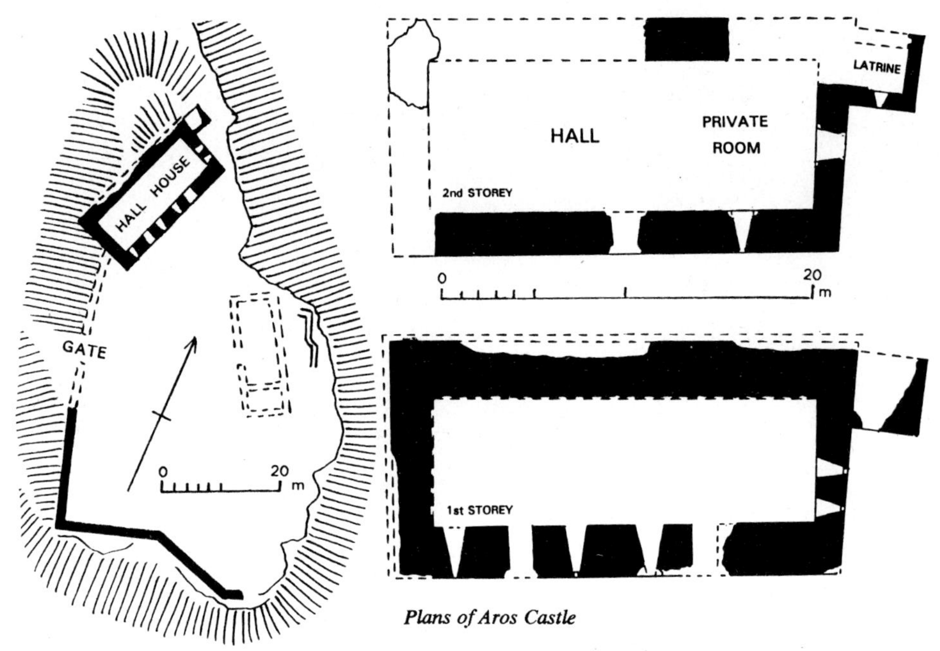

Plans of Aros Castle

ASCOG NS 106632

The existing building on east side of the Isle of Bute, now a holiday home, is dated 1678 and has a stair wing with a watch chamber above on one side of a main block of two storeys and an attic. There is an empty space for an heraldic panel. Ascog belonged to the Fairlies until 1584 when it passed by marriage to the Stewarts of Kilchattan, cadets of the Stewarts of Bute. It passed in the mid 18th century to the Murrays of Blackbarony and then to the MacArthurs, who adopted the Stewart name.

ASGOG NR 946705

On a low knoll by Asgog Loch are remains of a tower 14.2m long by 10.3m wide. A high section survives of the 2m thick NW wall with one basement loop and lower portions of the SW end wall, also 2m thick, and of the NE wall which was 3m thick and contained a pair of small vaulted rooms and a narrow stair. The tower may date back to the time of Robert Lamont, recorded as a witness in 1477, although the first mention of it, as a "fortalice" is in 1581. Most of the Lamonts of Asgog were killed or died in prison after the tower was burnt by the Campbells after a siege of four or five weeks in 1646, the place having been used as a base for raid on Campbell lands.

AUCHENBRECK NS 019814

West of a farmhouse on a stone revetted platform above the head of Loch Riddon is a platform 35m long by 18m wide with on the SE side a 25m long retaining wall 2.2m high and 0.7m thick. Here was a secondary seat of the Campbells of Kilmichael or Glassary, later designated of Auchinbreck, although Lochgair was always the principal seat. They were descended from Duncan, granted lands here in the mid 15th century by his father Duncan Campbell of Lochawe. The last inhabitant of the castle was John Fullarton, Bishop of Edinburgh, who purchased it in 1703 and renamed it Greenhall.

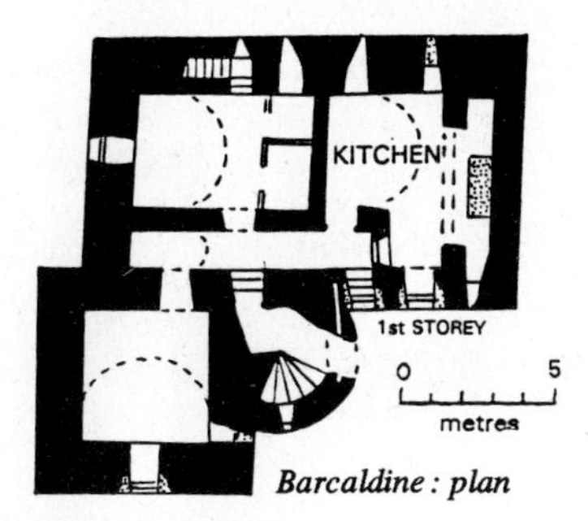

Barcaldine : plan

Barcaldine Castle

BARCALDINE NM 907405

Over the entrance is the completion date, 1609, and arms and initials of Sir Duncan Campbell of Glenorchy and his first wife Jean Stewart, daughter of the 4th Earl of Atholl. Jean died in 1593, perhaps before the building was begun, and it is likely that there was another panel with arms and initials of Sir Duncan's second wife Elizabeth Sinclair, whom he married in 1597. A wing about 7.4m square projects from the SW corner of a main block 14.5m long by 8.9m wide over walls mostly about 1.4m thick. In the main re-entrant angle to the east is a round turret containing the entrance and a staircase linking all four storeys, the highest being partly within the roof and having round bartizans on the wing SW corner and the main block NW and SE corners. The main block has below the hall a kitchen with its fireplace in the east end wall, and a wine cellar with a service stair rising to the NW corner. A passage links these rooms to the entrance and to another cellar in the wing, below which a pit prison was discovered in 1897 but sealed up again. The hall fireplace, and indeed all the fireplaces in the bedrooms, are of the period 1897-1911 when the then roofless building was restored for Sir Duncan Campbell, 3rd baronet of Barcaldine, whose arms also appear by the entrance. One window embrasure in the hall north wall is 18th century, the hall having then been partitioned. In the NE corner straight flights of steps link the hall and a bedroom at the east end on the third storey. This level originally formed two rooms, but is now divided into three with a connecting corridor, as is the top storey which now has three dormer windows on the north side, one for each room. Further bedrooms are provided over the private room at hall level in the wing. Two north windows have original grilles, the other grilles being modern replacements.

There survives an inventory of furnishings at Barcaldine in 1621. In the hall were two long tables with benches, a four-legged table with two small benches and a chair. The windows had shutters below leaded panes composed of small lozenges, a few of which needed replacing. The main chamber in the wing and the bedroom above it each had a bed of turned oak and a bed of fir. The kitchen contained a dressing board and a plank and had two iron hooks in the vault for hanging carcasses. The cellar in the wing contained a large chest of fir for containing meal, and there was a baking stool and trough and two iron hooks. At the entrance was an iron yett with a draw bar and a timber door with a lock and key (these still survive in place). There were also three lockable chests. Barcaldine Castle was garrisoned during the conflicts of the 1640s and 1670s. After the Earl of Breadalbane was told in 1698 of the poor condition of the castle he disposed of it to Alexander Campbell. Repairs were executed but a new house was built c1724, and the castle decayed after the estate was sold in 1842.

BREACHACHA NM 159539

This castle near the shore of the island of Coll has a tower of c1435-50 which measures 9.9m by 8.5m over walls 2.3m thick at ground level and is about 12.5m high to the wall-walks. A blocked doorway with a long draw-bar slot leads into the unvaulted and window-less cellar from which rises a staircase in the south wall, now also blocked. The second storey has narrow loops to the south, east and north and a latrine in the SW corner. A narrow spiral staircase beside this corner originally led up to the third and fourth storeys but there was considerable remodelling c1590 and a wider new spiral stair was then provided in the SE corner. The third storey has two loops and a narrow room in the east wall which originally extended round into the north wall. The fourth storey has original loops to the east and north, the latter now being blocked, and a later loop to the west. There was a chamber, now filled up, beside the old stairwell. The battlements are entirely early 17th century and feature a wall-walk around an attic and a roundel on the SE corner. The tower filled much of the space within a tiny court about 15m by 11m within a wall 1.4m thick to the east and south and much of the remaining space was taken up by a south range containing a single storey hall block with a wide firebreast in the north side and having an entrance lobby divided off at the west end. What little open court was left was filled in with earth in the late 16th century to make a gun platform and a new entrance with a machicolation over it was made on the east side. From this entrance steps rise to an upper storey added over the hall c1685. Both the courtyard wall and the round tower 5.5m in diameter at the SE corner retain original battlements although the court wall parapet has been heightened. Immediately north of the castle is a late 15th century detached kitchen, now joined to the tower by a ruinous 17th century gun battery.

The castle was built soon after Coll was granted by Alexander, Lord of the Isles, to John Garbh MacLean. During a feud between the MacLeans of Coll and the senior line of the family at Duart the latter captured Breachacha Castle in 1578. The Duart MacLeans again seized the then newly repaired castle in 1593 and held it until the end of 1596. Donald MacLean held the castle against the Earl of Argyll in 1679 but had to surrender on terms. His son Hector built a new house nearby c1750 but the tower was still roofed in 1843. The ruined castle was purchased in 1965 by Major MacLean Bristol and restored as a residence. It has recently been re-harled.

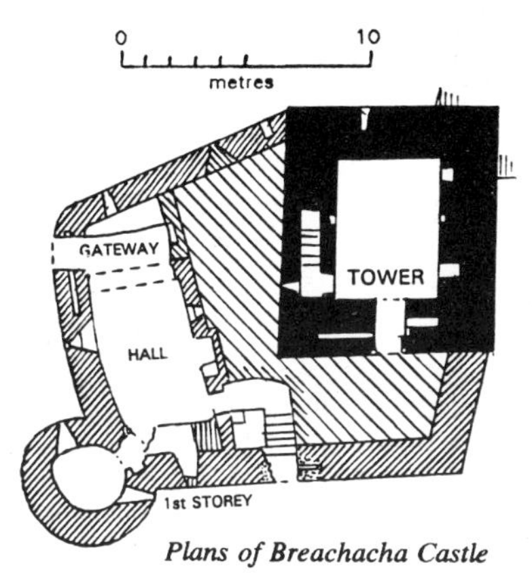

Plans of Breachacha Castle

Breachacha Castle

BRODICK NR 016378 NTS

A courtyard castle was probably built here c1220-40 by the Stewarts although in 1263 it was held against them in support of King Haakon of Norway by Angus MacDonald and Ruari MacRanald. The Stewarts then held Brodick until it was taken over by Edward I's forces and left in charge of John de Hastings. In 1307 he was able to hold out against an attack by Robert Bruce. It was returned to the Stewarts soon afterwards and in 1371 became royal when Robert II ascended the throne. After Robert III's death in 1406 an English fleet sailed into the Clyde and destroyed Brodick Castle. It was presumably rebuilt only to be stormed and destroyed by the MacDonalds. Arran was granted to Lord Hamilton c1470 and he and his son James, created Earl of Arran in 1503, rebuilt the castle in the form of a tower house 12m by 9m containing a hall over two cellars with a two bedrooms on the third storey and an attic within the parapet on triple continuously corbelled courses. Arran defeated the Stewart Earl of Lennox who was trying to free the young James V from the Douglas Earl of Angus. Sir James Hamilton of Finnart treacherously killed Lennox, precipitating a feud between the families who had rival claims to the throne. In 1528 Ninian Stewart, Sheriff of Bute, sent his sons to raid Arran and demolish Brodick Castle. After James V died in 1542 the 2nd Earl of Arran became Regent for the infant Queen Mary. The castle was destroyed yet again in 1544 by the Lennox Stewarts during an expedition in support of Henry VIII of England against the Regent. However the tower seems to have survived these vicissitudes so probably only the roof, floors, and outbuildings can have been destroyed. After Arran resigned the regency to the French Queen Mother, Mary of Guise, he was compensated with the title Duke of Chatelherault by the French King. He retired to Brodick and rebuilt it, the tower being lengthened 10.5m to the west, and he died there in 1575.

Brodick Castle

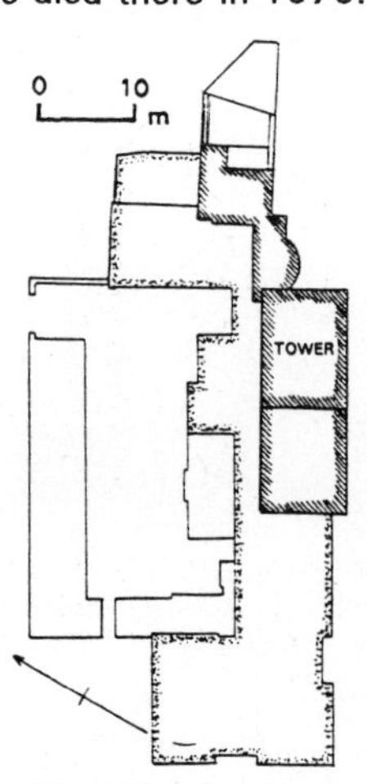

Plan of Brodick Castle

In 1570 Hamilton of Bothwellhaugh was sheltered at Brodick after he shot the Regent Moray in Edinburgh. The 3rd Earl (he assumed that title when his father became a Duke) was an unsuccessful suitor to Queen Elizabeth. In 1558 she sent the Earl of Essex to raid Arran and Kintyre, further damage being done to Brodick Castle. The Earl became insane in 1562 but lived until 1609. His younger brothers John and Claude were defeated by the Regent Morton and driven into exile but John later found favour with James VI and was created Marquis of Hamilton. James, 3rd Marquis was created a Duke in 1643 by Charles I and was executed in London in 1649. His successor was mortally wounded fighting for Charles II at Worcester in 1651. Brodick had been seized by the Campbells in support of the Covenant army in 1639 but was recovered by the Hamiltons during Montrose's campaigns of 1644-5. However by 1646 there was a Campbell garrison back at Brodick which was under siege by the loyal islanders. A relieving force arrived from the west and devastated the whole island. Brodick was back in Hamilton hands in 1651 and after the defeat at Worcester was one of four Scottish castles which held out for Charles II. The garrison yielded at the first summons by Captain Goldsmith, who had been sent with a detachment from Ayr to take the castle. The occupying Cromwellian forces then added a battery on the east side to cover the approach. For two centuries it contained the principal entrance.

After Charles II was restored he acknowledged William Douglas as 3rd Duke of Hamilton in right of his wife, daughter and eventual heir of the 1st Duke. In 1844 Archibald, 9th Duke built a block to the west which doubled the length of the south front and ends in an embattled tower. He added new corridors and a new entrance on the north side and a kitchen wing to the NE beyond a late 16th century wing. After the 12th Duke died in 1895 the title went to a branch of the family who live at Lennoxlove in Lothian while Brodick was inhabited by his daughter Mary Louise Hamilton. After she died in 1957 the castle was handed over to the Treasury in lieu of death duties and it is now administered by the National Trust for Scotland.

CAIRNBURGH NM 309440

A pair of separate islands in the Treshnish group, Cairn na Burgh Beg (the Little Castle), and Cairn na Burgh More (The Big Castle) have remains of thin loopholed breastworks of late date. That at Cairn na Burgh Beg survives only on the vulnerable SW side of an upper court 85m by 70m which overlooks a similarly sized lower court with traces of more massive defences. Cairn na burg More has a court 200m long by 95m wide on the southern half of its island, which is divided off by gullies. Here there are vertical cliffs 34m high all along the west side and the defences are concentrated around the NE end. An angular bastion flanks a gateway hidden behind a stack further south. Within the court are a 15th century chapel and a later barrack block, both ruined but complete to the wall-head. One of these islands was in 1249 one of four castles held by Ewen, Lord of Lorn from King Haakon on Norway. It was ceded to Alexander II of Scotland after his defeat of Haakon in 1263. The MacDougalls of Lorn kept the castle until their forfeiture in 1309, after which Angus Og of Islay was made keeper. In 1390 Donald of Islay, Lord of the Isles, made Lachlan MacLean of Duart keeper of the castle. After Lachlan MacLean was forfeited by James IV in 1504 Cairnburgh was besieged by a naval force. In 1513 Lachlan again rebelled and seized Cairnburgh but was restored after making terms. After General Leslie captured the castle in 1647, Hector Maclean of Torloisk and 30 men were installed to hold the castle against the Duart MacLeans. In 1679 Hector MacLean was busy provisioning the two islands when Archibald, 9th Earl of Argyll, demanded their surrender. They held out and were only given up to the 10th Earl in 1692. The castle changed hands more than once during the 1715 rebellion and was subsequently garrisoned by Hanovarian troops. It remained in use until after the 1745 rebellion.

Caisteal Nan Con (Morvern)

Nan Con: plan

CAISTEAL DUBH NAN CLIAR NM 473631

This building may have been a late 16th century outpost of Mingary Castle commanding Kilchoan Bay. It seems to have comprised a tiny two storey building upon a lip of rock the underside of which was enclosed by walling to make a small slab-roofed chamber with a doorway facing SE with a draw-bar slot.

CAISTEAL NAN CON NM 583486

On a promontory on Morvern within sight of Aros Castle is a house probably built by Allan MacLean, tacksman of Killundine in the 1670s. It measures 18m by 7.3m over walls 0.9m thick with the rooms connected by a spiral stair in a round turret on the SW side in which one shot-hole survives. Private rooms with fireplaces were partitioned at the SE end at all three storeys. The other parts are mostly ruined about the lowest level which contained an unheated central main room with a store beyond. Pennant suggests that the house was captured by a force of Camerons in 1719 who were dislodged by a bombardment by a warship and it probably lay derelict afterwards.

CAISTEAL NAN CON NM 765136

On a rock on the NE side of the island of Torsa are footings of a tower 13.7m long by 8.8m wide with a small court to the east with an entrance on the south and a round tower with a latrine shoot on the NE corner. External wall-faces survive but the interior faces are buried. Torsa was held by the Campbells of Lochawe from 1313 until the 1390s when it went to the Earl of Breadalbane. The castle may have been built either by the MacDougalls of Rarey, tenants here in the early 16th century and again in the 17th, or the MacLeans of Duart, who had possession in the late 16th century.

Caisteal Na Nighinn Ruaidhe

CAISTEAL NA NIGHINN RUAIDHE NM 916137

The name, which means "castle of the red-haired maiden" is said to refer to Bridget, the heiress of Loch Avich who married the first Campbell laird here c1200. The castle is probably two or three generations younger than that, but existed by 1414 when Duncan Campbell of Lochawe granted lands here to his kinsman Ronald of Craignish with the provision that Ronald would be constable of the castles of Craignish and Loch Avich on the understanding that he would build up and roof them. The remains lie on an island close to the NW shore of Loch Avich. They comprise the fairly complete SE wall of a tower 15.8m long by 11.3m wide over walls up to 2.3m thick, and traces of an accompanying court. The doorway facing SE at basement level was so low that it can have been little more than a hoisting place for supplies. The main entrance was probably at hall level on the opposite side. A fireplace survives in the SE wall at that level, and there are two window embrasures, one with seats, on the third storey which seems to have been divided by a cross-wall. There are also shoots of various now destroyed latrines in the south and east corners at the upper levels.

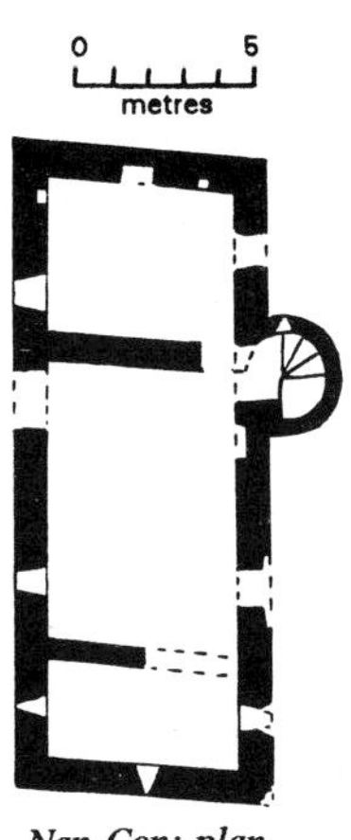

Nan Con: plan

Carnassarie Castle

Carnasserie Castle

Plans of Carnassarie Castle

CARNASSARIE NM 839008

This building is similar to Melgund in Angus in being designed to look like a hall block added to an earlier and more massive tower, but was actually built in a single campaign in 1566-72 by John Carsewell, Rector of Kilmartin and Bishop of the Isles, the lands having been obtained in 1559 from the 5th Earl of Argyll. In 1594 John Campbell of Ardkinglas was imprisoned in the castle, being suspected of complicity in the murder of John Campbell of Cawdor. Just 20m NE of the castle is a rocky knoll with slight traces of an earlier building of the Campbells of Lochawe on its summit measuring about 17m by 23m. To the NW are footings of outbuildings and to the west is a gateway with the keystone of the arch dated 1681 with initials of Sir Duncan Campbell of Auchenbreck (his family obtained Carnasserie in 1643) and his wife Lady Henrietta Lindsay. In 1685 Sir Duncan fortified the castle in support of the Earl of Argyll's rebellion. It is said to have been besieged that summer by the MacLeans and MacLachlans and that after the castle surrendered it was burnt, twenty of the garrison wounded, and the commander Alexander Campbell murdered.

The tower-like east end contained a withdrawing room with a service stair down to the large cellar below. This part measures 9.7m by 9.3m over walls 1.6m thick and has an external string course between the third and fourth storeys and corbel coursing at the top for a parapet and angle rounds within which was an attic. The upper rooms did not communicate with those below and were reached by a stair rising from the NE corner of the hall, a fine apartment 12m long by 6m wide occupying the rest of the building. The hall has a fireplace in the north wall and in the western corners are a pair of mural rooms (one probably a latrine) flanking the flue of the kitchen fireplace below. A passage runs along the north side at ground level to connect all the rooms there to the main entrance and wide main stair in a rectangular turret on the NW corner. The turret has a gunloop commanding the west wall and there are several other gunloops, whilst the eastern cellar under the hall has a loop with top and bottom roundels.

CARRICK NS 194944

On a rock by the mouth of Loch Goil is an unusually fine building probably of the 1390s built by the Campbells or possibly by Robert III as a hunting lodge. It seems to have been held by Duncan Campbell of Lochawe in the 1420s, but it is first mentioned as a "castle and fortalice" in 1529 and 1541 when Archibald, 4th Earl of Argyll granted it to his successive wives. The Campbells of Ardkinglass acted as hereditary captains and had custody there of the charters of the Earldom. The castle was burnt in May 1685 by Captain Hamilton during the rebellion of the 9th Earl of Argyll, but it is now to be restored. The building measures 21m by 11.3m over walls 15m high and 2.3m thick at the lowest of three unvaulted storeys (an intended vault in the basement was never built). There are no subdivisions although it is likely that each level once had timber partitions. The arrangement of the third storey, with each end having its own latrine and separate straight stairway up from the entrance at second storey level and what appears to be an oratory formed in the middle window embrasure suggests that there was a northern suite of two rooms with the most private in the middle of the building, whilst the southern room was quite separate. The stair serving the northern suite carries on up to the wall-walk, within which was an attic. The second storey formed a hall with a latrine in the NE corner, two large windows with seats facing west, and other single windows to the north and east. All these windows were closed by shutters secured by draw-bars. There was probably a narrow chamber partitioned off at the south end, there being another latrine in the SE corner. There are no fireplaces within the building so heating must have been by central braziers. The existing doorway between the tiny 16th century court to the east and the basement is modern, although a draw-bar slot suggests there was an original opening here. The basement has three loops facing east and one loop in each end wall, but none in the landward-facing west wall. The NW corner is recessed at the lowest level and chamfered above. The northern half of the court was later filled by a two storey range, now very ruined, with a polygonal stair turret in the angle between it and the main block.

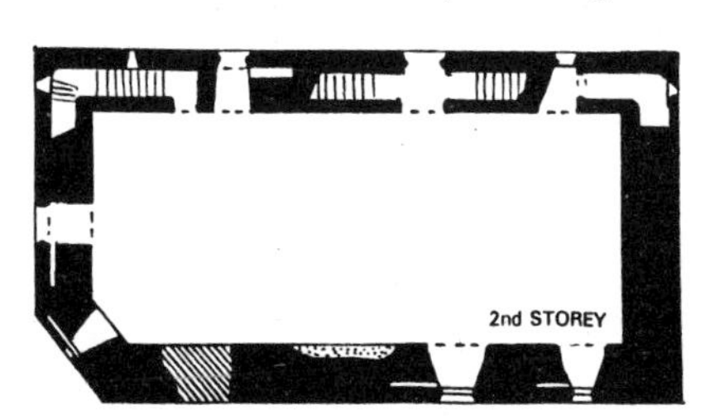

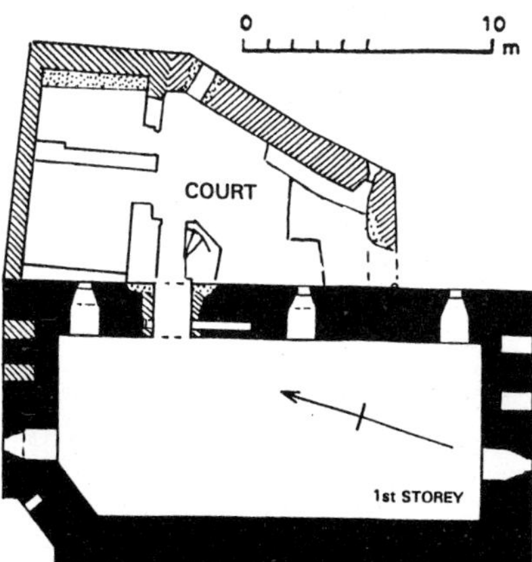

Plans of Carrick Castle

Carrick Castle

CASTLE COEFFIN NM 853437

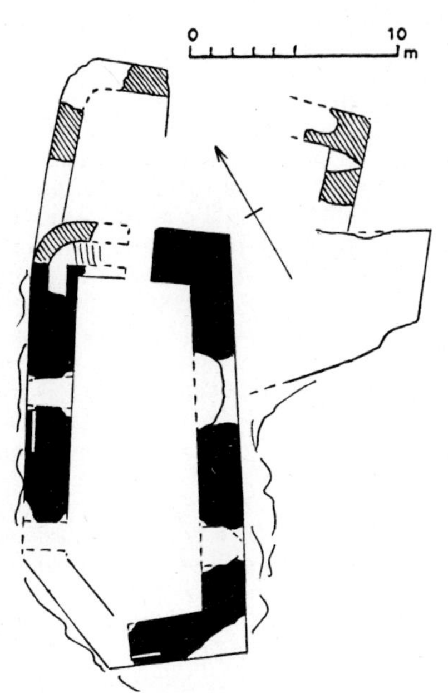

Plan of Castle Coeffin

This castle on a rock on Lismore commanding views up and down the Firth of Lorn was probably built by the MacDougalls a generation or two before their defeat and forfeiture by the Bruces in 1308-10. They regained Lismore under David II but in 1388 the estate was sold by the heiress Janet and her husband Sir Robert Stewart to John Stewart of Innermeath. An exchange of lands brought the lordship of Lorn to Colin Campbell, 1st Earl of Argyll, and his charter giving part of Lismore with the castle of "Chaben" to his uncle Sir Colin Campbell of Glenorchy in 1470 is the first surviving reference to the actual building. An anonymous account suggests the building was abandoned by the late 16th century and it is now much ruined. It was a two storey hall-house 20.3m long by 10.4m wide over walls up to 2.4m thick. The main entrance has a ground level at the NE end and had a stair rising up from it around the north corner to the hall. There were also entrances in the SW end wall and midway along the NW side, all three having draw-bar slots. It is unlikely the SW entrance remained in use after the collapse of the rock supporting the west corner and a new wall was built cutting off the angle. About the same time the northern corner was rounded off externally and a small court of irregular plan built in front of the steep NE approach. One basement loop survives in the SE wall. The upper storey had a private room divided off at the SW end with a latrine in the south corner and a window to the SE. The hall had a window in each side-wall near the partition wall, the NW embrasure also giving access to a latrine. Straight flights of steps around the east corner rose to the battlements.

Castle Coeffin

CASTLE LACHLAN NS 005952

Gilaspec MacLachlan seems to have had a castle here on a low knoll beside Loch Fyne in 1314 but the present building is thought to be 15th century. The castle was garrisoned by the Captain of Dunoon (a Campbell) in 1645, and was seized by the Campbells in the conflicts of 1715 and 1745, the MacLachlans being Jacobites (the then chief, Lachlan, died of wounds received at Culloden). It began to decay after the family built a new house to the NE and although the NE range was partly roofed in 1830 the building was much ruined by 1890, the north and south corners having collapsed. Much patching was then carried out by John MacLachlan. As originally built a wall 2m thick enclosed a quadrangular court about 17m by 13m entered on the SE side and containing wooden lean-to buildings for which latrines were provided in the NE wall. In the 16th century the internal ranges were rebuilt in stone leaving just a tiny dark central court with a well at the NW end under an arch carrying narrow rooms above. A stair between these rooms and the NE range provided access to pairs of upper rooms set over two vaulted cellars. The two third storey rooms formed a suite with the furthest room reached through that next to the stair but those below had individual access from the stair and also from the hall in the SW range via timber galleries. The hall has below it two cellars, one with an inserted double-splayed gunport looking out to sea, and a kitchen at the SE end. Next to the kitchen is a spiral stair from the court up to the service end of the hall, the musicians gallery above, and to the large apartment over the hall. There were probably attics above. The loopholed wall flanking the entrance approach is 17th century.

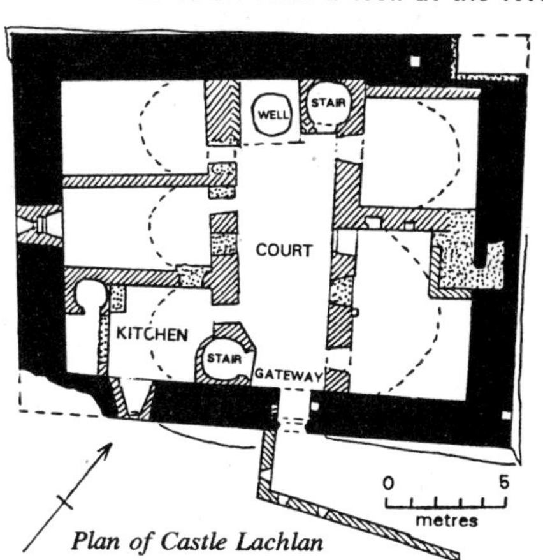

Plan of Castle Lachlan

Castle Lachlan

CASTLE SHUNA NM 915482

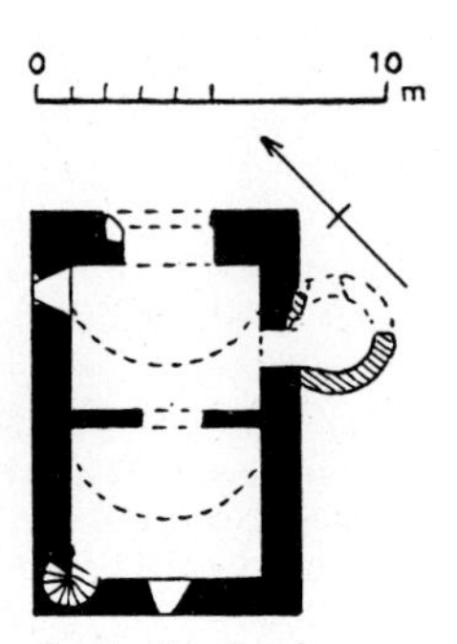

Castle Shuna: plan

This small ruined tower on the south end of the island of Shuna was probably built by John Stewart of Appin, who died in 1595, or his son Duncan. It measures 11.6m by 7.4m over walls 1.1m thick and contained a hall over a basement divided into a cellar on the SW and a kitchen on the NE. The kitchen has a fireplace in the end wall with its back broken out. Each lower room has one loop and a service stair leads up from the cellar. The hall has a fireplace in the SW end wall and a window embrasure on either side of the south corner. The NE and NW walls are broken down at this level and nothing survives of the upper levels. In the 17th century a round staircase turret was added to the SE side. The footings of a large building nearby may be an 18th century house and byre replacing the castle.

CASTLE STALKER NM 920473

During James V's expedition to pacify the chiefs in this area he is said to have ordered the construction of this castle on an islet at the mouth of Loch Laich. Alan Stewart of Appin had custody of the building and probably supervised and paid for its construction. Duncan Stewart, 6th laird of Appin sold the estate in 1620 and by 1627 Castle Stalker was possessed by Donald Campbell of Ardnamurchan, who had remodelled it by 1631. The Privy Council in 1684 ordered the castle to be handed over by the Campbells to Robert Stewart, tutor of his namesake the 8th laird of Appin. The Campbells beat off an attack by the Stewarts and the herald James Guthrie sent to execute the council's orders was waylaid, injured and his trumpet broken. The Stewarts finally gained possession in 1686 but were forfeited as Jacobites in 1689 although the castle was only surrendered on terms the following year. The castle was garrisoned by Hanovarian troops in 1745 and when surveyed in 1748 was said to be capable of holding a garrison of forty men if £500 were spent on repairs. No work was in fact executed and the castle fell into ruin in the early 19th century. However in the 1970s it was purchased and restored as a residence again.

Very little survives of the tiny barmkin to the east and south but the tower is a well preserved specimen of its period. Below it is a rock-cut pool apparently designed to catch rainwater from the roofs and forming the only water supply. The tower measures 14.8m by 11.8m over walls 2.7m thick. An original doorway with a drawbar slot leads into the largest of three cellars in the basement each having one loop. The NE wall is partly thickened to contain a pit prison with a loop and latrine reached by a hatch from above. The loop is now blocked by a later platform at the head of a still later flight of stairs up to another entrance at hall level with the royal arms above it. The hall has a fireplace positioned rather unusually at the south end of the NW wall, windows with seats in the embrasures to the SE and SW and a pair of narrower loops at the NE end. A spiral stair in the north corner leads down to the main cellar and up to the third storey and battlements. The third storey has a fireplace in the SW end wall, a window in each of the other walls, and a latrine in the NW wall. The insertion of a small second fireplace near the north end of the SE wall suggests the room was later subdivided. As rebuilt c1630 the top has an attic room surrounded by wall-walks intended to be roofed over and provided with various shot-holes, a latrine on the NW side, and machicolations over the two doorways. A rectangular cap-house contains the stair head and there is a round bartizan on the southern corner.

Castle Stalker

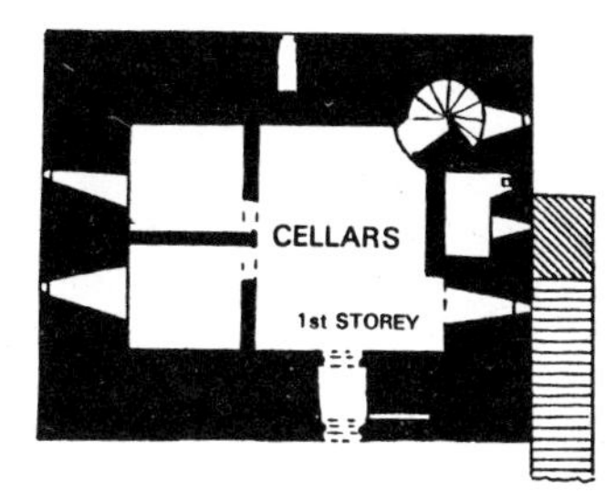

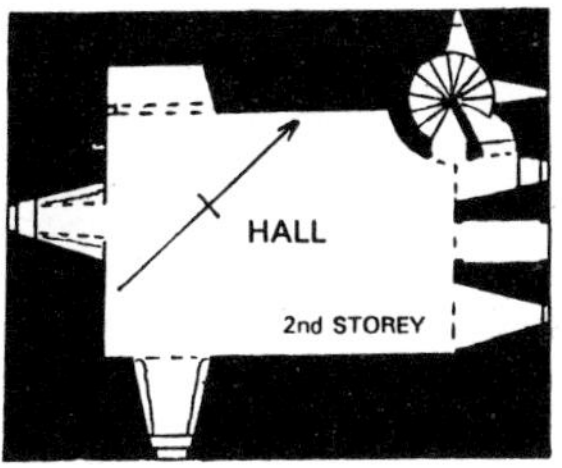

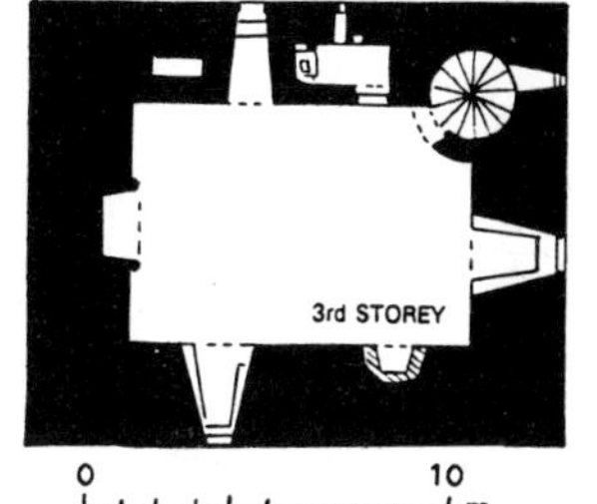

Plans of Castle Stalker

0 10 m

Castle Sween

CASTLE SWEEN NR 712788 HS

Castle Sween takes its name from the chieftain who is said to have built it at the close of the 12th century, Suibhne the Red. He also held land in Ireland where his descendants became noted mercenaries in the 15th and 16th centuries. Sween seems to have passed to Walter Stewart, Earl of Menteith, in the 1260s. He was succeeded in the 1290s as lord of Knapdale by his younger son Sir John Menteith who took the side of Robert Bruce in the Wars of Independence. Consequently Edward I and Edward II of England encouraged the MacSweens to recover Knapdale. They were ultimately unsuccessful in this although a Gaelic poem records a fleet led by John MacSween to this district. Despite an abortive grant to John MacDonald of Islay in 1336 the Menteiths retained possession and passed c1360 to Robert Stewart. As Robert II he seems to have granted Sween to John Macdonald, his son-in-law, now Lord of the Isles. The Macdonalds appointed the MacNeills as keepers with possession of the surrounding lands until c1473 when Hector MacNeill was succeeded by his son-in-law Alexander MacMillan. The mainland territories of John, Lord of the Isles, were declared forfeit in 1475, but the castle may not have been surrendered for in 1478 John was summoned to Parliament on charges of aiding and abetting rebels by provisioning and holding the castle. In 1481 James IV granted Castle Sween to Colin, Earl of Argyll. The Earls appointed the Campbells of Auchenbreck as keepers and there was squabbling among this family over possession in the 1590s when the widow of Duncan Campbell, forcibly ejected by a nephew, was restored by her son. In 1615 Castle Sween was the mustering point for the expedition by the 7th Earl of Argyll against the Macdonalds of Islay. In 1646 the castle was used as a distribution centre for meal imported from Ireland and supplied to other castles garrisoned by the Campbells. It is thought to have been captured and burnt in 1647 by a Royalist force led by Alaisdair MacDonald. It was left to decay and much of the west tower collapsed into the loch "many years" before 1830. A dense covering of ivy was removed after the ruin was placed in the guardianship of the Office of Works in 1933, and considerable repairs were executed in the 1980s by their successor Historic Scotland.

Castle Sween

Castle Sween originally comprised a curtain wall 2m thick and about 10m high surrounding a quadrangular open court averaging 21m long by 16m wide. All the sides have pilaster buttresses in the middle and other pilasters clasp three of the corners. The SE corner has a bolder projection in the form of a turret containing latrines which also served to flank the round arched entrance in the south wall. This entrance has a draw-bar slot and pierces one of the mid-wall pilasters. The wall is here thickened internally to carry a staircase rising up from the east. Within the court are a well in the NE corner and various confusing wall footings. There were eventually wide east and west ranges with just a narrow court between them. In the 13th century a range was added on the west outside the curtain, which is here pierced by an original postern doorway with a draw-bar slot. Later, probably during the Wars of Independence, this building, of which only the northern part survives, was heightened into a tower and a round tower 6.4m in diameter added against its northern side. The addition contains two latrines at second storey level and possibly once had a catapult on the roof to command the seaward approach from which assault was then most likely. The two storey block at the NW corner of the court probably dates from just before the castle was forfeited by the MacDonalds and their keepers the MacMillans. It is likely that two further storeys were intended but remained unbuilt because of the forfeiture. The block measures 14m by 11m over walls 2m thick. Each level has several narrow loops in the side walls and a doorway broken through the curtain to connect with the east range apartments. There was a narrow postern on the west side. In the late 16th century an oven was inserted in the NW corner and the side walls thickened internally and a spine wall built to carry vaults that were probably never actually built.

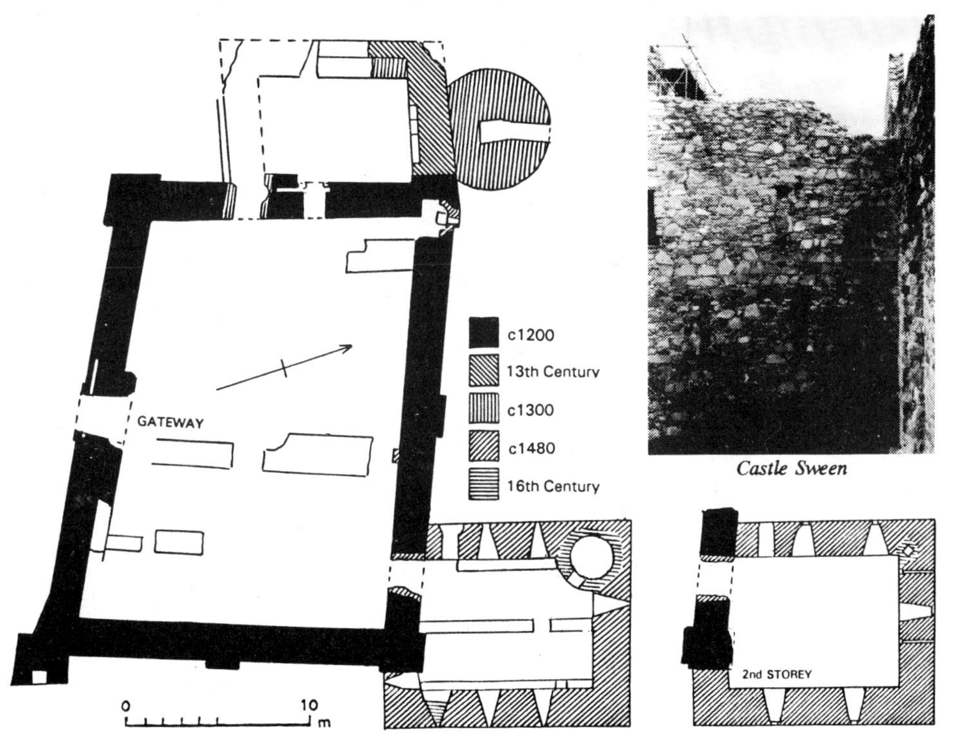

Castle Sween

Plans of Castle Sween

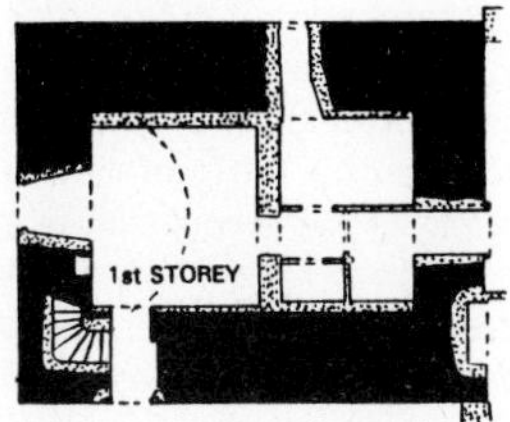

Plan of Craignish Castle

Craignish Castle

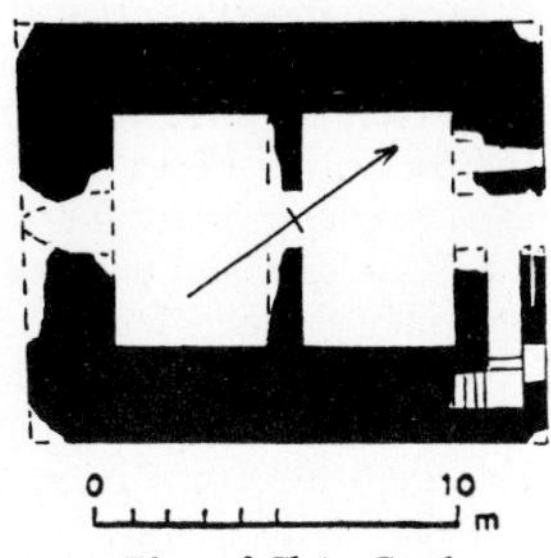

Plan of Claig Castle

CLAIG NR 471626

On Am Fraoch Eilean, a rocky islet 20m high lying off the SW end of Jura, lies the lowest level of a 15th century tower said to have been used by the MacDonalds for the incarceration of prisoners. It measures 14.2m by 11.2m over walls 2.6m thick and has remains of a crosswall separating two cellars, each with a single loop in an end wall. The NE end wall additionally contains the entrance and a straight mural staircase rising up around the east corner to the now vanished hall above. The NW wall overlooks a drop but there are traces on an embanked court on the other sides.

CRAIGNISH NR 772016

Only the vaulted basement and part of the hall above with a latrine in the NW corner survive of a tower 12.6m long by 10.2m over walls from 2 to 2.5m thick at ground level. There is a remodelled entrance at ground level at the south end of the east wall. No other old features remain in the basement, which has been subdivided. The upper storey was mostly rebuilt and subdivided in the 17th century and has outer walls just 1m thick to the south and east, whilst the third storey is entirely of that period. A new extension to the north was added c1837. This has been reduced in size and a modern stair wing added beyond what used to be a cross-wall, whilst the tower now has a high hipped roof. The original tower probably dates from about the time of a charter of 1414 in which Ronald MacDuill Campbell was recognised as holding Craignish in return for military service including provision of a twelve oared ship from Duncan Campbell of Lochawe. After the male line of the MacDuill Campbells failed in 1546, Craignish reverted to the Earl of Argyll. In 1614 part of the surrounding lands and the right to inhabit the castle were granted to Ronald Campbell, whose son Archibald, acting as tutor to his nephew, successfully defended the castle for three weeks in 1646 against an attack by a Royalist force under Alasdair MacDonald. In the 1670s Craignish was sold to George Campbell and date stones of 1693 and 1705 respectively at a cottage at Duine and the farmsteading at Craignish Mainswith his initials and those of Margaret Campbell of Lochnell whom he married in 1693 suggest that he added a range later replaced by that of the 1830s. The estate passed to the Campbells of Jura in the 1790s and was sold c1860 to the Gascoignes for whom the upper parts of the main tower were remodelled c1910.

DRIMNIN NM 547549

An estate map of 1836 shows a rectangular building with a possible stair turret on the east side near the south end standing on a rock overlooking the Sound of Mull. The building was probably built c1650-60 by the first of the MacLeans of Drimnin, successors here of the MacLeans of Coll. It was abandoned c1750 in favour of the predecessor of Drimnin House and was replaced in 1839 by a Roman Catholic chapel.

DUART NM 749354 OP

After his marriage in 1366 to Mary, daughter of John of Islay, Lachlan MacLean took possession of extensive estates on Mull and added a large and massive tower house on the NW side of a court built by the MacDougalls a century earlier. The court is 20m square with walls up to 2.4m thick, although the vulnerable landward SW wall was only 1.6m thick. This wall contains a modern entrance, although the original entrance may have faced NW and was flanked by a square turret on the west corner. The tower is built over the 7m high NW wall and measures about 20m by 14m over walls mostly 3.7 to 4m thick. The unvaulted basement has one original window embrasure and was entered from the court via a porch projecting from the NE end. The porch has a narrow postern facing the sea. The space above the porch was originally an open platform from which there is an upper entrance, but it was roofed in as a room during the restoration of 1911-12. A stair, now blocked, from the lower entrance leads to the hall. A spiral stair near the east corner then leads to the third storey, originally perhaps two rooms, but now three, and to an attic and wall-walk entirely of 1911-12. The hall has windows with seats either side of the west corner, a rebuilt fireplace in the NW wall which also contains a mural room, now filled up. A wide bay projecting from the SE wall was made in 1911-12. It carries a continuation of the wall-walk on the curtain wall around half of the side of the tower at third storey level.

The extensive possessions of the MacLeans of Duart were made into a barony for a later Lachlan MacLean by James IV in 1496, Duart Castle being its principal seat. Hector Mor, who died in 1568, built a two storey range against the SE curtain and the southern corner was rebuilt in a round form. His grandson Sir Lachlan, who died in 1598, added a NE range joining the other range with the tower house.

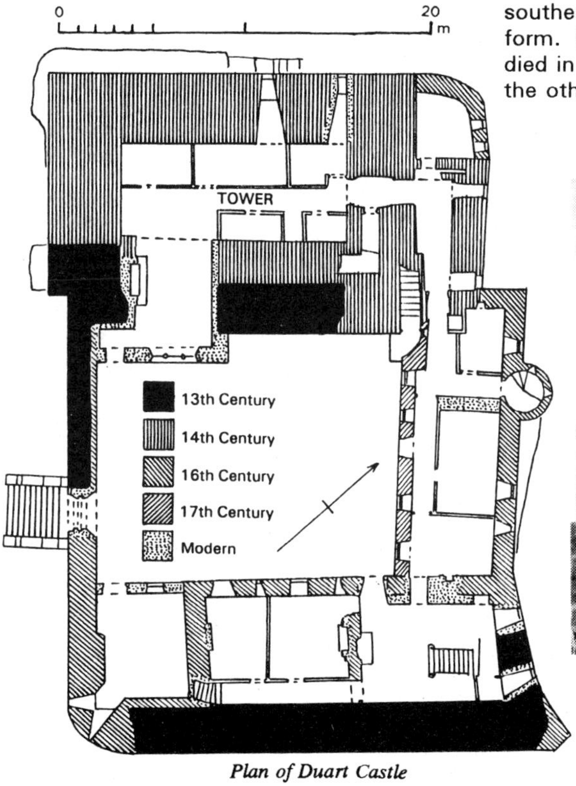

Plan of Duart Castle

Duart Castle

Duart Castle

Whilst Sir Lachlan MacLean was away supporting Montrose's campaign, the Campbells invaded Mull and besieged Duart Castle. It seems to have held out until General Leslie arrived in 1647. In September 1653 it was surrendered without a fight to the Colonel Cobbett and then garrisoned for Cromwell. Despite being impoverished by the recent wars, Sir Allan MacLean completed the remodelling of the NE range shortly before he died in 1674. The estates were then lost to Archibald, 9th Earl of Argyll, who took possession of Duart after a show of armed resistance by some of the younger MacLeans. At some point during the 1680s the MacLeans seem to have recovered the castle and they held it against the Campbells until 1692 when Sir John MacLean went into exile in France. The castle was garrisoned by Hanovarian troops during the 1745 rebellion and in 1748 it was surveyed and reported that for £1,500 worth of repairs it could provide a barracks for a peace-keeping force of 150 men. Duart was later sold by the 6th Duke of Argyll and passed to Colonel Campbell of Possil. It was sold to the Guthrie family in 1875, but in 1911 was acquired by Sir Fitzroy MacLean, 10th baronet of Duart, and restored and re-occupied the next year.

DUN AN GARBH-SROINE NM 803089

Remains of a drystone wall 2m to 3m thick standing up to 1.2m high enclose an irregularly shaped court 80m long with a maximum width of 32m on a ridge above Asknish Bay on the south approach to Loch Melfort. The entrance lies in a NE facing re-entrant angle and there is a narrow postern on the other side of the sharply pointed northern end of the court. There is a turret midway along the east side. A well recorded in 1843 has vanished. Despite a lack of internal domestic buildings it is likely that the McIver Campbells had their seat here from the 14th century until the 17th.

DUN ARA NM 427577

The MacKinnons held this part of Mull by 1354. Sir Lachlan MacKinnon was ordered in 1616 to reside at Kilmorie in Strathordell on Skye but his son and successor John is said to have died at Dun Ara. Remnants of a wall 1.3m to 1.8m thick enclose an irregularly shaped court 40m long and up to 15m wide occupying the whole of the summit of a rock 15m high near Sorne Point. The entrance lies in a re-entrant angle on the east side. A building assumed to have formed a hall 12.3m long by 5.7m wide within walls 1.3m lies towards the north end. There are doorways in the sidewalls near the west end which has later been divided off by a thin wall. Two other buildings of drystone construction lie behind (north of) the hall and one more lies to the south.

DUN ATHAD NR 284407

A thick drystone forework 18m long controls the narrow approach to a promontory 90m long and up to 23m wide with vertical sides descending over 100m to the sea 2km SE of the Mull of Oa on Islay, with views of the Antrim Coast and the Mull of Kintyre. The MacDonalds are thought to have held it in the 16th and 17th centuries.

DUNAVERTY NR 688074

Minor fragments of walls up to 1.5m thick remain on the site of an early castle of enclosure on a rock at the south end of the Kintyre peninsular. The east and south sides with vertical cliffs to the sea were probably undefended. In the 8th century Dunaverty was the main seat of Graban, grandson of Fergus of Dalriada. It was seized by a party of English and Scottish rebels but was recovered by the Crown in 1240 and it was garrisoned against Haakon of Norway in 1263. It was later held by the MacDonald lords of the Isles. A royal garrison was installed by James IV in 1494 but it is said that the castle was stormed and the new governor hanged by Sir John MacDonald of Duniveg within sight of the departing royal ship. The castle was repaired by James V in 1539-42 and was damaged by the Earl of Sussex, sent by Elizabeth I to make a raid on Kintyre in 1558. A garrison commanded by Archibald MacDonald was massacred after submitting to the Covenant General Leslie in 1647. It was then decribed as "a house on top of a hill...environed with a stone wall". The defences are thought to have been dismantled during Argyll's rebellion of 1685.

DUN BAN NM 384416

A causeway 2.7m wide leads 60m off the coast of Ulva to give access to a sheer sided rock 10m high with remains of a round-cornered drystone building 11m by 6m on top. Access to the top is only by a steep gully and a section on the west side where the cliff gives way to a steep slope has a drystone blocking wall at the foot. A minor branch of the MacQuarrie family of Ulva is assumed to have lived here.

DUN CHONAILL NM 671681

This island in the Garvellachs between Jura and Mull was probably fortified by Ewen MacDougall after he obtained it from King Haakon of Norway in the mid 13th century. In 1343 David II gave custody of it to John, Lord of The Isles. From the 1490s until c1630 it was held by the MacLeans of Duart and then passed to the Earl of Argyll. There are traces of both mortared and drystone parapets on the summit, which is divided by gullys into three sections and has traces of ten buildings on uncertain date.

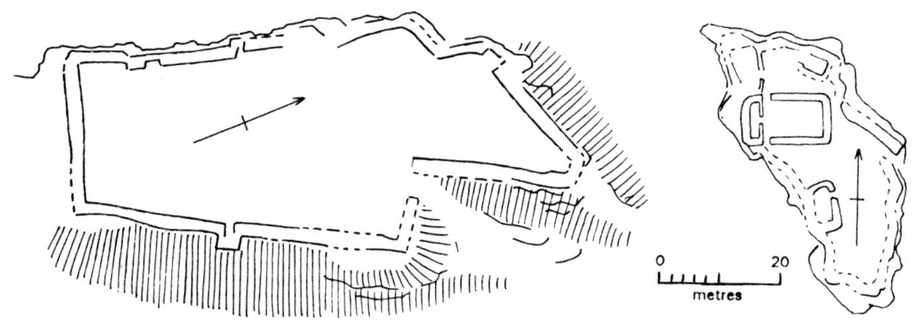

Plan of Dun An Garbh-Sroine

Plan of Dun Ara

Dundarave Castle

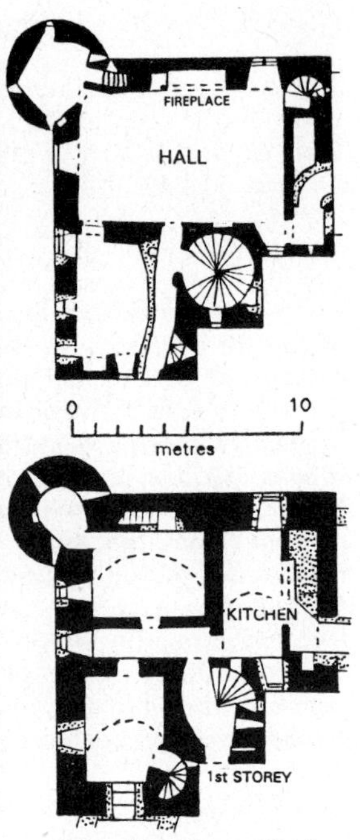

Plans of Dundarave Castle

DUNDARAVE NN 143096

Over the entrance is a reset stone with the date 1598 and initials of the builders John MacNaughton and Anna MacLean. The original seat of the MacNaughtons seems to have been at Glen Shira and they are first designated of Dundarave in 1501. John MacNaughton was forfeited as a Jacobite in 1689 and the estate passed to the Campbells of Ardkinglas. In 1748 the castle was occupied by a party of military road-makers under Major Cawfield and was probably abandoned soon afterwards. It was a ruin throughout the 19th century but in 1911-2 was restored by Sir Robert Lorimer for Sir Andrew Noble, and relatives of the latter held the estate until c1950.

The L-plan castle has a main block 12.1m long by 8.5m wide from which a wing 6.2m wide projects 5.2m from the southern end of the SE wall. A round tower 4.7m in diameter projects from the outermost angle and contains quadrangular rooms with shot-holes over a round basement with three more. In all the castle has 25 loops for discharging fire-arms. A square stair turret in the re-entrant angle contains the entrance and a staircase serving five full storeys in the wing and four storeys and a dark attic in the main block. At ground level a passage separates cellars in the wing and the SW part of the main block, both with service stairs, whilst the remainder of the main block forms a kitchen with its fireplace in the end wall, the flue being flanked higher up by mural chambers in the corners and a secondary stair from the hall to the room above. The private room in the wing has been much altered as a result of the insertion of a passage from the hall to the upper storey of a modern range beyond the wing. The hall itself is little altered and has a fireplace on the NW side. A chamber leading off one of three window embrasures now forms an access passage to an L-shaped modern extension beyond the NE wall. The main block contained two rooms on each of the third and fourth storeys originally, although the fourth storey as restored was divided into three rooms. There are bartizans on the wing outer corners.

DUNIVAIG NR 406455

A rock on the south side of Islay bears the SE wall of a 16th century tower about 13.5m long by 10m wide. The original thin walling was thickened in an irregular manner later in the century. The tower occupied about half the interior of a triangular court extending down the NW slope and connecting with a polygonal outer court 37m long by 22m wide. This court has a very ruined wall more than 3m thick and probably of 13th century date on the vulnerable east and north sides. The landward gate in the middle of the north side had a tower above, which was battered by cannon when the Earl of Argyll besieged Dunivaig in 1615. A wider gate, probably intended to enable ships to be brought up into the court, faces to seaward on the SW. Within the court are turf covered remains of several buildings, that nearest the north side probably being a bakehouse with an oven within the curtain wall.

Dunivaig Castle is first mentioned by Fordun as a stronghold of the Lord of the Isles in the late 14th century. It passed to a cadet branch, the MacDonalds of Dunivaig and The Glens and after their rebellion and forfeiture in 1494 was granted to John Maclan of Ardnamurchan. He garrisoned the castle against a MacDonald attack in 1514-16. After he died in 1519 the Earl of Argyll made his brother Sir John Campbell of Cawdor keeper of Dunivaig. It later reverted to the Crown and was granted to James MacDonald of Dunivaig whose lands in Scotland were made into the barony of Barr in 1545 (he also held an estate in Ireland). The castle was besieged during the family feud with the MacLeans in the 1580s and in 1596 was taken into royal custody. The MacDonalds forcibly repossessed the castle in 1614, leading to the siege already mentioned by the Earl of Argyll. Although reputed to be impregnable it was reduced to ruins by a few days' heavy bombardment. However it still held a Campbell garrison in 1630 when demolition was recommended by the Privy Council after an attack by local rebels, although the place continued to be garrisoned throughout the 1640s, being surrendered after a short siege in 1647 to General Leslie, who was impressed by its strength and described it as "weel furnished and manned". Hugh Campbell finally abandoned it in the 1670s in favour of the newly built Islay House.

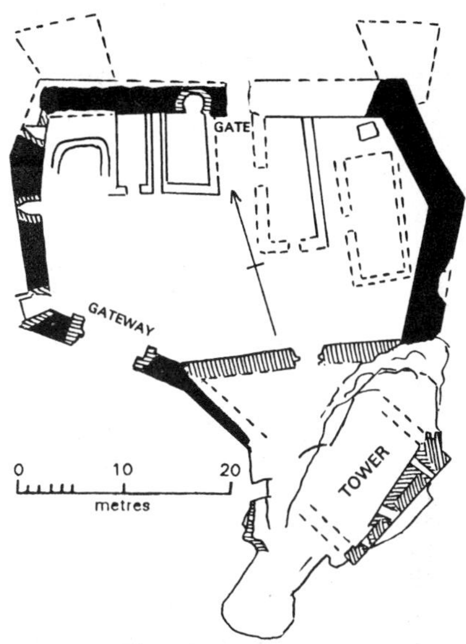

Plan of Dunivaig Castle

Dunivaig Castle

DUNOLLIE NM 852314

A stronghold stood on this promontory 24m high north of Oban from an early date. It was captured and burnt in 698 by Irish raiders and was rebuilt by Selbach, ruler of Northern Dalriada. There is no certain evidence of the site being in use during the 13th and 14th centuries and the probability is that the exiting tower and court date from after 1451 when John Stewart of Lorn granted to John MacDougall lands here which had formerly belonged to the MacDougalls before their defeat by the Bruces in 1309. The castle was captured from the MacDougalls by the Marquis of Argyll in 1644 and John MacDougall was only restored to his estates in 1661. The castle was garrisoned against the MacLeans in 1675. John MacDougall, 22nd laird was forfeited after the 1715 rebellion but Dunollie was later restored to his son Alexander who then transferred to a new house nearby.

The tower projects diagonally from the NE corner of a court about 24m square with sheer drops on the south and west sides. On the west there survives the footings of the outer wall of a 16th century outbuilding; to the south there was just a breastwork of which little remains. On the north and east sides the court has walls 2.3m thick. The main entrance faces east and has a draw-bar slot, whilst on the north is a postern in the form of a zig-zag passage through the wall. The tower measures 12m by 11.3m over walls 2.7m thick. The tower has an entrance from the SW into a vaulted cellar with SW and SE loops opening onto the court. Steps from the entrance ascend round the south corner to the second storey with has a narrow window to the NE, a similar window and a latrine to the NW, another window and a fireplace either side of the stair head in the SE wall. A fourth window towards the SW has been modernised and has another stair rising towards the south corner. This stair leads to the base of a spiral stair and to the hall on the third storey which has a fireplace and latrine to the NW and a window on each other side. Above was a attic room from which there was access to a wall-walk about 14m above the ground.

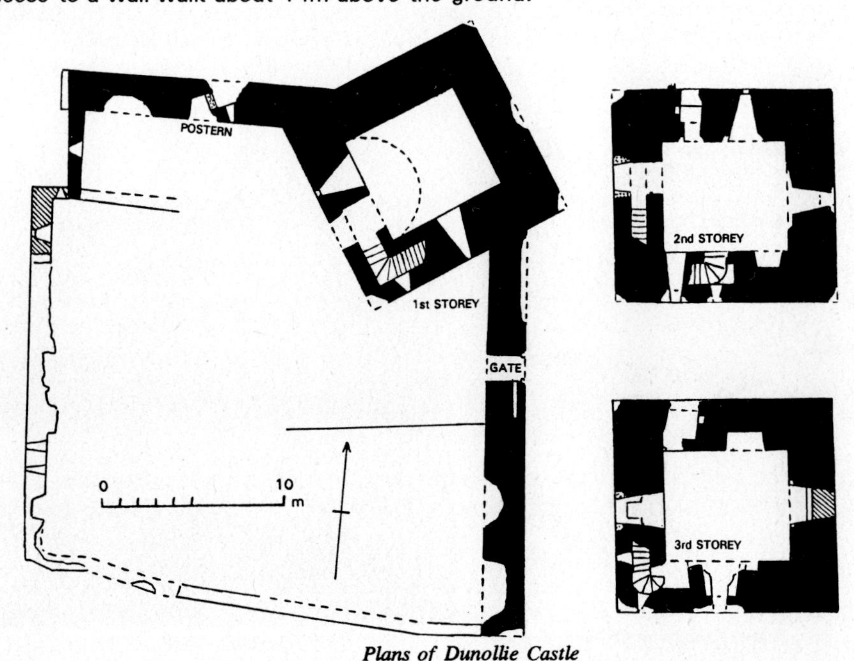

Plans of Dunollie Castle

Dunollie Castle

Plan of Dunoon Castle

Dunollie Castle

DUNOON NS 175763 F

On a 27m high rock at the end of a promontory beside the Firth of Clyde are the last traces of a wall about 1.3m thick around a court about 24m by 15m. Parts remain of the east corner and of a stepped gateway passage at the west corner. A castle here existed by the mid 13th century, it then being held by the Stewart family. It was surrendered to Edward Balliol in 1334 but was soon recaptured for David II by Sir Colin Campbell and Robert Stewart after a siege in which they used "engines of war". It was retained as a royal castle in the 15th century (it may have originally been founded by Alexander II) and the Bishops of Glasgow and Argyll were constables respectively in 1451-4 and 1455-60. Custody was then given to Colin Campbell, 1st Earl of Argyll, this being made hereditary in his family in 1473. The Earls frequently used the castle and dated many charters from it. In 1544 the Earl of Lennox burnt the township below the castle despite his fleet being fired upon by the garrison led by the 4th Earl of Argyll. In 1563 Queen Mary spent two nights here and in subsequent years the Campbells of Ardkinglas were keepers. Pont's map of c1590 suggests there was a tower house which has now vanished. After a new house was built at Innellan in the 1650s the castle was allowed to decay and little remained by 1820 when James Ewing of Castle House had the wall bases exposed. In 1924 the site was handed over to Dunoon Burgh Council and it now lies within a public garden.

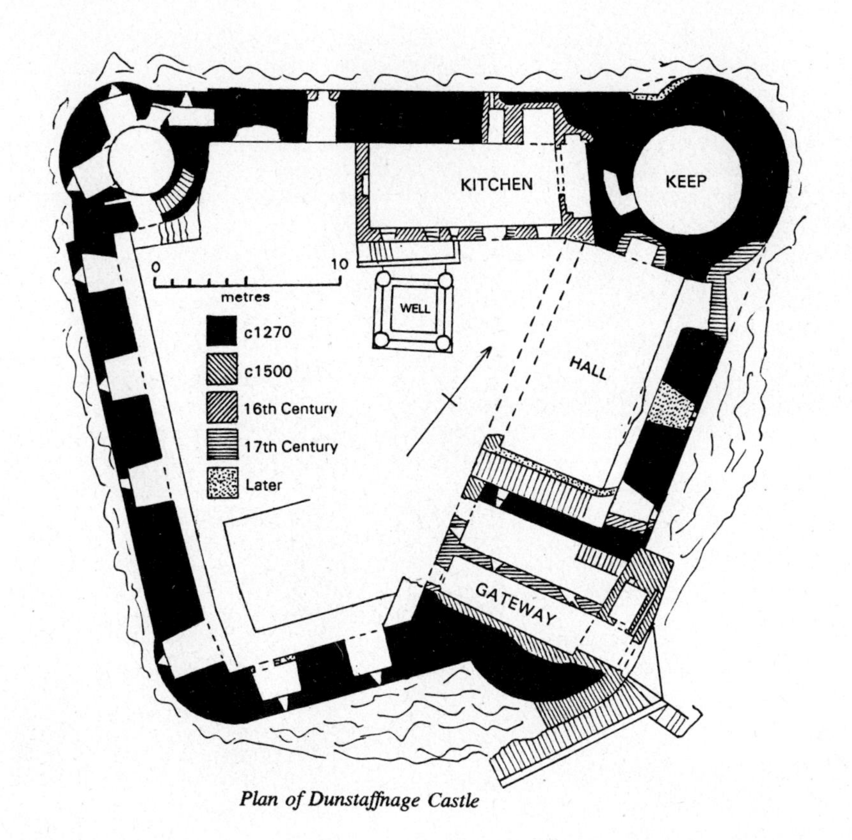

Plan of Dunstaffnage Castle

DUNSTAFFNAGE NM 882344 HS

On a vertical sided outcrop of rock 9m high on a peninsular at the mouth of Loch Etive stands a castle of enclosure probably built by Ewan MacDougall, Lord of Lorn c1240-75. The castle was besieged and captured by Robert Bruce after his defeat of the MacDougalls in the Pass of Brander in 1309 after which they were forfeited. Arthur Campbell, a kinsman of the Campbells of Lochawe was made captain of the castle c1321. Part of Lorn was restored to John MacDougall by David II and passed by marriage to John Stewart of Innermeath. In the 1470s it passed to the Earl of Argyll. He and his successors appointed a series of kinsmen as hereditary captains who took the title of Campbell of Dunstaffnage and who inhabited the gatehouse as converted into a tower house. The place was regarded as a useful base for operations against rebel chiefs during the 16th and 17th centuries and it was garrisoned throughout the conflicts of the 1640s and the 1670s and 80s, finally being burnt in 1685 by the Marquis of Atholl after the defeat and forfeiture of the 9th Earl of Argyll. A proposal to erect a large fort around the castle in 1689 was not acted upon. After a fire gutted the gatehouse in 1810 the captains left the castle which was occupied by tenants until the late 19th century. In 1962 custody was handed over to the Department of the Environment (now succeeded by Historic Scotland) and the ivy was stripped off and considerable repairs put in hand which were only completed in the 1980s.

Walls up to 3.2m thick at courtyard level surround a quadrangular court about 30m by 28m. At a height of about 2m the walls are stepped back internally to a thickness of about 2.7m and contain deep embrasures on all sides, one of which on the SE has been later made into a chamber. Round towers of 8.5m and 10.8m diameter respectively at the west and north corners lie mostly within the court rather than projecting to flank the walls because of the nature of the site and there is a very shallow roundel projection at the south corner. A hall 14m long by 6.5m lies on the upper floor of a two storey range extending from the north tower to a round fronted eastern tower of slightly bolder projection which contains the gateway. The thin hall inner wall rebuilt c1475-1520 is destroyed but a pair of two light windows remain in the curtain wall. The present entrance is also of the time of the rebuilding and is reached by a modern flight of steps up to a platform in front of it. There is a small room in the wall thickness just inside the doorway. A 17th century cross-way divides the lowest level of the gatehouse into a long narrow cellar and an entrance passage. The room above was remodelled in the late 16th century, the wide window embrasure with seats being of that period, although the windows towards the court in the thin west wall are 17th century. The top storey is mostly late 16th century and the curtain wall-walk and parapet are continued around the thick walled south and east sides. The north tower is much ruined and patched and has little interest although it probably originally formed the keep or lord's residence. West of this tower, and having a kitchen fireplace built against it, is a house created in 1725 from the shell of a late 16th century range extending between the two towers. In front of this building is a large well. The west tower has a prison at court level and is entered at the stage above which has two deep embrasures with loops towards the field, a latrine, and a stair curving up to the third storey, also with two loops and a latrine. The topmost storey was rebuilt in the 17th century.

Dunstaffnage Castle

Duntrune Castle

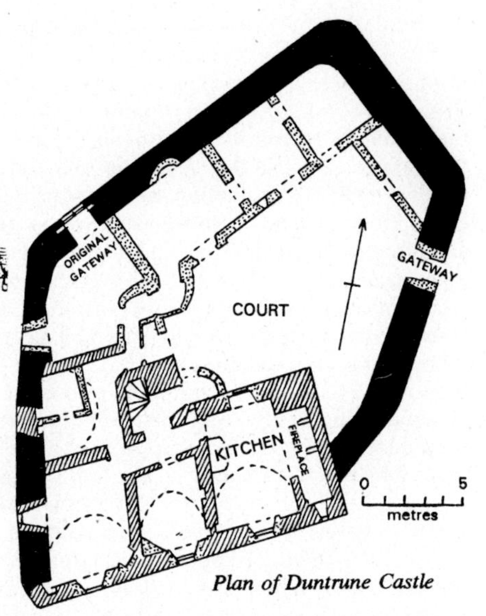

Plan of Duntrune Castle

DUNTRUNE NR 793955

The castle is first specifically mentioned in 1640 when it was garrisoned against an attack by Alasdair MacDonald, although in 1615 Duntrune was a mustering place for the attack on Islay by the 7th Earl of Argyll. The curtain wall averaging 1.5m thick around irregularly shaped court and having maximum dimensions of 29m by 17m was probably built after the lordship of Araskeodnish was granted in 1423 by Duncan Campbell of Lochawe to his brother. A new L-plan house of three storeys was fitted awkwardly into the acute southern corner c1600. A square turret in the re-entrant angle contains the entrance and a staircase linking all the rooms. The main block contains a hall over a kitchen and the smallest of the three cellars, and there are private rooms at the SW end of the hall and in the wing. After John Campbell got into financial difficulties in the 1660s Duntrune passed to a kinsman, Neil, who was allowed by his superior the 9th Earl of Argyll to garrison the place during the unrest of the mid 1670s. After a later Neil Campbell died in 1796 Duntrune was sold to Neil Malcolm of Poltalloch for whom considerable remodelling was carried out, including the addition of the embattled wall enclosing an approach made to a new entrance formed on the east (the original entrance, now a window, faces west). The outbuildings on the NW and NE sides of the court are also of this period. This family lived here until Poltalloch House was completed in 1853, but in the 1950s the latter was abandoned and the family moved back to Duntrune which was then modernised.

EILEAN DEARG NS 008770

On a small island 150m from the east shore of Loch Riddon near where it opens to the Kyles of Bute are the slight and much overgrown remains of a castle which was described an impregnable castle of the Lord of Lochawe by Bower in the 1440s. In 1685 it was used as the main arms depot for the 9th Earl of Argyll's rebellion but was abandoned when a naval force arrived under Captain Hamilton who removed some of the stores and then fired the 500 barrels of powder, which completely wrecked the buildings. Excavations in 1964-7 identified the footings of a tower either built by the Mores of Abercorn c1370 or by Colin Campbell c1440 which measured about 14m by 12m over walls 2.4m thick. It lay on the west side of a court measuring about 25m by 22m. In the SE corner of the court was what was probably a hall range 14.5m long by 4.7m wide within walls 1.1m thick, and on the north side was a thinly walled building identified as a chapel. A hollow which contained a spring on the east edge of the island, outside the court, was revetted with masonry to form a well.

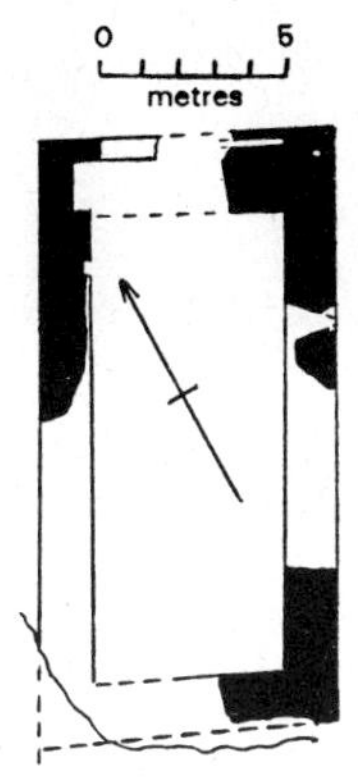

Fincharn: plan

Fincharn Castle

FINCHARN NM 898043

The summit of a rock overlooking the SE side of Loch Awe is filled with the ruins of a 13th century hall-house 8.2m wide with an average length of 16m (it is irregularly laid out). The walls were 1.4m thick except for the north end wall which was 2.2m thick and contained the entrance with a mural chamber leading off in the NW corner. The building is much damaged and the basement is partly filled with rubble. One east loop survives on the lower level whilst the upper level has one complete east facing loop, single jambs of two others in the same wall, and jambs also of others to the south and west, plus what was probably a latrine in the NW corner. There are traces of a small walled court slightly wider than the hall-house and 11m long beyond the north wall. The castle was probably built soon after lands here were granted or confirmed to Gillascop MacGilcrist by Alexander II in 1240, the charter being the oldest surviving document relating to property in Argyll. The castle is may be that of "Glasrog" captured in 1297 from the Stewarts in the interest of Edward I in 1308, and is almost certainly the castle of Glassery held for Edward I by John MacDougall of Lorn in 1308, and which in 1374 was re-granted to Gilbert of Glassery. It subsequently passed to his son-in-law Alexander Scrymgeour, Constable of Dundee, and was held by his descendants until 1668. The castle was in later years occupied by tenants and this may explain the lack of any obvious extensions or alterations to the fabric.

FINLAGGAN NR 388681

Finlaggan was an important seat of the Lords of the Islands and remained a MacDonald possession until the 17th century. Although described as a castle it had neither a tower nor a curtain wall, just a cluster of unfortified domestic buildings on the islet of Eilean Mor at the NE end of the loch. Ruins stand high of a hall block 18m long by 8.8m wide and divided by a cross-wall containing two doorways, plus a chapel to the east. There are lesser remains of several other buildings. Excavations have recently been carried out on the island for several seasons, and a trench cut on the shore opposite in 1994 by archeologists as part of the Time Team television series revealed a wall assumed to be part of one of the two 17th century guard houses which covered the access to a causeway. No buildings remain on the 30m diameter Eilean na Comhairle close to the SW, where courts are said to have been held.

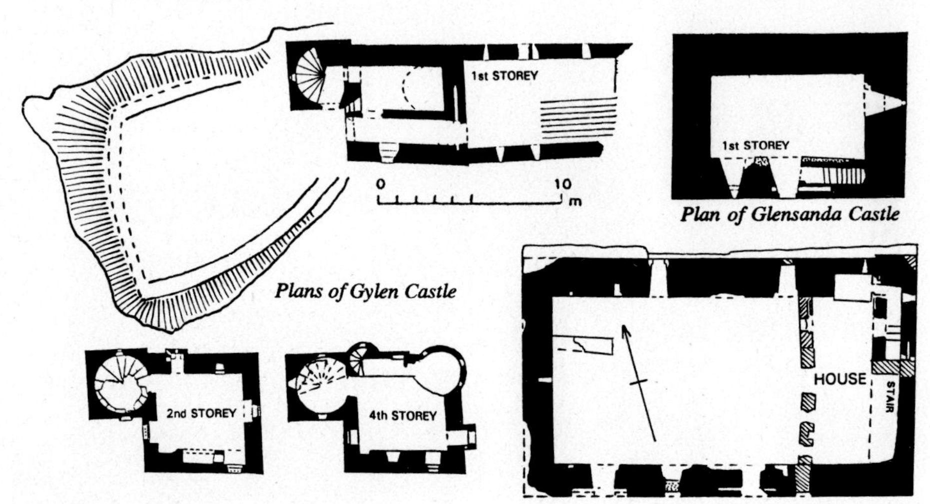

Plans of Gylen Castle

Plan of Glensanda Castle

Plan of Fraoch Eilean Castle

FRAOCH EILEAN NN 108251

A charter issued by Alexander III to Gillechrist MacNaughton in 1267 suggests that the ruined hall-house on an island near the north end of Loch Awe was then under construction at the King's expense and was to be held by MacNaughton as part of the policy of consolidation of royal power in the Western Highlands after the Treaty of Perth made with the King of Norway in 1266. The MacNaughtons later became vassals of the Campbells of Lochawe who in the 17th century built a modest house in the eastern part of the building, then a ruin. The island was sold to Robert Campbell of Monzie in 1765 but later passed to the Campbells of Dunstaffnage. In 1960 the ruin was repurchased by one of the Inverawe Campbells and some repairs carried out.

The hall house measures 21.7m by 12.6m and has a north wall 2.1m thick above a plinth, an east wall 2.4m thick which contained a staircase leading up from an entrance (now blocked) above ground level, and south and west walls 1.7m thick. The basement has another entrance, also with a draw-bar hole, on the south and two windows in each of the south and north walls. It was presumably divided into a number of rooms and there was a prison in the NE corner reached from a stair leading down from the east entrance. The hall may have had a private room divided off at the west end. The north wall contains a window embrasure and a stair to the former wall-walk, and the south wall has two very damaged window embrasures corresponding to each of the supposed divisions. The east end has been altered as a result of the creation of a two storey house there, also now ruined. A later medieval court extended 14m west of the hall-house and 8m south of it. Part of the wall 1.3m thick remains 3m high on the south side with a gap for the gateway overlooking a boat-house and traces of a round SW corner tower. Footings of two buildings remain in the court.

GLENSANDA NM 823468

On an outcrop above the mouth of Glen Sanda far from any public road stands a ruin 12.8m long by 8.8m wide over walls 2.3m thick. Probably built c1500 by Ewen MacLean, it contained a single living room with a fireplace and latrine in the NW wall and three windows, and a cellar with two loops and an entrance in the SE wall from which rises the stair connecting the two storeys. A stair in the north corner then leads to the parapet which is still fairly complete on the SW and SE sides. There are no vaults. Footings of an outbuilding 12m long by 6.5m wide lie nearby to the south.

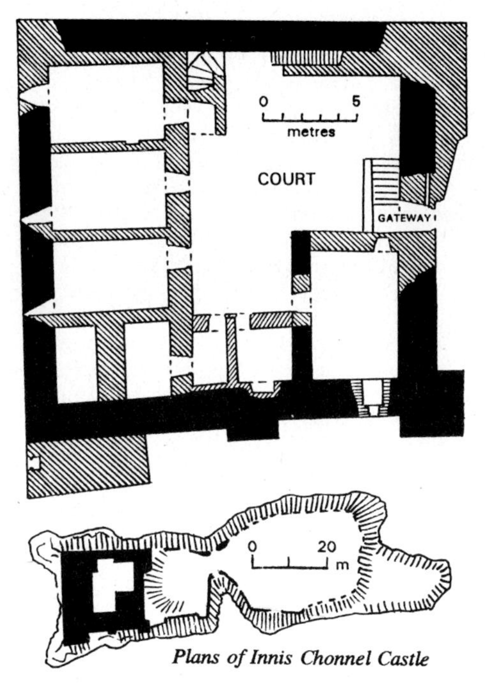

Plans of Innis Chonnel Castle

Gylen Castle

GYLEN NM 805265

Dramatically poised on a sheer-sided promontory 17m high near the south end of the island of Kerrara is a tower thought to have built completed in 1582 by Duncan MacDougall of Dunollie. It was not restored after being burnt in 1647 by the MacDonalds. The tower has a wing containing the entrance and a staircase serving all four storeys of a main block 6.4m square and 9.5m high to the eaves. The basement contains a cellar by the stair and a narrow passage connecting an outer court 55m long by 20m wide with a tiny inner court. Only footings remain of the court walls. The upper storeys have fireplaces in the SE wall and latrines in the NW wall. The top storey has an oriel with machicolations defending the passage and a round bartizan on the north corner. A secondary stair then leads up to a caphouse over the main stair.

INNIS CHONNEL NM 976119

This castle on an island on the east side of Loch Awe was probably built by the Campbells in the first half of the 13th century. It is first mentioned in 1308 when John MacDougall of Lorn was holding it for Edward II. Loch Awe reverted to the Campbells after the defeat of the MacDougalls in 1309 and was rebuilt by Sir Duncan Campbell, who died in 1453. It was his chief seat, but his grandson Colin, created Earl of Argyll, transferred to Inverary. Innis Chonnel was then used as a prison for criminals and political prisoners, having a series of hereditary captains. The MacArthurs filled this post until 1613 when the honour passed to the MacLachlans after Duncan MacArthur was convicted of theft. The captains had an estate called Ardchonnell on the shore opposite and were expected to keep the castle buildings in repair. The MacLachlans had a house ashore by 1704 and the castle was ruinous by 1806, although arrangements for the keepership continued to be made until at least 1801.

Three courts entirely fill the island of Innis Chonnel. A narrow isthmus with landing places on either side and a wide gateway to the north separates a very ruined oval outer court 35m by 25m from a better preserved middle court roughly 16m square, both apparently being 15th century. The well preserved 13th century inner court 18m by 19m with walls 2m thick lies at the west end. The SE corner has a square turret and there is a pilaster buttress in the middle of the south side. In the 15th century a turret containing small vaulted rooms was built against the SW corner, the NW and NE corners were rebuilt (a stair from the court rises to the latter), and the gateway on the east was renewed. The building in the court SE corner is partly original but the whole of the west range is 15th century. A rather poorly lighted hall with a private chamber at the south end and a kitchen and an anti-room at the north end lie over three vaulted cellars, plus, at the south end, a smaller cellar and a prison tucked into the SW corner. The kitchen appears to be the result of a 17th century remodelling. An outside stair from the court leads up to the anti-room. At the wall-walk level 8m above ground the SW and SE turrets contain rooms. The parapet on the south side is 17th century, and 15th century parapets remain on the west and north sides.

INVERARAY NN 096093

Three concrete pillars above the west bank of the River Aray mark the site of a tower built by Colin Campbell about the time of his elevation to the Earldom of Argyll in 1457. Traces of the tower were found by excavation in 1966 and it is known from old drawings to have been 15.5m long by 10m wide over walls 2.2m thick. The building was remodelled by Archibald, 7th Earl of Argyll after he attained his majority in 1592. The battlements were removed and the main block then had a basement divided into three cellars, a hall above, two storeys of private rooms above and an attic on top, whilst further rooms were provided in a wing 6.1m wide projecting 5.5m and in a new SW range. There was a turret stair corbelled out over the re-entrant angle and a scale-and-platt stair led up to the hall, possibly as a result of further remodelling in the 1660s. On the corners at the summit were bartizans with conical roofs. In 1650 there were twenty furnished rooms and another eleven are mentioned in a later list as a result of additions by the 9th Earl. By the 1740s the tower was badly cracked, partly as a result of land-slip towards the river, and the new building (outside the scope of this book) was begun in the forecourt. The old tower was finally demolished c1774.

Inverary formed the chief seat of the Earls of Argyll and was kept for them by the MacIvers of Stronshira. James V stayed for a month in 1533 and Queen Mary paid a brief visit in 1563. Several attacks were made upon the adjacent township by Montrose and Alasdair MacDonald in 1644-47 but the castle probably remained untaken. After the 9th Earl was forfeited for rebellion in 1684 Inverary was granted to the Marquis of Atholl and was used as a munitions store and base against the Earl's invasion of 1685. At some point the castle was damaged as in 1689 orders were given for it to be reglazed and slated, whilst in a hearth-tax assessment of 1693 the old tower is noted as ruinous. New pavilions were built in the 1720s by the 2nd Duke of Argyll.

ISLAND MULLER NR 756224

The lower part of a 15th century tower 13.3m long by 12m wide over walls up to 2.8m thick lie on a low rock connected by a causeway 90m long on the north side of Kilchousland Bay, NE of Campbeltown. This may be the castle of Smerby in which Sir James MacDonald imprisoned his father Angus MacDonald of Dunnyveg in 1597.

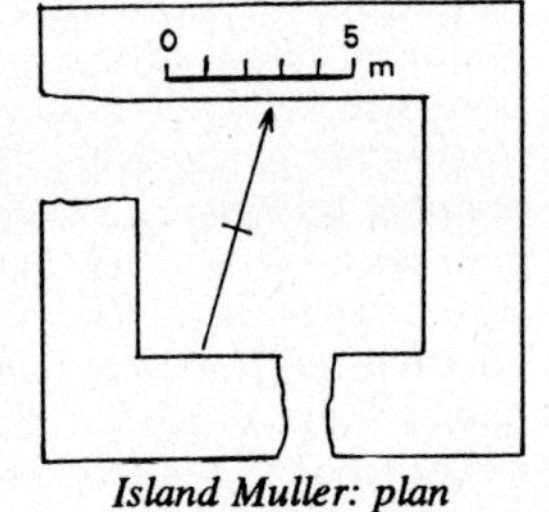

Island Muller: plan

Innis Chonnel Castle

KAMES NS 064676

The Bannatynes are first mentioned in the time of Alexander III and served the Stewart kings as Chamberlains of Bute. They are first noted at Kames in 1334, but the tower is more likely to be of the 1390s, whilst the wing containing a scale-and-platt staircase can hardly be earlier than the 1590s. The tower measures 11m by 7.7m externally and contains a low cellar, a hall with two large modern windows facing west, two upper storeys, and an attic within a mostly rebuilt parapet upon a single row of corbels. There are no stairs within the main body of the tower and it seems that originally there were separate entrances to each of the two lowest levels. A burn flows past the south and east sides and a moat was tracable on the other sides in the late 19th century. None of the extensive outbuildings appear to be ancient. The Bannatyne direct male line failed in 1786 but a MacLeod nephew adopted the Bannatyne name. His successor Judge Lord Kames went bankrupt and sold Kames to James Hamilton. It is now a holiday home belonging to the Scottish Coucil for the Care of Spastics.

KILBERRY NR 708641

Some walling of the main block of an L-plan tower of the Campbells of Kilberry may survive in a mansion of the 1840s extended in 1843. The original tower was remodelled in 1727 and gutted by fire in 1772. Plans were then made in connection with an insurance claim. It had a wing 7m wide projecting 6.1m eastwards from a main block 11.8m long by 7.8m wide over walls 0.9m thick. The entrance was in the re-entrant angle but the stair lay on the opposite side at the junction of wing and main block. Two diagonally opposite corners of the main block and one corner of the wing had bartizans with conical roofs. They were of greater diameter than their modern counterparts. There were three storeys and attics. Pediments bore the initials of Colin Campbell and Helen Wood with a date that was probably intended to be 1595. Descendants of this Colin Campbell, a grandson of Archibald Campbell of Auchinbreck and first of this family here, still own the property.

KILCHURN NN 133276 HS

This celebrated castle lies on a rocky peninsular, originally an island, at the north end of Loch Awe. Lands here formed part of the lordship of Glenorchy granted by Duncan Campbell of Lochawe to his son Colin in 1432. The tower house is thought to have built during the 1440s, whilst the "laich hall" which stood beside the one surviving section of the original barmkin wall was added by Sir Duncan, 2nd laird of Glenorchy (1475-1513). Kilchurn was then the principal family seat and the 3rd and 4th lairds died within it in 1523 and 1536 respectively. During this period the MacGregors were keepers of the castle, charged with providing a watchman and maintaining the wall-walks. Sir Colin, 6th laird, who died in 1583 added the four round bartizans to the tower, one of which has fallen and now lies upside down in the court. A range of rooms called the "north chambers" were also then added. However, Sir Colin built a new seat at Balloch by Loch Tay in Perthshire, and his son Sir Duncan, d1631, built Finlarig Castle at the other end of the loch and these then became the principal residences. By this time the Campbells and MacGregors were at war and Kilchurn was neglected, the "laich hall" being ruinous when Sir Duncan began rebuilding it as a two storey block in 1614. In 1643 the tower was re-roofed and the castle was garrisoned against the Royalists. The expected attack did not take place until 1654 when General Middleton besieged Sir John Campbell of Glenorchy and the Marquess of Argyll at Kilchurn for two days before being drawn off by the approach of General Monck.

In 1685 Glenorchy, now Earl of Breadalbane, suggested Kilchurn as a mustering point for loyal troops mustered against the rebel Marquis of Argyll. The Earl was less keen on the castle being garrisoned against Jacobites in 1689, but in 1690 work began on reconstructing it for use as a barracks, the north and east ranges being rebuilt and round turrets with gunloops being added to the north, west, and south corners. In July 1693 "ane iron yeatt weighting fortie aught ston" for the castle was made in Glasgow and brought by sea to Bonawe. Plasterwork, probably in the SW range, was being executed late in 1694, and other work continued until 1698. It does not appear that a garrison was installed until the rebellion of 1715. The castle was abandoned shortly after the 1745 rebellion and was unroofed c1770. The ruin was patched up c1900 and again in the 1970s after being taken into state care.

Kilchurn Castle

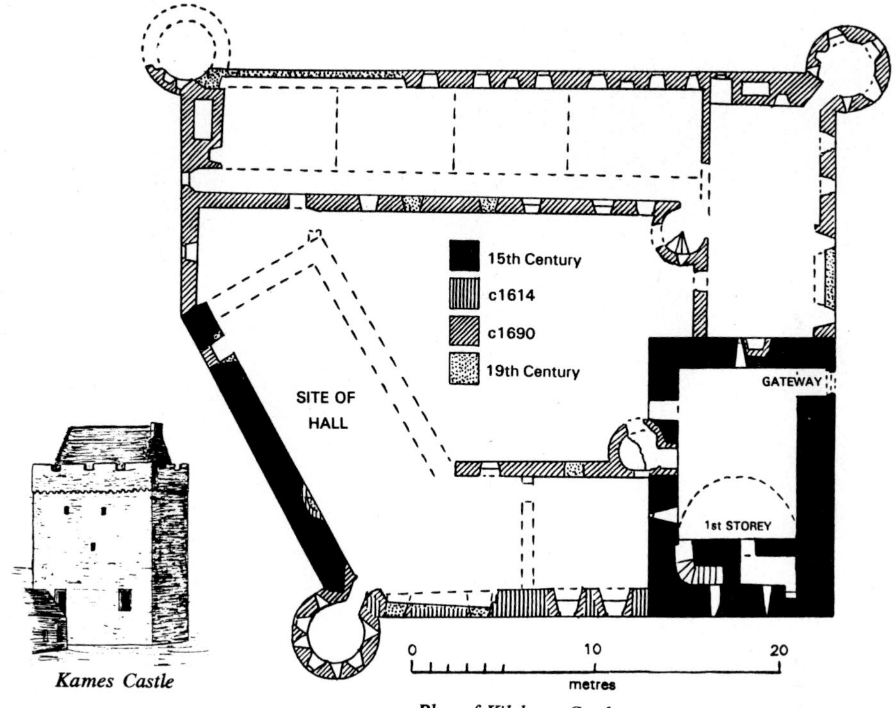

Kames Castle

Plan of Kilchurn Castle

The tower house measures 14.7m by 10.4m and contains four storeys and an attic, all the rooms being served by a stair turret added in the 1690s in the re-entrant angle between the tower and the SE range. The landward NE wall is 2.3m thick and contains a doorway at the north end which is the only entrance to the castle. There is another doorway to the court nearly opposite in the 17m thick SW wall. No entrance passage is divided off from the single vaulted cellar lighted by two loops. The far SE wall is 3.2m thick and contains a prison reached from the cellar and a service stair which rises up to come out between a pair of vaulted rooms, one with a latrine, at the south end of the hall. The original upper entrance to the hall in the SW wall now looks into the much ruined upper storey of the SE range and has been patched in modern times. The hall has been much altered and now lacks a fireplace but it has two windows facing the approach and a doorway leads into the upper storey of the NE range. A stair rising up round the south corner leads to the suite or two poorly lighted rooms on the third storey. The fourth storey was a dark sleeping loft later divided into two rooms each with a tiny inserted fireplace.

The tower lies in the east corner of a court 32m long by 26m with ranges on all sides. The north range comprises four barrack rooms linked by a corridor on each of two storeys, and there were service rooms below courtyard level. Each room had two windows towards the field with a fireplace in between, and there were latrines at the east end, between it and the NE range which contained pairs of larger rooms, also with a kitchen and service room below. In the angle between the two is a stair turret. The round flanking tower at the west corner and the adjacent part of the NW wall have mostly fallen but the other two flankers remain intact. Most of the walling of the 1690s is barely a metre thick but the remaining fragment of the original 15th century barmkin wall on the south side is 1.8m thick. It contains a blocked postern.

Kilchurn Castle

Kildonan Castle

Kilmartin Castle

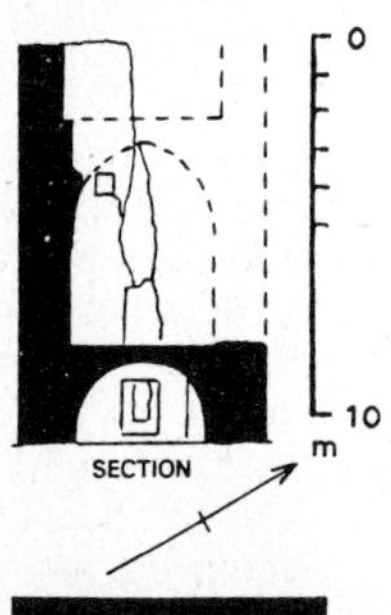

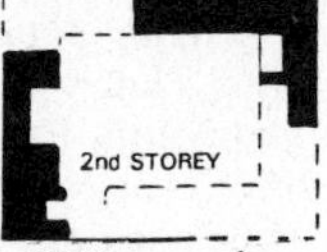

Kildonan: plans

KILDONAN NR 037210

In the garden of a house at the south end of Arran is a ruined tower probably built shortly before 1406, when Robert III granted his illegitimate son John of Ardgowan parts of southern Arran including "Kildonan, with the castle". Dean Munro refers to James Stewart holding Kildonan castle and lands around it inherited from his father Ninian, Sherriff of Bute, but the same year he was dispossessed by the Hamiltons in retribution for an attack on Brodick in 1544. The tower and its outbuildings were probably burnt by the Earl of Sussex in his raid of 1558 and it is not heard of again. The tower is 8.6m long by 6.9m wide and stands 11m high. The vaulted cellar has a loop at each end and a doorway with a drawbar slot. The broken down east corner beside the entrance contained a spiral stair. The hall above had a lofty pointed vault, although it is likely it was subdivided with a loft under the vault. A fireplace remains at the SW end and there were probably windows adjoining in the sidewalls. Little remains of the top storey but either it or the hall had a latrine at the south corner. The tower lies by a cliff and had a tiny court between it and a hollow to the south.

KILKERRAN NR 729194

A section of walling 6m high, 6m long and 1m thick remains in a cottage garden opposite the churchyard. James IV erected a castle here c1498 and it was garrisoned by James V at the time of his expedition to the west in 1536.

KILMARTIN NR 835991

This building, now being restored, is thought to have been built by Neil Campbell, Rector of Kilmartin from 1574 to 1627, and Bishop of Argyll from 1580 to 1608. It was probably erected in the 1590s after the 7th Earl of Argyll attained his majority, Neil having been a curator of his estates. In 1674 Kilmartin passed to the Campbells of Inverawe who occupied the castle until a new house was built elsewhere c1750. A room in the castle was temporarily accommodating the parish school in 1800. The building was in "disrepair" by 1825, and was a ruin by 1844. The castle has round towers 3.9m in diameter at the east and west corners of a main block 15.3m long by 7.4m wide with walls up to 1.2m thick. The west tower contains the main stair and has shot-holes commanding the adjacent entrance in the NW wall. A passage connects the doorway and stair, and runs past two cellars to a kitchen with its fireplace, now very ruined, in the NE end wall. The laird's room lies over the kitchen and is connected to it and the room above by a secondary stair in a small round turret rising from ground level projecting from the NW wall. The hall has two windows in each side wall, a third window on the SW with access to a vaulted room in the south corner, and there is a big fireplace in the NW wall. There was just a single room above reached from the main stair. The upper rooms in the east tower are too small to have been proper bedrooms. They were either closets or wardrobes or were used by servants.

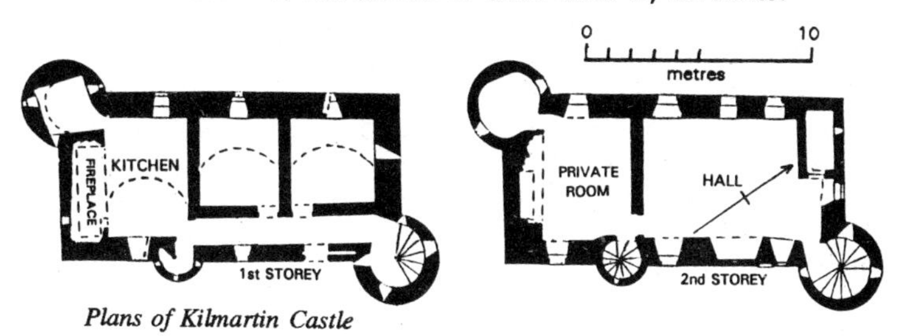

Plans of Kilmartin Castle

Kinlochaline Castle

Plans of Kinlochaline Castle

KINLOCHALINE NM 697476 OP

This tower measuring 13.3m by 10.5m over walls 2.8m thick is thought to have been built in the 15th century by one of the MacLeans of Duart although it is not mentioned until 1557 when Hector MacLean gave his wife Janet, daughter of the 4th Earl of Argyll a liferent of lands in this area. Originally the tower had a single cellar below a hall with a fireplace at the north end, both levels having entrances in the south wall and there being no staircase between them. A stair from the upper entrance then led via an entresol gallery in the south wall to the upper parts. Except for a mural room in the NE corner all the features of the third storey and battlements were remodelled c1890, when the lower entrance was blocked and a forestair built to the upper entrance. It was either John Dow MacLean or son his Allan, sucessive Baillies of Morvern in the late 16th century who subdivided the basement and introduced vaults plus a pair of service stairs down from window embrasures in the hall west wall. There is a well in the south wall, originally accessible at two levels, but the lower access to it was blocked by new walling in the late 16th century. In July 1644 the castle was captured for the Royalist cause by a 400 strong force of MacDonalds and others. John MacLean of Kinlochaline was involved in the feud between the MacLeans of Duart and the Earl of Argyll in consequence of which his castle was attacked by the Argyll in 1679. It was surrendered after the Earl threatened to undermine the tower or blow it up after blockading it for a week. MacLean got his castle back when Argyll fell into disgrace in 1681 but in 1690 it was occupied in the interest of the 10th Earl by Donald Campbell and fifteen men. In 1730 the then roofless castle was purchased by Sir Alexander Murray of Stanhope. He intended to restore it in conjunction with mining in the vicinity but it is clear from the fabric no work was carried out until 1890 when T.V.Smith, owner of the Ardtornish estate, had it made habitable.

KNOCKAMILLIE NS 152710 F

A fragment of probably early 17th century walling 7m high, 7m long and 0.9m thick with a stub of an adjoining cross-wall lies on the SE corner of a platform about 16m square with traces of another platform to the east. The site lies above Innellan Pier, commanding the Clyde coast and Bute. The house belonged to the Campbells of Auchinbreck and was assessed in 1693 for three hearths. In 1864 the building was reported as having been robbed for materials in the last thirty years.

LOCH AN EILEIN NL 986435

Fordun in the late 14th century noted a strong tower on the island of Tiree and it is mention in 1549 by Dean Munro as "ane auld castell". The tower must have been built by the Lord of the Isles but from 1390 was held by the MacLeans until 1674 when it was annexed to the Earldom of Argyll. In 1678 Archibald, 9th Earl of Argyll captured the castle from the MacLeans and it was then abandoned, probably being dismantled for materials to build Island House in 1748. There are no remains of the tower which in the late 17th century was "surrounded with ane trintch of stone and earth". The site was originally an island but later an embanked causeway was built out to it.

LOCH AN SGOLTAIRE NR 386972

A summer house serving nearby Colonsay House has been erected in the middle of a court about 10m square on one of several islands on a loch near the NW coast of Colonsay. The court is surrounded by a wall about 2m thick pierced on the north by a much rebuilt entrance. On the NW a mural stair leads onto the top of one of four corner bastions about 4m in diameter. The building lies within a pentagonal outer court about 33m by 30m with a drystone wall 2m thick having twin rounded bastions flanking a gateway on the north and other slightly larger bastions at the NW, NE, and SE corners. The other corner and adjacent sides rise directly from the waters of the loch. To the west and south of the other walls is a level platform ending in a kerb at the water's edge. The defences could be late medieval in origin but in their present form are mostly the work of Sir James MacDonald during his rebellion of 1615.

LOCHGAIR NR 929913

The Campbells of Auchinbreck had a house here by 1583 and it was plundered in 1685 by Government troops, Sir Duncan Campbell having taken part in the recent rebellion. There are indications that by 1748 it was a building of considerable extent, but it was demolished about the time Asknish House was built in the 1780s.

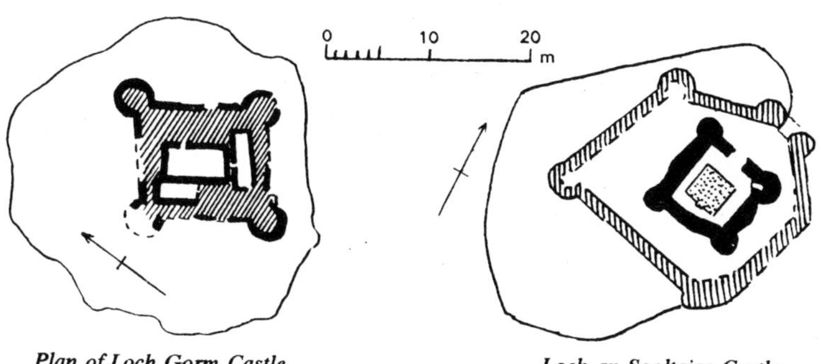

Plan of Loch Gorm Castle

Loch an Sgoltaire Castle

LOCH GORM NR 234654

A castle here on a natural island about 45m diameter in a freshwater loch on Islay is first referred to in 1549 by Dean Munro as a MacDonald stronghold then occupied by the MacGillans of Doward. The site was occupied in 1578 by Lachlan MacLean who was besieged there by the MacDonalds and Campbells. It was described as a ruin in 1586, but must have soon been repaired by the MacDonalds, being "ane strengthe castell" in 1596, although in 1608 it had just been "demolishit and kaist doun to the ground" by a royal force under Lord Ochiltree. In 1614 it was repaired by Sir James MacDonald for use as a base during his rebellion of that year. The stronghold was captured in January 1615 but by April Sir James had retaken it and his forces held it until they surrendered to the Earl of Argyll in October, after which it held a Campbell garrison until the 1640s. Drystone walls 2m thick with corner bastions 5.5m to 6m diameter enclose a turf filled area 20.5m by 17m at wall-top level 2.4m above the ground. Into the court are let three buildings with floors at a lower level. The largest building measured 7.5m by 4m within drystone walls about a metre thick with slots for three cruck-trusses to carry the roof.

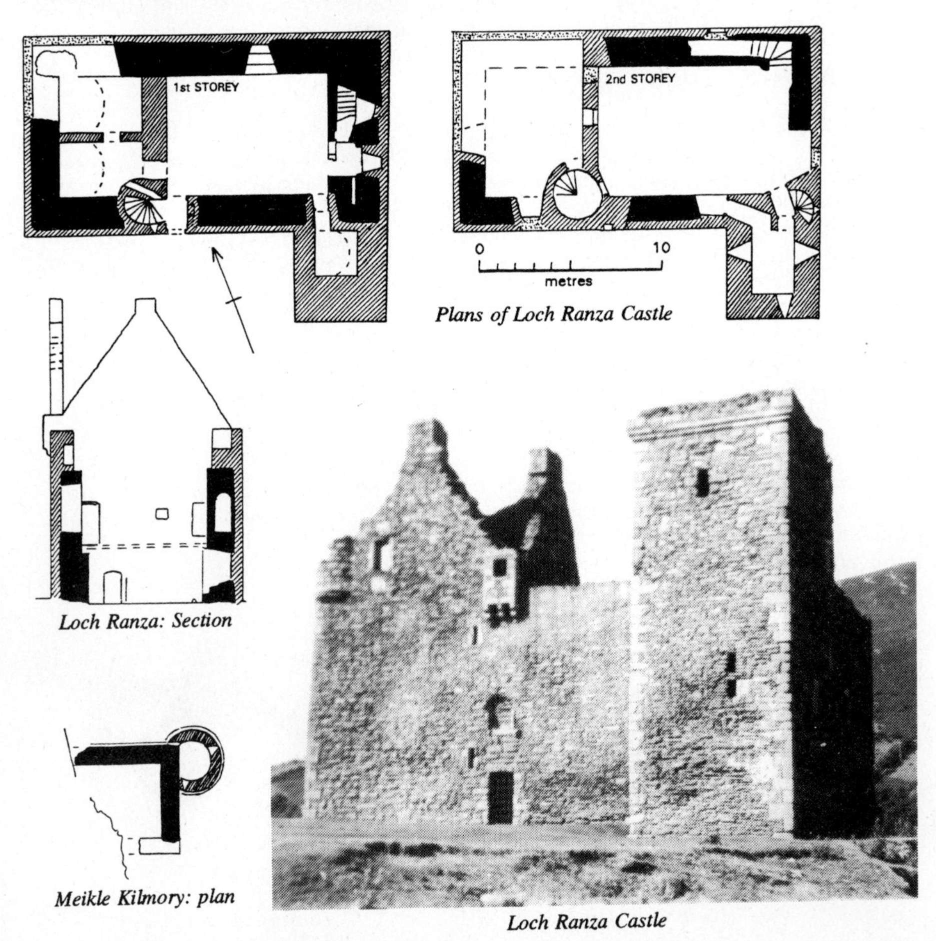

Plans of Loch Ranza Castle

Loch Ranza: Section

Meikle Kilmory: plan

Loch Ranza Castle

LOCH RANZA NR 933507 HS

This hall-house was built either by Alexander the High Steward or his successors in the late 13th century, or by a kinsman, John of Menteith, created Lord of Arran and Knapdale c1315. Robert Stewart, later Robert II, took these lands back in the 1360s, compensating the heiress of John's grandson. In the 15th century the Lord of the Isles claimed Arran and encouraged the MacDonalds of Kintyre and the MacAlisters of SW Knapdale to raid the island. James II's response was to hand over the castle and lands of Loch Ranza as a military holding to Alexander, Lord Montgomery, in 1452. This failed to prevent the devastating raid by Donald Balloch in 1455. The castle was probably damaged during the many raids and invasions during the late 15th and early to mid 16th centuries, and eventually it was remodelled and a wing added. In 1614 royal forces mustered here for an expedition against the rebel island chiefs. In the mid 17th century the Montgomeries at Loch Ranza supported the Covenant and found themselves isolated among Royalist families. No attack is recorded but there was consternation among the islanders when Alister Colkitto MacDonald ran amok on Arran in 1647. On the foreclosure of a mortgage the castle passed to the Duchess of Hamilton in 1705 and was abandoned soon afterwards.

The present external details and internal layout are entirely of c1575-90 but it is clear that much survives of the shell of the original hall-house which was about 7.5m high to the wall-walk. It now measures 20.1m by 10.6m over walls mostly 2m thick and is entered on the south side close to the foot of a spiral stair beside an inserted crosswall. It is likely that there was formerly a timber division here, closing off a private room at the west end of the main hall on the upper storey. Over the entrance is a space for a lost heraldic date-stone and high above it is a box-machicolation. The original entrance was in the east end wall and stairs rise from it around the NE corner. The larger eastern part of the building has no windows still in use and it is possible that this part was left as an open court after the remodelling. Access from the room over two vaulted cellars west of the crosswall to a small rooms over what was probably a prison in the added wing could have been by means of a wooden gallery. The west part contained a third storey and was roofed with its axis north-south, but the north gable and much of the walling adjoining the NW corner has fallen. There is a round bartizan on the SW corner. The wing also has a third storey and has the stump of a parapet carried on corbelled coursing.

LUNGA NM 795064

A gunloop remains in the 17th century central section of the house built by the Campbells of Craignish near an inlet at the approach to Loch Melfort. It takes its name from John MacDougall of Lunga (an island 8km to the west), who acquired it c1780.

MACEWAN'S NR 915795

Excavations have shown that the ancient dun with a 3m thick drystone wall around a court up to 22m across on a promontory at the north end of Kilfinan Bay was refurbished in the 16th century, probably by the MacEwans of Otter, although they had lost their status as principal landowners in favour of the Campbells by c1500.

MEIKLE KILMORY NS 051611 V

The lower parts of three sides of a small and feeble block of c1600 with walls 1m thick adjoin a farm outbuilding on a crag overlooking Inchmarnock SW of Rothesay. To one corner has been added a tiny round turret 3.2m in diameter containing three shot-holes, but without any obvious means of access to the room inside.

MINGARY NM 502631

On a promontory overlooking the Sound of Mull, the Island of Coll and the mouth of Loch Sunart is a small 13th century court probably built by the MacDonalds of Islay. In the mid 14th century it was granted along with Ardnamurchan to Angus MacIan, a kinsman of John MacDonald, Lord of the Isles, and first of the MacIans of Ardnamurchan. The castle was occupied by James IV during two of his expeditions to the Western Isles. Sir Donald MacDonald of Lochalsh besieged the castle in 1515 whilst trying to lay claim to the Lordship of the Isles. He finally captured and dismantled it in 1517. In 1588 John MacIan was captured by Lachlan MacLean of Duart during the latter's feud with the MacDonalds. The MacLeans and a force of Spaniards from an Armada galleon then besieged Mingary Castle but had to withdrew after the neighbouring clans appeared in force to relieve it. By this time the Earls of Argyll were the feudal superiors of Ardnamurchan and in 1612 the 7th Earl allowed his brother-in-law Donald Campbell to occupy the castle and install a keeper within it. The MacIans were unable to withstand Campbell usurpation of their territory and were virtually wiped out. In 1644 the castle was besieged and captured by Alisdair MacDonald and was occupied by his forces until captured in 1647 by General Leslie. In 1696 Archibald, 10th Earl of Argyll granted Ardnamurchan to Alexander Campbell of Lochnell and his son Duncan. They built the north range of buildings. The estate was sold in 1723 to Alexander Murray who resided in the castle whilst supervising his programme of agricultural improvements and mineral exploitation. He died in debt in 1743 and the Campbells re-occupied the castle, which held a Hanovarian garrison 59 strong early in 1746. Ardnamurchan passed c1770 to James Riddell whose descendants held it until 1848. The north range was probably habitable as late as 1838 but the castle must have been abandoned soon afterwards.

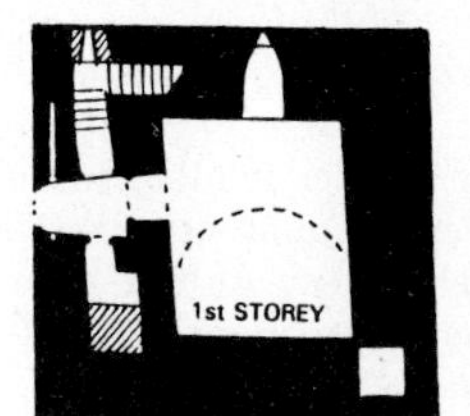

Plans of Moy Castle

Moy Castle

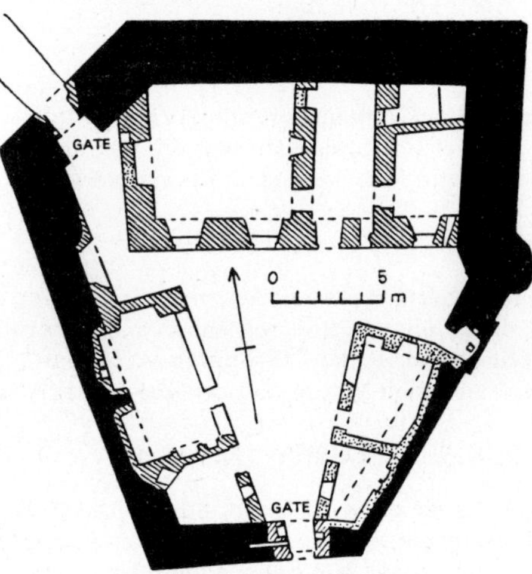

Plan of Mingary Castle

Mingary Castle has a hexagonal court about 18m across enclosed by a wall which is 1.8m thick and 8.5m high on the southern seaward sides but is thickened and heightened to 2.7m and 14m respectively on the north, where a ditch up to 9m wide isolates the site. A narrow entrance with a renewed outer opening lies in the short NW side and there is a late 16th century postern with a draw-bar slot in the south wall. The north side now contains an 18th century house with a scale-and-platt stair between pairs of rooms of uneven sizes on each of three storeys, but is clear from the original second and third storey north windows and east latrines, and the provision of a third storey mural chamber lighted by a twin-lancet window, that there has always been a range in this position. Other 18th century service ranges, probably of the 1720s and 1770s respectively lie on the west and east sides of the court, the curtain on the east side having been thinned at the lowest level to make more space for the latter. The west range contained an apartment over a kitchen and adjoins an original latrine in the curtain. On the north side the original parapet has been thickened against cannon-fire in the late 16th century. To seaward the parapet was entirely rebuilt and bartizans provided on the southern corners.

MOY NM 616247

This tower on a rock at the head of Loch Buie on Mull was probably built in the early 15th century by Hector, brother of Lachlan MacLean of Duart. The castle is first mention in a charter of 1494 confirming John MacLean of Loch Buie in possession of lands here previously held from the Lord of the Isles. It was probably Hector MacLean, who died c1614 who remodelled to upper parts of the tower. In 1679 Hector MacLean, aided by the Campbells, seized Moy Castle from his father Lachlan, who was imprisoned in Duart Castle under Campbell custody for several months. In 1690 the castle was garrisoned by the Earl of Argyll with 24 men under Colin Campbell of Braglen, the Jacobite MacLean laird having recently submitted to the government. The castle was abandoned in favour of a new house nearby c1752. Some years later John MacLean of Lochbuie was fined for imprisoning two neighbouring lairds in the castle, an incident recalled by Boswell in his journal on his visit with Johnson in 1773.

The tower is 10.7m square and contains over a vaulted cellar a hall and bedroom, plus an attic within a parapet with added angle rounds on the east corners. From the entrance on the east side, where there are very slight traces of an oval barmkin 27m long by 15m wide, straight flights of steps ascend around the SE corner to the hall. A spiral stair in the SW corner then rises to the wall-walk. The hall has three windows, a latrine in the NW corner, and a tiny chamber in the SE corner. There was no fireplace either in this room or that above, but one was later provided in the upper room, which has two original windows.

RAREY NM 831206

NE of the 18th century house is a promontory rising 28m above the River Euchar. A ditch 11m wide and 2m deep on the NW isolates an area 30m by 22m. Excavations in 1957 found only a layer of charcoal from burnt-out buildings. Rarey was given in 1313 to Dugall Campbell of Lochawe but later passed to the MacDougalls.

Mingary Castle

Rothesay Castle

ROTHESAY NS 086646 HS

A castle at Rothesay is first mentioned c1228-30 when a garrison installed by Walter, High Steward and Justiciar of Scotland, was besieged by Norsemen contesting his possession of Bute. The defenders threw down burning pitch and lead on the assailants but the castle was captured when the Norsemen made a cover of boards and hewed their way through the castle wall "because the stone was soft". This probably means that the now-missing jambs of a postern doorway on the west side were hacked away, as it is highly unlikely that a solid wall 2.5m thick could be breached with hand-axes. In 1263 the castle was again occupied by Norsemen until King Haakon's defeat later that year. It was strengthened after being returned to the Stewarts, the postern being blocked and four round flanking towers added. Rothesay was occupied by the English during the Wars of Independance and was taken by them for John Balliol in 1334. It was recaptured shortly afterwards by Sir Colin Campbell after the governor Sir Adam Lisle was killed in a battle on the slopes of Barone Hill.

With Robert Stewart's accession to the throne in 1371 Rothesay became a favoured royal residence. The castle was besieged c1455 by the Lord of the Isles during James II's struggle with the Black Douglases. Royal interest in it was revived under James IV when courts were held there and the castle used as a base for naval operations against the MacDonalds and other turbulent clans in the Western Isles. Ninian Stewart was made hereditary keeper and work begun in 1512 on extending the gatehouse to provide a spacious upper hall. The work was left incomplete when James IV was killed at Flodden and was only completed long after his son James V came of age. During his troubled minority the Master of Ruthven burnt the town although the castle managed to hold out. The work was probably still unfinished when James V died in 1542, and in 1544 the castle was captured by the Earl of Lennox for Henry VIII of England. Under James VI the castle was little used and it was probably in a neglected state when James Stewart, Sherriff of Bute, garrisoned it for Charles I against the Covenanters in the 1630s. He later fled to Ireland and the castle held a Cromwellian garrison until it was withdrawn in 1659. The castle was burnt by Argyll during his rebellion in 1685. The Stewart Sheriffs of Bute became Earls of Bute in 1703 and were later elevated to Marquis. They lived in the Mansion House nearby, now the Bute estate office. The ruined castle was partly patched up by the 2nd Marquis in 1816-17, and by the 3rd Marquis in 1872-9. Finally in 1900 the collapsed eastern side of the hall was rebuilt, although the room was not opened to the public until 1970, the ruin then being a monument in state care (now Historic Scotland).

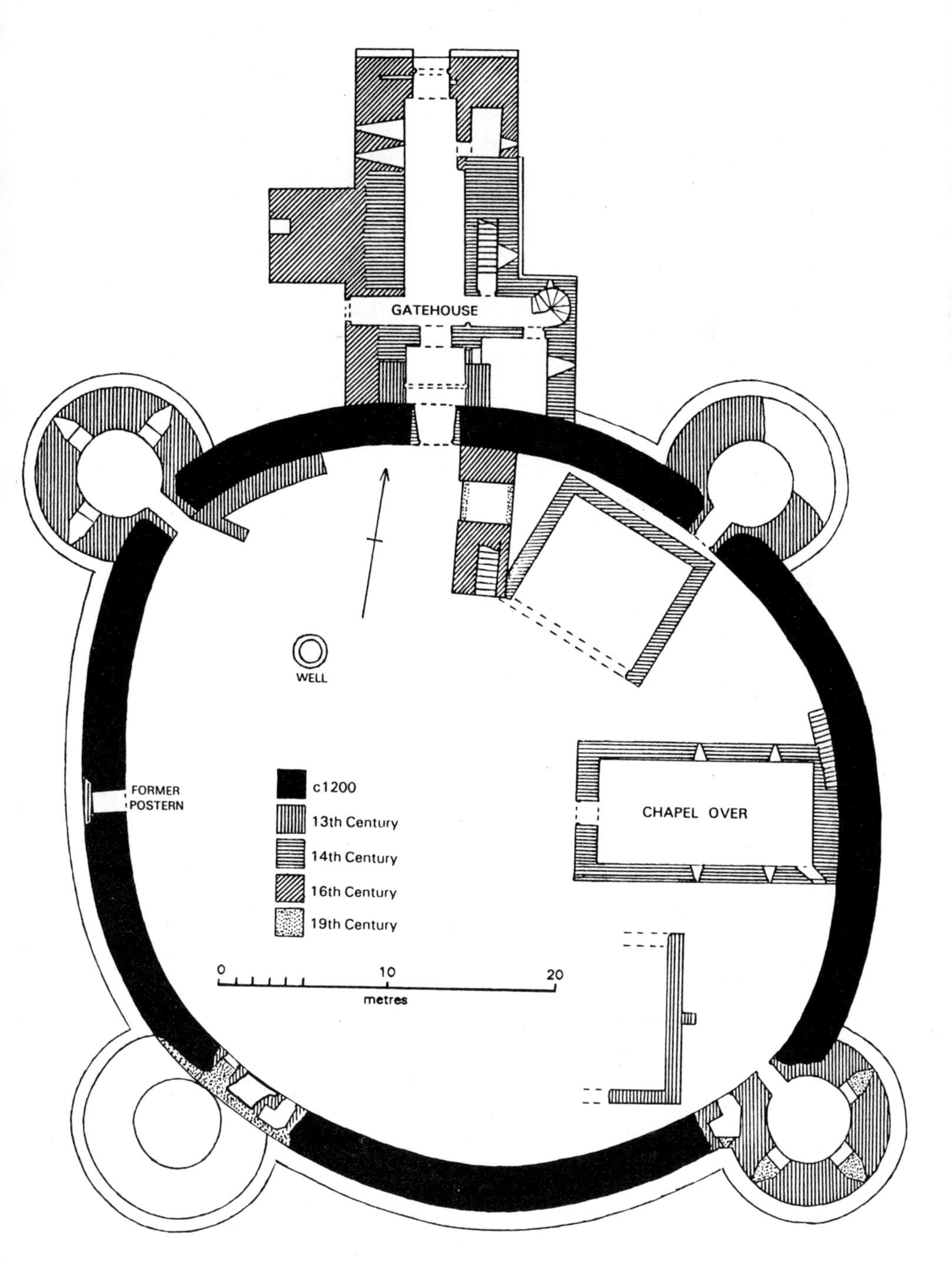

Plan of Rothesay Castle

Rothesay Castle

The castle consists of an ovoid court with an average diameter of 42m. There are round towers to the NE, SE, SW, and NW, and a north gatehouse extending out across a level berm and half the width of a wet moat. The towers have battered bases and a similar base has been added to the western and southern sections of the curtain wall. The NW tower is called the Pigeon Tower as its fourth storey has been adapted later as a dovecot. The lowest storey has three arrow-loops, all blocked. Much less has survived of the other towers. There are latrines made in the curtain wall beside those to the SE and SW. None of them contains a stair and the upper levels must have been reached from the wall-walk which was itself reached from the court by stairs on the NW and east sides. Abutting against the east steps is a ruined block containing the chapel of St Michael over an undercroft. The chapel was reached by an outside stair on the south side and retains several windows, a piscina, a sacrement house and evidence of the screen which separated the nave from the chancel. Although early Gothic in style, the chapel must be of the time of Robert II or III (1371-1406). Within the court are the lower parts of two other buildings and a well, now mostly filled in.

A modern timber bridge crosses the outer part of the moat to the gatehouse. This is a composite structure of several periods. Originally the court was entered through a simple arch. Later this was narrowed with jambs opening the other way and a small projection added on just big enough to contain a room from which a portcullis was operated. The crossloop opening off the wide stair leading up to the hall indicates that this survives from an extension of c1290-1310 which would have been large enough to contain the lord's residence, whilst the great hall of that period was probably on the west side of the court. As rebuilt in the 16th century the gatehouse was lengthened northwards, widened, and a latrine turret and postern provided on the west side. The area at the south end of the hall has not been re-roofed. This part communicated by passages formed by roofing over the curtain wall-walks with the adjacent drum tower rooms. The third storey of bedrooms over the hall is also open to the sky.

SADDELL NR 789315

This building, now a holiday home owned by the Landmark Trust, was erected in 1508-12 by David Hamilton, Bishop of Argyll, to replace Achadun Castle on Lismore. It was burned by the Earl of Sussex during his raid on Kintyre in 1558, then being held by the MacDonalds of Dunivaig. After they were forfeited Saddell passed to the Campbell Earl of Argyll. In 1650 it was leased to William Ralston on condition that he carry out various repairs which are still evident in the structure. In the late 18th century a new mansion was built nearby for the Campbell laird of Glensaddell and the barmkin was then made into an office court, being in later years used to accommodate estate workers. Incorporated in the group of 18th and 19th century outbuildings lies a 17m long section of the barmkin east wall 1.4m thick and 3.7m high, including a blocked gateway with a draw-bar slot. The fine tower house is 14.5m long by 8.5m wide over walls up to 1.6m thick and 14m high. The tower has four storeys and an attic within a parapet carried on a chequer arrangement of corbelling. There are angle rounds and another round beside the caphouse over the stair. Each storey is divided into two rooms both served by a staircase by the cross-wall. The entrance at the foot of the stair is somewhat above the ground floor level so that there is room for a pit-prison reached from a hatch in the passage floor. The upper levels have rooms in the west corners flanking the fireplace flue of the kitchen at the level of the modest hall.

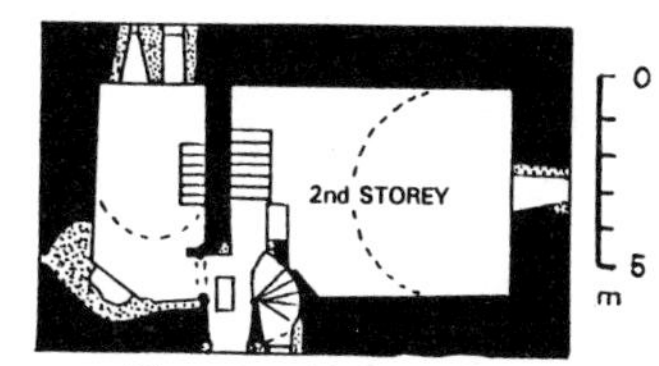

Plan of Saddell Castle

Doorway at Saddell

Saddell Castle

SKIPNESS NR 907577

In 1261 Dugald, son of Sween, held a castle at Skipness, presumably with the MacDonalds of Islay and Kintyre as overlords and it is likely that he had built the hall house and the chapel of St Columba lying just 17m to the south of it. Skipness passed to Walter Stewart, Earl of Menteith in 1262. In c1300 the hall and chapel were incorporated into a walled court probably representing an attempt by the MacDonalds, now back in possession, to defend themselves against the MacDougalls of Lorn, who were in alliance with Edward I of England. After John MacDonald, Lord of the Isles was forfeited in 1493, James IV granted the castle and barony to Sir Duncan Forester, although they quickly passed to Archibald, 2nd Earl of Argyll. The Campbells repaired and garrisoned the castle in the 1640s and held out against the raids led by Colkitto MacDonald. In 1685 the castle was ordered to be destroyed but the then laird, Walter Campbell, successfully petitioned against this. However the castle seems to have been abandoned as a laird's residence not long afterwards. In the late 18th century it became a farm steading, the internal walls of the hall and chapel then being dismantled and offices, removed in 1898, built against the walls.

The hall-house measured 17.2m by 11.2m over walls 2.2m thick above a battered plinth. No features survive in the lowest storey which is now pierced by a later archway but the upper storey living room, which was probably undivided, has a latrine in the NW corner and a window in each of the three surviving walls. The chapel was 19m long by 8m wide. Three lancet windows remain in the surviving south wall. West of them lies the gateway of the castle as rebuilt with a court 20m wide enclosed by walls 2m thick. The gateway projects slightly enabling flanking fire from side loops in a the tiny guard room from which the portcullis was operated. East of the chapel a tower 10m wide projects 5.8m beyond the curtain. It appears that a hall built over the east end of the chapel projected into the tower at second storey level. The west curtain has a series of cross-loops at second storey level and has a square latrine tower projecting where it meets the SW corner of the hall-house. A new private room with a projecting latrine turret at the NE corner was built east of the hall-house. In the early 16th century this became the second storey of what was raised up into a four storey tower, and a postern was opened in the east curtain immediately beside it. The tower has a vaulted basement and a corbelled parapet with angle-rounds around an attic which is still roofed. The parapet contains shot-holes and rises 15.7m above the ground. A former range against the east curtain has left few traces.

Skipness Castle

Skipness Castle

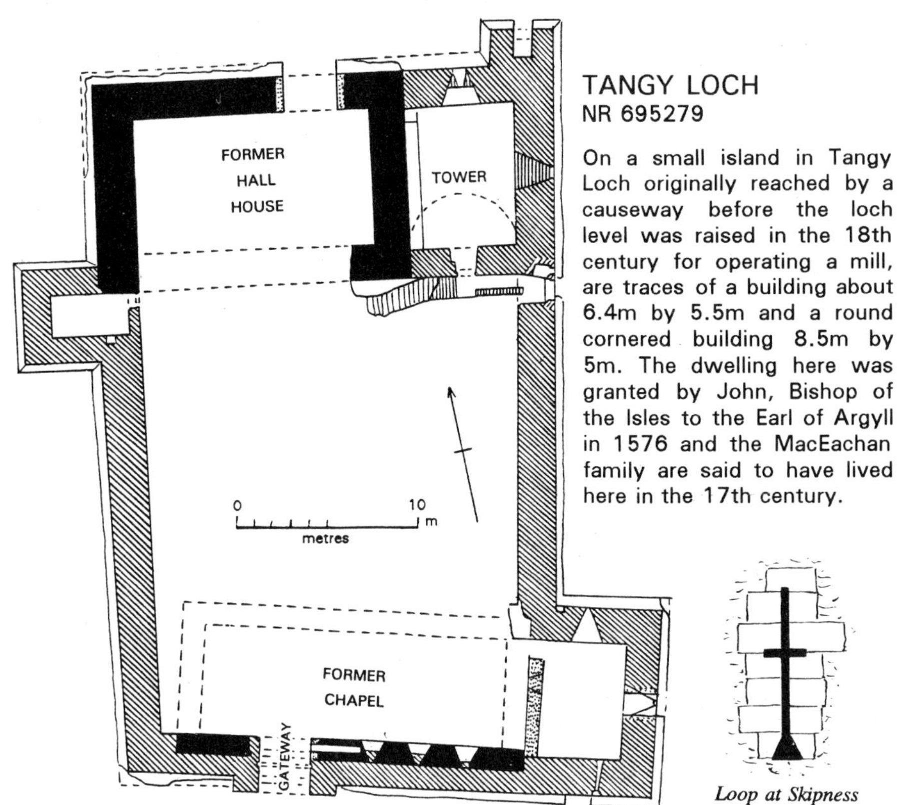

Plan of Skipness Castle

Loop at Skipness

TANGY LOCH
NR 695279

On a small island in Tangy Loch originally reached by a causeway before the loch level was raised in the 18th century for operating a mill, are traces of a building about 6.4m by 5.5m and a round cornered building 8.5m by 5m. The dwelling here was granted by John, Bishop of the Isles to the Earl of Argyll in 1576 and the MacEachan family are said to have lived here in the 17th century.

TARBERT NR 867687 F

The original 13th century castle here was either built by a dependent of the MacDonalds of Islay or by Alexander II. Certainly the plan form, a towerless rectangle 43m by 38m with thick walled ranges on all sides and a gatehouse in the middle of the NE side resembles that of the royal castle of Kincardine, probably of c1220-40. Only slight traces of this building, which had a round SW corner, now survive. A large outer bailey was added by Robert Bruce in the mid 1320s. It contained a hall with timber posts and a thatched roof and extended nearly 90m to the NE, ending with a wall with a pair of wide spaced round towers 9m in diameter probably with a gateway between them. Traces of the SE and NE defences of this court and of the short SW wall with two square towers also remain, but the long NW side has vanished. Tarbat was then the largest castle in Argyll and was regarded as a place of strategic importance. In the 1490s James IV recovered the castle from the MacDonalds and the Earls of Argyll were made keepers of it from 1504 until the 1680s, although the MacAlisters became hereditary constables. During the rebellion of 1685 Walter Campbell of Skipness captured the castle from a garrison installed by the Earl of Argyll. Probably the only part of the site then in occupation was the 16th century tower house built midway along the SW side of the outer bailey. It measured 12.5m by 8.3m over walls 2.1m thick which still partly stand four storeys high on the NE and NW. It is entered on the NE side through a later forework beside a short section of the old curtain. The vaulted basement with a loop at each end remains intact. The hall had its own separate entrance above that below. A big window embrasure remains at the far end of the same wall, and there was probably another opposite, with perhaps a fireplace in the SE end wall between them. A stair lighted by a loop with a bottom roundel rises around the west corner. The third storey has windows on the NW and NE and a passage with dumbbell-shaped loops runs eastward from the latter. A fireplace remains in the NW wall at the 4th storey level.

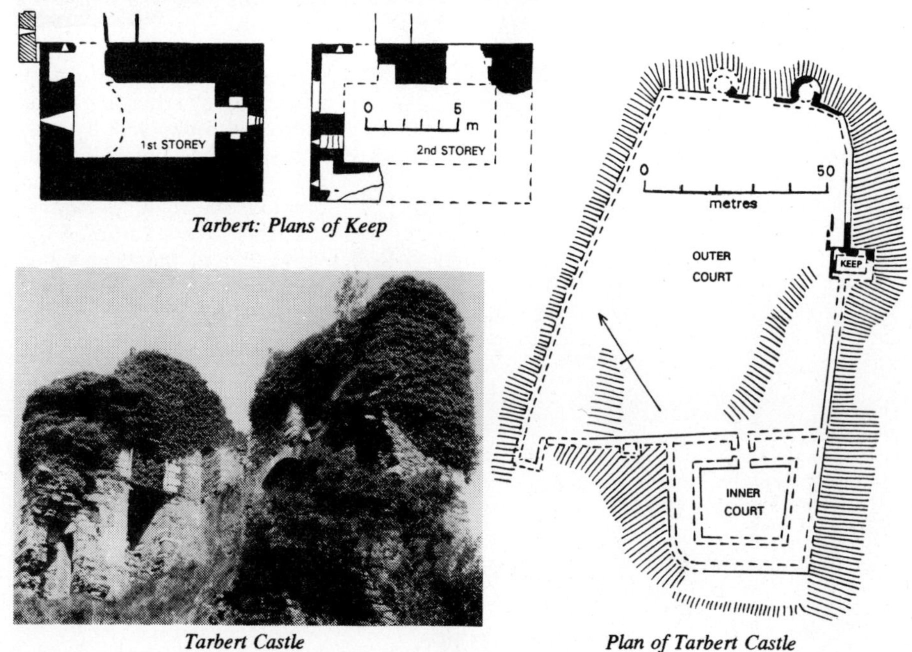

Tarbert: Plans of Keep

Tarbert Castle

Plan of Tarbert Castle

TORRAN NM 878044

On a rocky knoll rising 13m above the north side of the narrows of Caol Chaorann are footings of a late building 14.5m long by 7m wide with what was probably a latrine turret 4.5m wide projecting 3m from the east end of the south side. To the north was a small court roughly 13m square apparently containing a clutter of buildings. The structures are likely to be of the period immediately after "Mekill Torrane" was sold to John Campbell of Inverliever by the grandson of Sir John Campbell of Calder, who had obtained the estate in 1529 from the Campbells of Argyll.

TOWARD NS 118678 F

The Lamont family had their chief seat here although they were originally styled "of Inveryne". The tower at the south end of the promontory at the south end of the East Cowal peninsular was probably erected after a charter was granted in 1472 confirming him in possession of lands here and making those of Inveryne into a barony. The tower measures 11.8m by 8.8m over walls mostly 1.7m thick. The SW corner still stands 13m high to the parapet corbelling. The entrance is in the east wall at hall level beside this corner, and there is a latrine nearby in the south wall. Little else survives of this storey, which was vaulted and had a spiral stair leading up in the NE corner, and service stairs in the northern corners leading to the two vaulted spaces below which are much better preserved. Just one south window with seats remains of the third storey. The smaller western part of the lowest storey was divided into two levels each with its own separate entrance through the cross-wall from the larger east chamber. The northern half of the lowest level was later divided off, perhaps to create a prison.

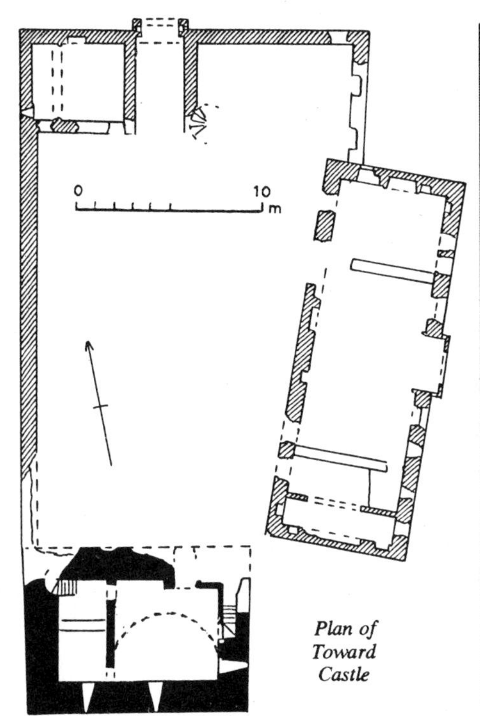

Plan of Toward Castle

Toward Castle

Sir John Lamont purchased further lands at Toward from James V in 1535 and in 1563 entertained Queen Mary at the castle. His grandson Sir James is thought to have built the court 17m wide extending 27m to the north. In the north wall, which is just 0.9m thick is a finely decorated gateway arch projecting very slightly and having loops looking along the walls outward of the main gate. West of the gate, filling the NW corner, are remains of a kitchen or bakehouse. The single storey house on the east side of the court was probably added c1620 by Sir Coll Lamont. It has a central hall with a fireplace in a breast on the east side, a kitchen on the south with the fireplace area almost as big as the modest working area, and a private room at the north end. Sir James Lamont supported Alasdair MacDonald's attacks on the Campbells and in consequence his seat at Toward was besieged in May 1646 by a large force of Campbells. After the wall was breached by cannon Sir James agreed to surrender on honourable terms but in fact the garrisons of Toward and Asgog were massacred in Dunoon churchyard, this being one of the charges laid against the Marquis of Argyll and leading to his execution in 1661. The Lamonts subsequently lived at Ardlamont, and ruined Toward was sold in 1809, being acquired by Kirkman Findlay c1818.

WESTER KAMES NS 062681

Not far north of Kames Castle is the tower of Edinbeg or Wester Kames built by the Spens family c1600. It passed to the Grahams c1670 and then to the Stewarts of Bute, being restored from ruin in 1905 to serve as a residence for the family of the Marquis of Bute. It measures 7.5m by 6.3 and contains a hall over a vaulted kitchen and cellar, and two upper storeys. The three lowest levels are connected by a stair in a round turret engaging the NW corner. A narrower stair is then corbelled out in one of the re-entrant angles to serve the top storey mostly in the roof and a much restored square caphouse on the main turret. There is a round bartizan on the SE corner.

OTHER CASTLES, MOTTES, & HOUSES IN ARGYLL

ACHADUNAN NN 200135 Mound 6m high with summit 28m long but only 2m wide as a result of erosion by River Fyne. 10m wide ditch on south and east.

ACHANELID NS 006873 Rectangular platform 5m high with River Ruel to east, and ditch to south. Foundations on summit 28m long by 12 to 18m wide.

A'CHRANNOG NR 294674 Moated platform 16m square with 4m diameter corner bastions on Islay. Perhaps built by Sir James MacDonald in 1615.

ARDFERN NM 791028 Footings of building 10m by 6m over walls 1.3m thick on a hillock NE of Duine cottage, near Loch Craignish. Campbell of Corranmore seat.

BALLIEMEANOCH NS 102999 This 7m high platform with a summit 24m by 20m half filled with footings of a house on the SW side is perhaps late medieval.

BALYMORE NR 922833 Mostly natural mound rising 9m from ditch to summit 24m by 15m with two burial enclosures. Seat of the MacEwens of Otter.

CASTLE CRAWFORD NS 179786 23m long mound 2m high by Dunoon golf course.

CASTLES FARM NN 137296 Mound by the farm may be the site of a 16th century MacGregor castle said to have been burnt in 1611 by Sir Duncan Campbell.

DUN AN OIR NS 006878 Mound rising 15m to top 30m by 24m near Achanelid Farm.

EILEAN NA CIRCE NR 767892 A drystone parapet encloses the SE and SW sides of a court 33m by 15m with two buildings on the summit of a rock 100m offshore.

EILEAN TIGHE BHAIN NN 043249 The lower part of a building 9.5m by 7m of c1600 lies in the middle of a natural island 25m in diameter in Loch Tromlee.

GARVIE NS 036903 There are no remains of a 16th century castle of the Campbells.

GLEN SHIRA NN 113107 Much altered mound beside Dubh Loch with possible buried stonework. Pont's map c1590 shows a residence named Ylendow here.

LARGIE NR 708483 A fragment of the side wall of the house of the MacDonalds of Largie survived by High Rhunahaorine farm until the late 19th century.

MACHARIOCH NR 726094 Natural mound 800m west of farm rising 2m above ditch on west, south and east to a summit 7.5m in diameter.

OLD AUCHAVOULIN NS 116681 One wall 1.1m thick and 14.5m long stands 6m high of a Campbell house. Pont (c1590) shows a tower house amd court here.

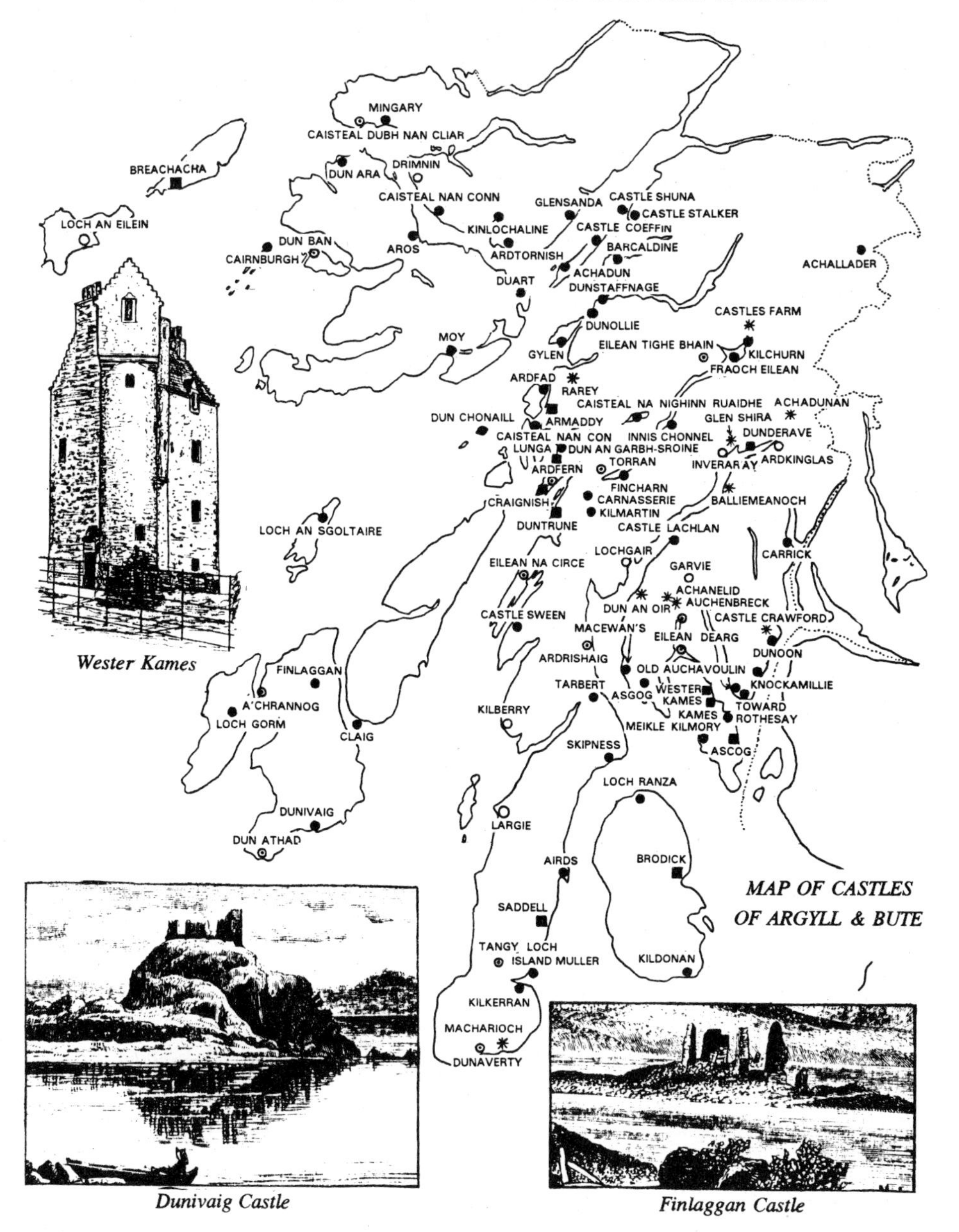

Wester Kames

MAP OF CASTLES OF ARGYLL & BUTE

Dunivaig Castle

Finlaggan Castle

CAITHNESS, SUTHERLAND, ROSS & CROMARTY

ACHASTLE ND 116227

Cordiner's engraving of c1788 shows Achastle as having two towers connected by a curtain wall crowning cliffs above two streams. The remains indeed lie close to a steep drop to the confluence of the Berriedale and Langwell Waters. The north and west sides facing gently rising ground towards Langwell house are protected by a ditch. The castle is said to have been built by John Beg, a younger son of the Earl of Sutherland and lies just 0.5km NW of Berriedale Castle, seat of a neighbouring estate of the Oliphants. Footings of walls about 1.3m thick surround a court 21.7m long by 14m wide with a pair of rectangular turrets 4m wide on the northern corners. There was also a rectangular building projecting from the east half of the south wall.

ACKERGILL ND 352547

In 1354 Ackergill passed to John Keith of Inverugie on his marriage to one of the two heiresses of Reginald Cheyne. The late 15th century tower is first mentioned in 1510 in a document naming Gilbert Mowat of Brabister Myir as its captain. By 1538 the male line of the Inverugie Keiths had failed and Ackergill was granted to William, the Earl Marischal, head of the senior branch of the Keiths. The Keiths were frequently at loggerheads with their close neighbours at Girnigoe, the Sinclairs. In 1547 the Crown granted remission to George Sinclair, Earl of Caithness, and some of his kinsmen for the treasonable capture and holding of the castle and the detention of Alexander Keith, its captain, and his servant John Skarlet, in the castles of Girnigoe, Braal, and elsewhere. In 1593 the Earl Marischal complained to the Privy Council that his brother Robert Keith had forcibly occupied his house of Ackergill with the intention of molesting the neighbourhood. Robert Keith was thus proclaimed a rebel. In 1598 the Earl complained again to Privy Council that John Keith of Subster and his two sons and others had come by night "and ledderit (scaled with ladders) the walls of his place at Ackergill" and spoiled the house and harmed his servants and now "keeps the place". Ackergill was neglected after it passed to the Sinclairs in the early 17th century. It was garrisoned and provisioned against the invasion by Sir Robert Gordon against the Earl of Caithness in 1623, but was surrendered without a fight. The tower is said to have been garrisoned for Cromwell in 1651. Ackergill later passed to the Dunbars of Hempriggs, being in 1726 referred to as a "strong house yet in repair and with a new house lately built between it and the sea". The new house has since been much modified and extended, and the tower itself was remodelled in the 19th century with a new entrance, enlarged hall windows, and the battlements much rebuilt.

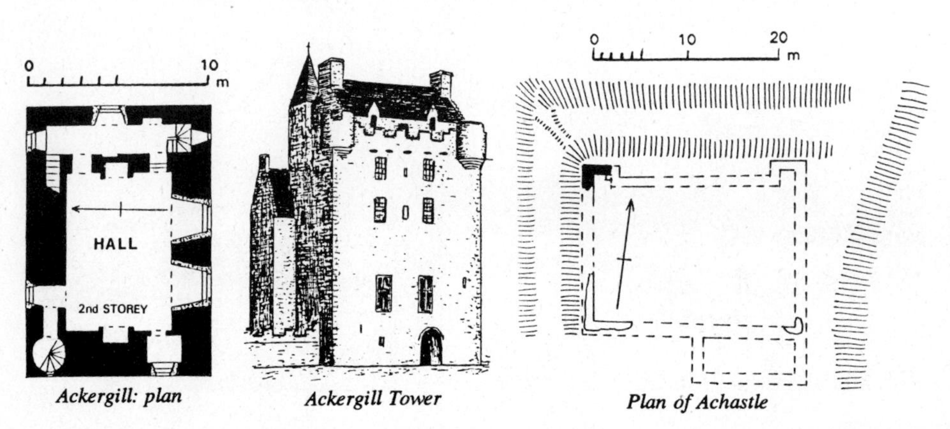

Ackergill: plan *Ackergill Tower* *Plan of Achastle*

Ackergill Tower stands on flat ground sloping gently towards the sea. There are no remains of any outer walls or buildings, although we can be sure such existed as the walls scaled with ladders in 1598 can hardly have been those of the lofty five storey tower. It measures 14.7m by 10.3m and has vaults over the cellar and the 7m high hall above with a musicians' gallery at the east end. These two levels are connected by a straight stair. A spiral stair at the other end rises to the battlements and ends in a caphouse which is modern in its present form. There are rebuilt roundels on the other three corners and gargoyles drain the wall-walk. The cellar was later given a fireplace and windows and in 1762 was being used as a kitchen. The pairs of rooms on each of the third and fourth storeys have closets contained within the walls.

ARDVRECK NC 240236

This ruined tower on a peninsular extending from the northern shore of remote Loch Assynt was built c1600 by the MacLeods of Assynt. In 1646 Domhnall Ban MacLeod successfully held out against a Royalist attack. The Marquis of Montrose took refuge with Neil Macleod, the 11th chief, here in 1650 after his defeat at Carbisdale, but was was betrayed to the Covenant authorities. In revenge the loyalist MacKenzies, the MacDonalds of Glengarry, and the MacLeods of Skye descended on Assynt and ravaged Neil's lands. In 1654 the MacKenzies returned again and seized a ship lying off Lochinver carrying much needed victuals and animals for Neil and his clansmen. He was denounced a rebel by Charles II in 1672 and the Earl of Seaforth obtained a commission of Fire and Sword against the MacLeods of Assynt. The castle was burnt and, after taking over the estate, the MacKenzies built a new, purely domestic, house called Eddarcalda at the SE end of the loch. In 1760 Assynt was put up for sale. Hugh MacLeod of Geanies, the rightful heir, was outbid by the Earl of Sutherland, but shortly afterwards the new house was itself burnt by a party of Jacobite MacRaes.

The tower is 10m long and was about 9m wide (the north wall has gone). The basement had a pair of vaulted cellars linked by a passage on the south side. Originally the passage connected with a round tower on the SE corner. The tower contained a now-vanished entrance and a stair to the third storey. Above it are remains of a square caphouse containing two levels of rooms reached by a stair corbelled out over the western re-entrant angle. The second storey of the main block has signs of a vaulted passage along the south side, but the upper rooms are too ruined for us to be certain of their arrangements.

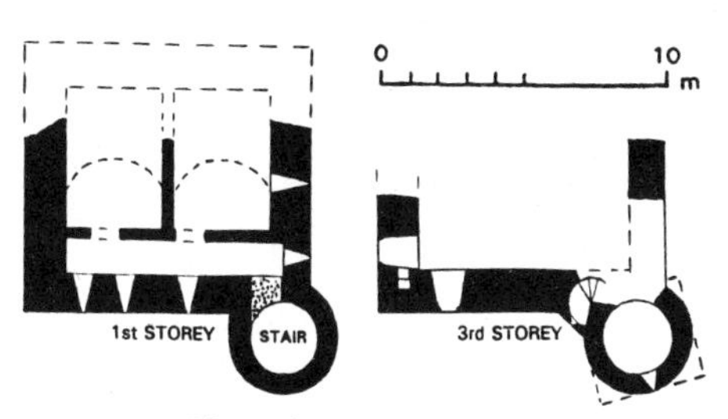

Plans of Ardvreck Castle

Ardvreck Castle

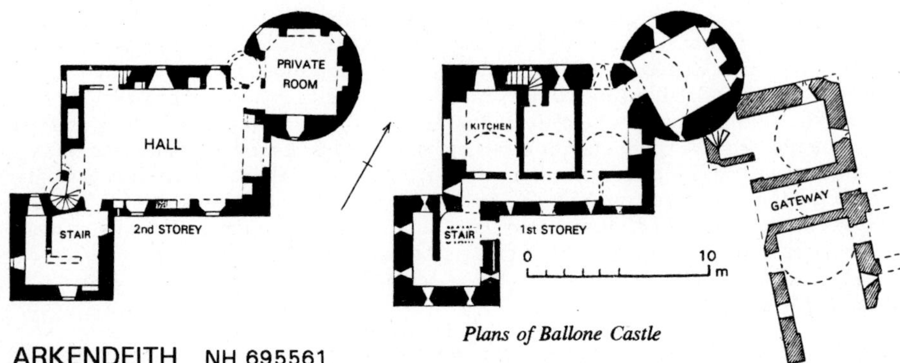

Plans of Ballone Castle

ARKENDEITH NH 695561

Beside the farmhouse is a small fragment of a late 16th century tower of the Bruces of Kinloss, ancestors of the Earls of Elgin. The place name is derived from the Gaelic Airc-Eoin-Dubh meaning the refuge of Black John, a noted freebooter. The lowest storey remained complete in 1883 but only a 6m long end wall 1m thick and just 2m high now remains. It shows traces of a loop and a cellar vault. A short length of an adjacent side wall retains a rectangular doorway with a draw-bar slot in the jamb.

Balnagown Castle

ASSYNT NC 195250

Fragments of dry-stone walling up to 1.5m thick, and traces of a retaining wall round the edge of an island, are relics of a fortress recorded as having been given c1343 to Torquil MacLeod of Lewis. It was superseded by Ardvreck Castle (page 75).

Ballone Castle

Bartizan at Ballone Castle

BALLONE NH 929837

This Z-plan castle above the North Sea at the north end of the Tarbat peninsular was built c1580-1600 by the Dunbars of Tarbat. It later passed to Rory Mor MacKenzie. The castle seems to have only been occupied until the 1680s and has been a ruin ever since, although it is currently being restored by Lachlan Stewart. The entrance (with a draw-bar slot) lies at the foot of a former main stair contained within a tower 5.9m square boldly projecting from the south corner of a main block 11.8m long by 8m wide. The stair only took up part of the interior of the tower, leaving space for L-plan rooms along the outer sides, the lowest of which has six double splayed gunports covering all four sides. There are five more such gunports in a square vaulted cellar in the base of a round tower 6.9m in diameter projecting from the north corner. From the entrance a passage runs along the SE side of the main block to connect a kitchen with a fireplace in the SW end wall, a wine cellar in the middle with a service stair and another gunport, and another cellar beyond, from which that in the round tower is reached. At the end of the passage, tucked in the east corner, is a vaulted strong-room. The hall was a fine apartment with two windows in each side wall, one in each end wall, a fireplace to the SE, and a latrine in the west corner. The round tower contains a withdrawing room plus a suite of two other rooms for the laird reached from the hall by a stair in a turret corbelled out over the western re-entrant angle. This stair also served the rooms at this end of the third storey and the attic in the main block. A similar stair, also facing west, gave access to two upper rooms over the main stair and the upper rooms at the SW end of the main block. The outermost corner of the stair tower has a round bartizan of the usual kind. On the west and east corners of the main block are bartizans of a kind rare in Scotland, although they have square counterparts in Ireland. They are set below the eaves of the main roof and are furnished with shot-holes and have machicolations ingeniously worked in between wide corbels ornamentally arranged in alternate rows. At a slightly later date a now much damaged two storey block was added to one side of the round tower to enclose a small court between the main building and the edge of the drop to the sea. The range contained offices flanking an entrance passage with a spiral stair in a wing next to the tower leading up to sleeping accommodation above.

BALNAGOWN NH 763752

Lands here were given by William, Earl of Ross, to his half-brother Hugh Ross c1350. The family were often at odds with their neighbours and in 1569 it was reported to the Privy Council that Alexander, 8th laird, kept the neighbourhood in terror, and so "herreit and wrakkit" some adjacent Crown tenants that they were unable to pay their rents. When the 18th chief died in 1711, Balnagown went to another family called Ross, but unconnected, being descendants of the de Roos family from Renfrewshire. A castle here is first mentioned in 1490 and the vaulted basement of the west range is of about that period. It was a tower house with its NE corner slightly projecting to contain the staircase. In the 1590s this part was remodelled and given a bartizan at the SE corner and a SW stair turret corbelled out just above ground. In 1668 David Ross added a NE wing to make an L-plan with a stair tower in the re-entrant angle. His initials and arms and those of his wife Lady Anne Stewart appear on a fine second storey fireplace in the main block and on the south gable is a stone dated 1672. Soon after Admiral Sir John Lockhart Ross came to Balnagown in 1763, he added a three storey block in the re-entrant angle, the stair tower there being removed. He also had a new entrance made in the middle of the west front. In 1818-27 Sir Charles Lockhart Ross added a verandah and a round NW turret, and in 1832-5 the entrance was moved to the south end and a new range added. Further work was executed in 1840-1.

BERRIEDALE ND 122224 F

Berriedale formed part of the third of Caithness which belonged to Reginald Cheyne in the first half of the 14th century and which later passed to the Sutherlands and then to the Oliphants. The castle may be of 15th century origin but is not mentioned until the 16th century when Laurence, Lord Oliphant, purchased it from his nephew Andrew. In 1606 it was sold to the Earl of Caithness. The castle stands on a sheer sided rock which shelters an anchorage at the mouth of Berriedale Water. The valley is isolated and was difficult to reach overland but the castle owners would have mostly travelled by sea. Only slight remains exist of the buildings which stood on either side of a long narrow court 53m wide by 17m in maximum width. On the landward side are footings of a thick screen wall some distance below which is a ditch once crossed by a timber bridge.

BORVE NC 725642

On a promontory projecting from the east side of Farr Point on the remote north coast of Sutherland are footings of a wall 2m thick of a tower built by the MacKays in the late 15th or early 16th century, and other slight remains.

Berriedale Castle

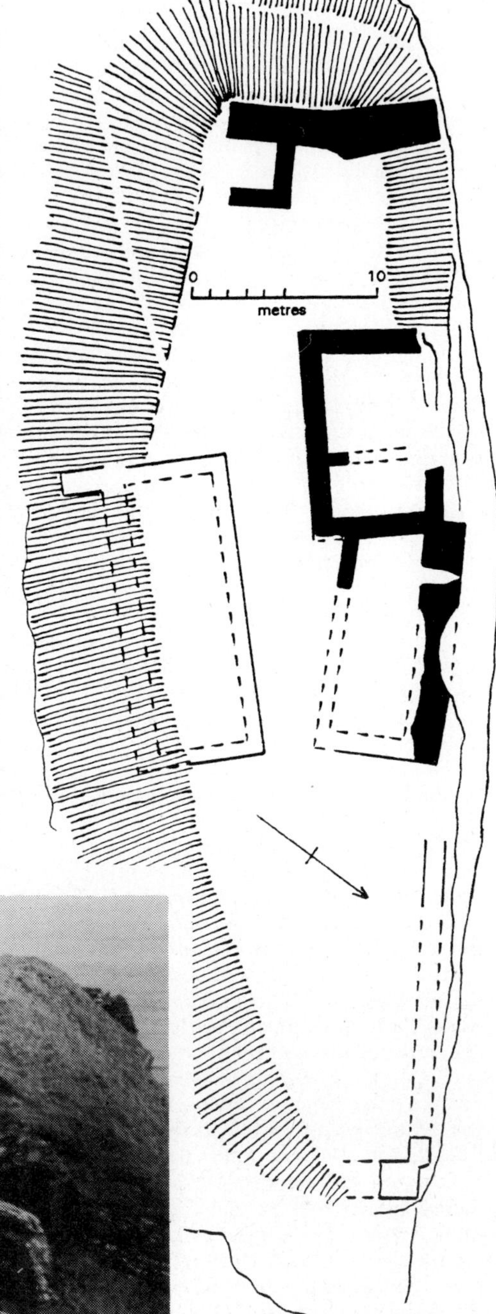

Plan of Berriedale Castle

BRAAL ND 139601 V

The ruined tower house near the west bank of the River Thurso 1km NE of Halkirk is probably early or mid 14th century. In 1375 it was resigned by Alexander of Ard to Robert II, who gave Braal to his second son, David Stewart, created Earl Palatine. James II granted Braal in 1452 to Admiral Sir George Crichton but by 1547 it had passed to the Sinclairs. In the early 17th century they began building a new mansion close to the tower. It is said to remained unfinished, construction being perhaps interrupted by Sir Robert Gordon's expedition of 1623. Everything above the cellar vaults appears to be of 1856 and later, and the block now forms several flats. The tower measures 11.5m by 10.6m over walls averaging 2.4m thick faced with long thin slabs. The entrance lies in the south wall at hall level. This room has two large and two small window embrasures, all fitted with seats and one having access to a latrine. The stone slabs in the NE corner may have been intended to form a fire-proof base for a brazier as there is no fireplace. The cellar below could only have been reached by a trap door in the wooden floor, and has a ventilation shaft to the south and loops with wide embrasures to the west and north. A stair in the south wall rises from the entrance to the lord's room on the third storey via an ante-room in the SE corner. This room has a fireplace but was not as well lighted as the hall. Both the southern corners have been altered, that at the SE having a buttress, whilst that to the SW is now rounded below and splayed off above. There was once a surrounding wet moat.

BRAHAN NG 512546

As predicted by the celebrated Brahan Seer, this castle has now vanished (it was demolished in 1953) and the present laird, a Matheson, lives in house created out of the old stables. The estate lies on a shelf to the north of the confluence of the River Conon and River Orrin. The castle was reconstructed c1600-10 by Kenneth MacKenzie of Kintail, whose son became the first Earl of Seaforth in 1623, and it was extended by their descendants in the 18th century.

Braal Castle

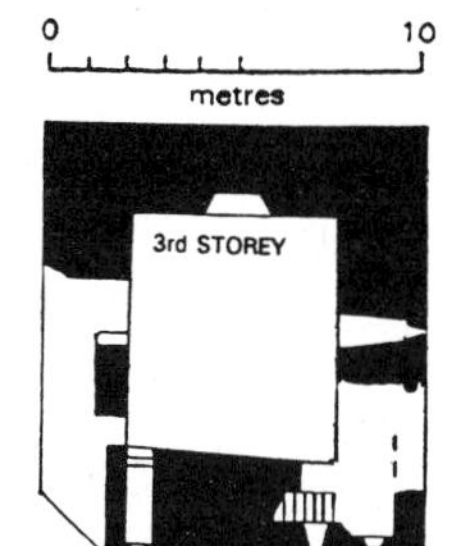

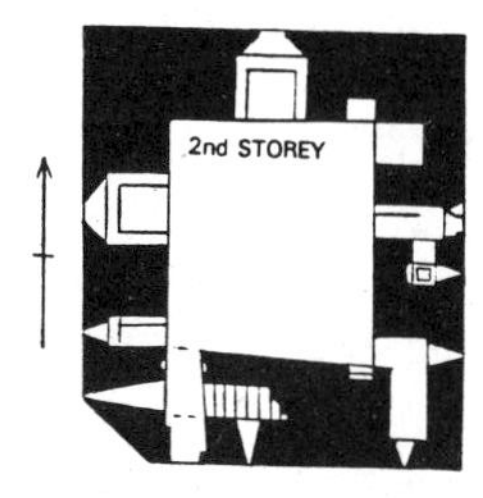

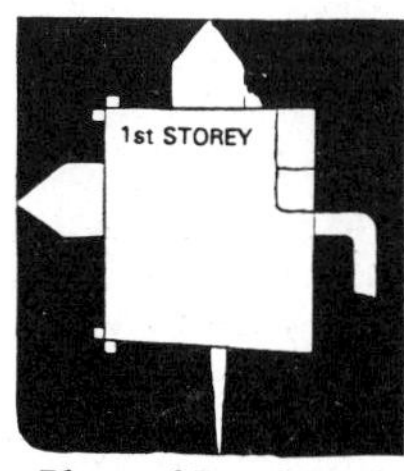

Plans of Braal Castle

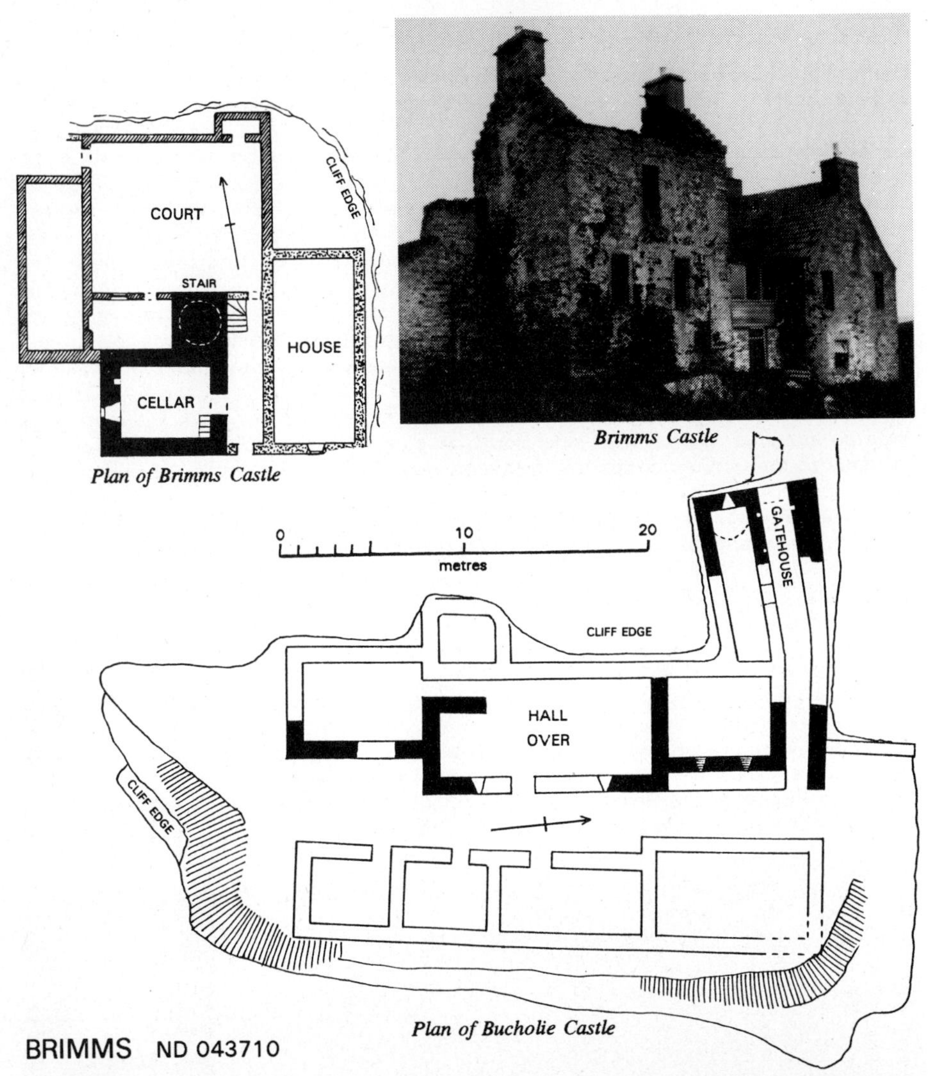

Plan of Brimms Castle

Brimms Castle

Plan of Bucholie Castle

BRIMMS ND 043710

This castle was built c1600 by a cadet branch of the Sinclairs of Dunbeath. It was inhabited until the 20th century but is now derelict, although some later farm buildings remain in use. It consists of a tiny L-plan tower with a court just 9.5m wide extending 8m between the wing and the cliff edge to the sea. The court has a round arched NW gateway and a building on the west plus a turret on the NE corner. To the SE is a 19th century house overlooking a rocky inlet. The tower house measures 7m by 5.7m and had four storeys, the highest of which lay mostly in the roof. The opening in the east wall of the vaulted cellar looks like a later insertion. Originally access was from above by means of a narrow service stair in the SE corner and a hatch in the vault. The 3m wide wing appears to have a solid base unless there is a pit now without access. It contains the original entrance at hall level and a stair leading up from it. A round turret corbelled out over the entrance contains a closet entered off the top of the stair.

BROUGH ND 228741

A sheer sided coastal promontory 2.5km north of Dunnet bears the last traces of buildings and has a neck defended by a ditch 12m wide and 3m deep.

BUCHOLIE ND 383658

Sweyn the Horsepirate's stronghold of Lambabourg in the 12th century may have been on this impregnable site with sheer cliffs descending 50m on all sides except for a narrow approach on the NW. Nothing of the present building predates the 15th century, when the Mowats transferred here from Aberdeen, although they may have had a grant of lands here by Robert Bruce. The castle was sold in 1661 to William Sinclair of Rattar but was abandoned about that time in favour of a more accessible new house at Freswick. A 16th century gatehouse containing two storeys of living rooms over a long narrow entrance passage flanked by a guardroom faces the approach. The outer wall still partly stands up to the parapet corbelling and indicates that the top storey was vaulted. The 6m wide approach causeway has a higher level on the south in line with the entrance and a lower level on the north. A gap in the higher level was spanned by a drawbridge, behind which there was a strong door for which a drawbar slot remains. Access to the castle is now only by scrambling up from the lower level. The entrance passage leads to a narrow court with a fragmentary west range and an east range now reduced to footings. The west range had a central hall about 12m long by 5m wide over an unvaulted basement. A turret projects from the SW corner and a range likely to have contained a chamber for a household official over a kitchen extends to the south. The laird's private room lay in a block beyond the north end of the hall and from it there was access to a second storey room of the gatehouse which has two windows facing the approach.

Bucholie Castle

Bucholie Castle

CADBOLL NH 879776

Cadboll belonged to Fearn Abbey until the mid 16th century when Abbot Donald Denoon managed to pass the estate to his "nephew" (illegitimate son) John. Either of these two may have built the castle. John was at variance with his brother-in-law, the 9th Ross laird of Balnagown, who was accused of "cassin down the fortalice and barrailed tower of Cadboll". In c1680 Aeneas MacLeod, Town Clerk of Edinburgh, purchased the estate and built a three storey L-plan house (still inhabited) alongside the castle. The ruined main block measures 15.5m by 7.9m over walls 1.3m thick. On the outermost corner is a round tower 4.7m in diameter. The main block shows no signs of having ever contained a hall or any private rooms suitable for living and sleeping in. There is a low and unlit vaulted basement above which are one large and two smaller rooms which also look like cellars, being vaulted, originally lighted only by cross-shaped loops, and lacking fireplaces or latrines. The entrance lies at this upper level, being reached by a short flight of external steps up to a slight projection in a re-entrant angle between the main block and a wing 7m wide and of unknown length. The wing was added by William Sinclair, who acquired Cadboll c1592. From the entrance a straight stair led up across the width of the wing. There is also a narrow service stair leading up from the adjacent room. The present top of the main block has a string course below it and a round bartizan on one corner. Only the stairs and the lack of any state rooms as the building now stands suggest a further storey was intended. Various doorways and windows have been opened through the walls in the 19th and 20th centuries to adapt the ruin as a farm store.

CAISTEAL BHARRICH NC 581587

Caisteal Bharrich or Castle Varrick stands on a spur overlooking the Kyle of Tongue on the north coast of Sutherland. The Bishops of Caithness are thought to have used it as a lodge when in transit between Scrabster Castle and Balnakiel House. The ruin measures 7.2m by 6.4m over walls 1.5m thick. It contained a living room with a fireplace and window, and reached by a ladder or steps, above a vaulted room which was probably a stable, having its own entrance and one loop. There was also an attic within the parapet. It was probably built in the 16th century.

CAISTEAL NA COIRE
NC 466012

Two walls now just 1.5m high and originally 2m thick, but now defaced externally, remain of a late 15th or early 16th century tower measuring 8.7m by 6.9m. The ruins lie on the east edge of a remotely positioned site enclosed by ditches and the main stream and a side creek of the River Oykell.

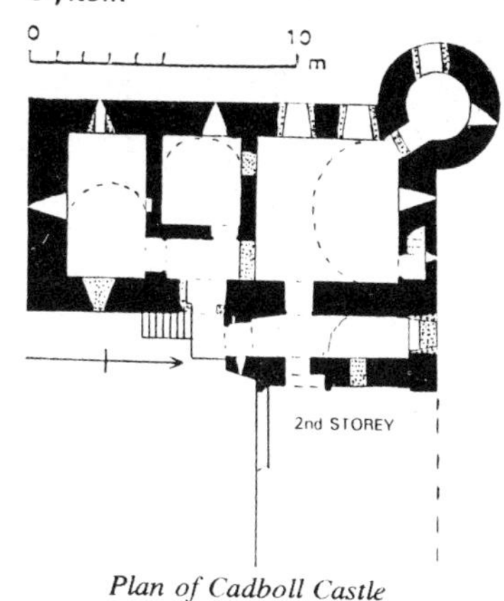

Plan of Cadboll Castle

Cadboll Castle

Cadboll Castle

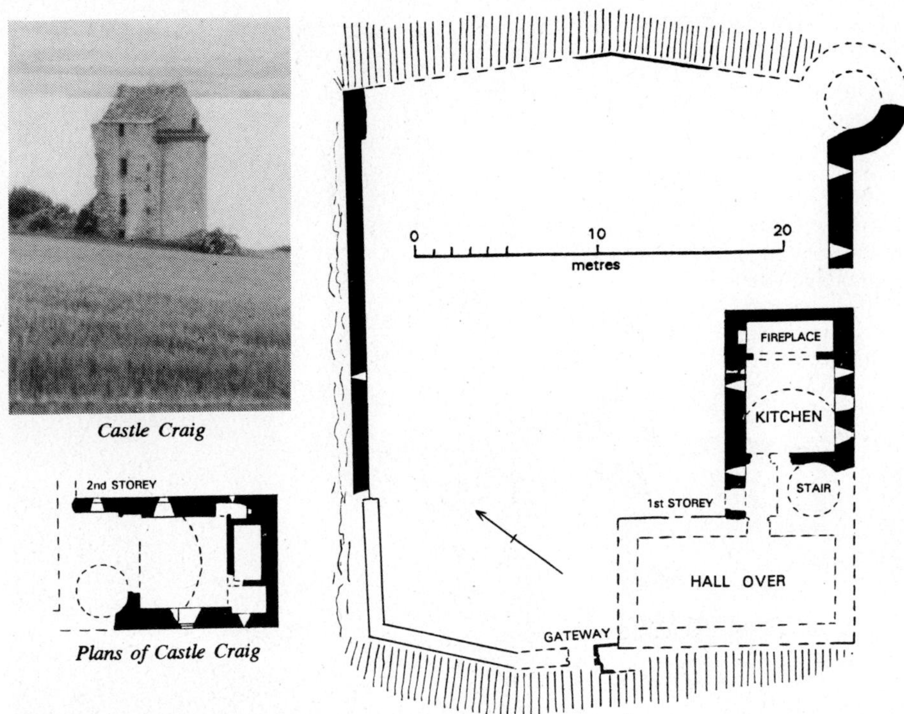

Castle Craig

Plans of Castle Craig

CASTLE CRAIG NH 632638

Castle Craig lies at the bottom of a gently sloping field above Cromarty Firth, far from any road. It was a retreat of the Bishops of Ross, whose cathedral lay at Fortrose on the other side of the Black Isle, but was granted in 1561 to Thomas Urquhart of Culbo. A court about 30m long by 25m wide has a low wall 0.8m thick containing two loopholes above a drop to the sea on the north side. The east and west sides were slightly angled in the middle so that the court was actually an irregular hexagon. One jamb of a gateway remains on the west and there is a fragment of a round flanking tower 6m in diameter at the SE corner. Adjoining this tower is a section 6m long and 1.3m thick of the landward facing south wall having two loops with bottom roundels.

The SW corner of the court was filled with an L-planned building probably of the 1540s or 1560s. The western part formed the main block containing a hall over two or three cellars, but the whole of this part is now no more than a pile of rubble and all that can otherwise be said of it was that it measured about 13m by 7m and that it appears to have been partly built on top of, and partly within, the footings of the earlier courtyard wall. The eastern part of the building comprised a wing 7m wide and projecting as much as 11m. It still retains vaulting over each of its four storeys and has remains of a roof laid directly on the top vault. The end wall contains a flue rising from a huge fireplace serving the kitchen on the lowest storey and is surmounted by a wall-walk and parapet with corner roundels. The roundels have corbelling ornamented with dog-tooth and rope-mouldings and there are machicolations. A kitchen window facing the field has been broken out to give access to that room. Between the kitchen and the rooms above it and those in the main block was a spiral stair about 2.8m in diameter and a series of lobbies, the lowest of which contained the entrance to the building. Over the entrance is a blank space for an armoral panel.

CASTLE LEOD NH 485593

On the building are the date 1616 and the initials of Sir Roderick (Rory Mor) MacKenzie, who acquired Castle Leod in 1606, and his wife Margaret MacLeod. It is still occupied by their descendant the Earl of Cromartie, the family having regained the estate in 1777 after being forfeited as Jacobites in 1746. As built c1560-80 the castle had a square wing engaging one corner of a main block containing a hall over three cellars with a connecting passage, two storeys of bedrooms, and an attic within a wall-walk and parapet with ornamental chequerwork corbelling with angle rounds. The wing would have contained the entrance and a main stair up to the hall, as usual. In the remodelling by Roderick and Margaret most of the main re-entrant angle was filled in to provide space for a new scale-and-platt staircase to the hall and several extra private rooms above. This part rises directly to the roof eaves with dormer windows and a bartizan with a conical roof instead of an open parapet. The back of the main block, facing north, was remodelled to match the new extension, the original parapet being roofed over, dormers with the date and initials referred to above added, and the roundels there converted into bartizans with conical roofs.

Castle Leod

Castle Craig

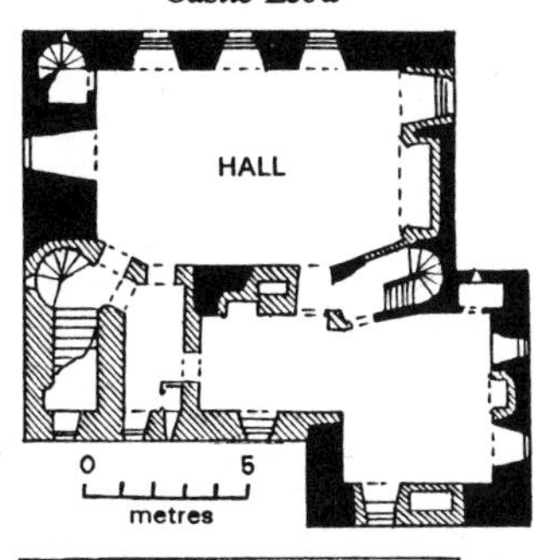

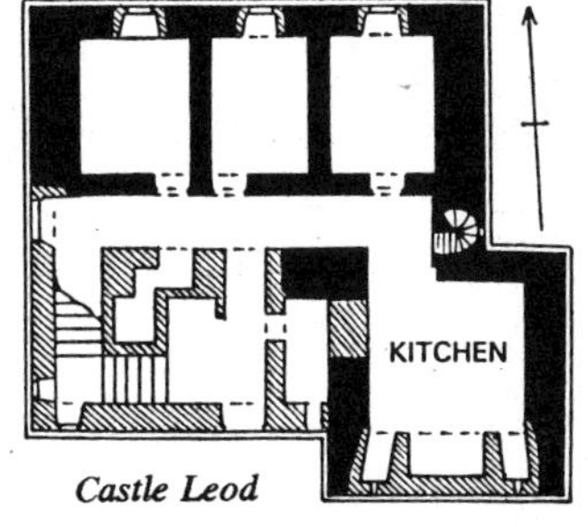

Castle Leod

CASTLE OF MEY ND 290739

The barony of Mey was acquired in 1549 by George, 4th Earl of Caithness, and the castle, then known as Barrogill, was built soon afterwards. It formerly had a stone inside dated 1566 with initials of the Earl and his wife Elizabeth Graham. By the 1660s the castle was in a neglected state, and in 1726 was "going to ruin", but was presumably repaired soon afterwards, being described by Pennant in 1769 as "a beautiful strong castle". The old Statistical Account of 1793 refers to additions then being made. Further work was carried out in 1819 and again after it was purchased in 1952 by H.R.H. Elizabeth the Queen Mother, whose arms appear on a west wing.

The castle lies on flat ground overlooking Pentland Firth. It has a long four storey main block with rectangular towers at diagonally opposite corners. The larger tower may be older than the rest of the building. The smaller tower contains the main stair around a central well with the entrance at its foot. A passage runs off and zig-zags past two vaulted cellars and a kitchen to a further cellar below the laird's apartments in the larger tower. The kitchen has a large fireplace contained in a projection at one of the remaining corners, this being carried up as a shallow wing balancing the stair tower at the other corner on this side. There are numerous bartizans on chequerwork corbelling. One contains a stair connecting the two highest storeys of the laird's tower. The original conical caps shown in a view by Daniel published in 1821 have gone. The building is much altered and extended but retains a series of widely splayed gunports in the lowest two levels. Some pierce the quoins at corners, an unusual feature also found in the similarly planned castle at Noltland in Orkney, also of the 1570s. North of the main block is a compact court with offices on its east and west sides. The main building was originally approached through this court but there is now an entrance in an extension on the south side.

Old print of the Castle of Mey

The Castle of Mey or Barrogill Castle

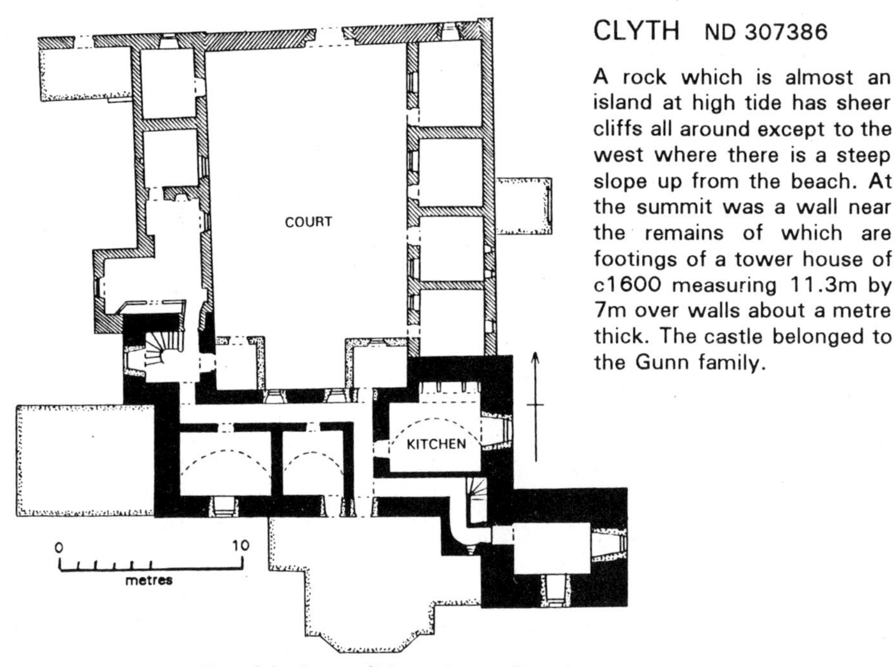

Plan of the Castle of Mey or Barrogill Castle

CLYTH ND 307386

A rock which is almost an island at high tide has sheer cliffs all around except to the west where there is a steep slope up from the beach. At the summit was a wall near the remains of which are footings of a tower house of c1600 measuring 11.3m by 7m over walls about a metre thick. The castle belonged to the Gunn family.

CROMARTY NH 792671

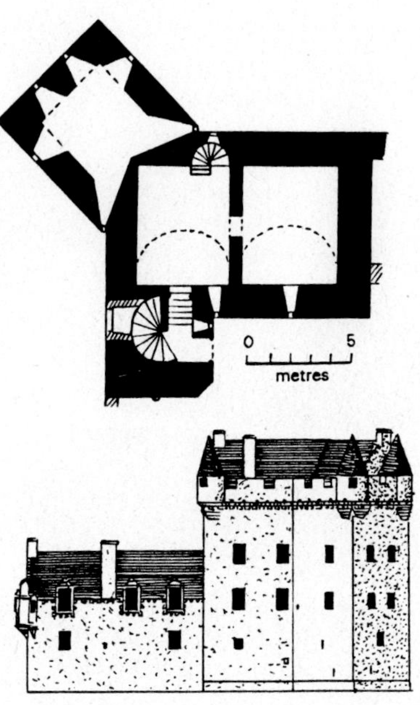

Old drawings of Cromarty Castle

It was probably in the late 12th century that what is now known as the Black Isle was formed into a small sheriffdom administered from a royal castle at Cromarty, which thus became the county town. The earliest mention of the sheriffdom is in a charter granted by William de Monte Alto (or Mowat) sheriff in the 1250s and 60s and one of several of this family to hold the office. The Earls of Ross later held the office until in 1364 Earl William resigned it to Adam Urquhart. In 1470 James III made over to Sir William Urquhart and his heirs "the Mote and Mansion mound of Cromarty in perpetual fee and heritage with licence to build a tower or fortalice on the Mote and equip it with suitable defences". This indicates that the original castle probably built by King William the Lion was of the motte and bailey type, and that although the site had remained in use the defences and main buildings were still of wood. Sir William died in 1475 and it seems to have been his grandson Sir Thomas who built a tower c1500-7.

In 1670 Sheriff Sir John Urquhart managed to transfer all the lands of the burgh of Cromarty to himself. His son later got into debt and lost his Cromarty lands to Sir George MacKenzie of Tarbat, afterwards Earl of Cromartie. His grandson also got into financial difficulties and sold the lands to Sir William Urquhart of Meldrum in Aberdeenshire. This branch of the Urquharts rebuilt the then much decayed castle but in 1763 sold it to Lord Elibank, who in turn disposed of it nine year later to George Ross of Pitkerrie. Ross was a minor Ross-shire laird of who had made a fortune in England as a supply agent for the army. He greatly improved the estate and in 1772 had the abandoned castle pulled down and replaced by a new mansion.

A set of drawings survive from 1746 showing the appearance of the castle both before and after it was drastically remodelled. It had a roughly rectangular court measuring about 43m by 26m with a tower house in one corner with a three storey block continuing the line of the tower main axis as far as the adjacent corner. This block had dormer windows and bartizans with conical roofs. At the other end of the court one corner was chamfered off by a short section of wall whilst the other was composed of the outer two sides of one of many former outbuildings which had by then vanished, although loops for them remained in the outer wall. The five storey tower had a stair wing at one corner, whilst the corner facing the field had a larger square wing projecting diagonally, a most unusual feature at any period. The drawings show both wings as badly cracked from top to bottom, probably the result of building on top of an at least partly artificial mound with consequent settlement problems. Both wings were removed in the remodelling, along with the whole top of the tower, to produce a domestic looking and symmetrical mansion. Originally the tower had parapets supported on a chequerwise arrangement of corbels. The corner roundels were not open as one might expect but had conical roofs. They may have been remodelled later but it is possible that they were roofed from the start as Sir Thomas is said to have employed a French architect who may well have introduced new ideas.

DINGWALL NH 553589

King William the Lion (1165-1219) established a castle here supposedly on the site of an earlier stronghold in which MacBeth is said to have been born c1000. It consisted of a motte by the mouth of the river with a bailey defending the landward approach to it from the west and south. The original timber defences and buildings were gradually replaced in stone although the chronology and layout of the buildings is unknown. Dingwall became the principal seat of the Celtic Earls of Ross and when the male line failed the castle became involved in the long dispute over possession of the Earldom, being occupied several times by the Lord of the Isles. The Regent Albany imposed a governor of the castle during his usurpation of the Earldom in James I's reign, but this unfortunate was assassinated by one of the Munros and replaced by a MacKay. After the Earldom of Ross was finally taken from the Lord of the Isles in 1477 by James III, Sir John Munro of Foulis was made governor of the castle and Chamberlain of Ross. He was succeeded in 1480 by Sir Andrew Munro, and in 1488 by Sir James Dunbar of Flowerburn. The castle was then being held for Prince James, second son of James III, and Duke of Ross until he resigned the Dukedom in 1503 on being elected Abbott of Dunfermline. In that year his elder brother James IV visited Dingwall Castle and had a new hall built in the court.

Between 1507 and 1516 the castles of Dingwall and Redcastle were held by Andro, Bishop of Caithness. He carried out repairs at Dingwall necessitated by assaults on the castle by the MacDonalds and MacKenzies. Land adjacent to the castle was purchased, probably with the intention of clearance to improve the field of fire from the walls. Other governors following this period were: John, Earl of Atholl (1516-22), John, Earl of Moray, brother of James V (1523 onwards), David Sinclair (1550), the aged George Munro of Docharty (1561 onwards), Sir Andrew Keith, Lord Dingwall (1584 onwards), and Sir John Preston, Earl of Desmond (c1605 onwards). The castle ceased to be maintained after James VI's death (1625) but continued to have nominal governors in the Munros of Foulis, then the Bains, and later the Davidsons of Tulloch. In 1750 the ruin was acquired by the Reverend Colin MacKenzie, Minister of Fodderty, who had much of the stone removed to build new farm houses at Fodderty and Millmain, while his son used large quantities of limestone from the ruin to make fertiliser to improve the lands of those farms. Much of what remained was robbed in the 19th century for building new houses in the town and all that now remain are three shapeless and ivy-mantled fragments in the garden of Castle House at the end of Castle Street, near to the mouth of the River Peffery.

Old postcard of Dirlot Castle

DIRLOT ND 126486

On the summit of a precipitous crag by the west bank of the River Thurso in a remote and barren area south of Halkirk are foundations of a tower which may have been built in the 14th century by Donald Cheyne. It measures 9.5m by 6.5m over walls 1.6m thick and had a court 13m by 7m wide on the SE which needed only a parapet to defend it. In 1464 Dirlot was held by George, chief of Gunn family but it was held by Alexander Sutherland at the time of his execution in 1499 for killing Alexander Dunbar, after which James IV granted the castle to the MacKays.

DOCHMALUAG NH 521601

Hidden under a heavy disguise of ivy close to a bend in a track near Brae Farm is a thinly walled rectangular block measuring 6m by 4.9m containing three unvaulted storeys, two superimposed doorways, and unusual windows with pairs of lights separated by a transom. The building only begins to make sense when one realises that there is a vaulted cellar on a lower level 7m away above the gully of a stream. It would thus appear that the ruin is only a wing, perhaps added or remodelled later, having probably a vaulted cellar now buried by earth and debris beneath it. It lies on one side of an assumed main block over 15m long by about 8m wide containing a hall over several cellars (mostly now buried) linked by a passage on the other side.

DORNOCH NH 797897 A

The 13th century cathedral and Bishop's palace were both much damaged by fire in 1570 during a feud between the Murrays of Dornoch and the MacKays of Strathnaver. Only the south range with cross-loops in its basement remains of an early 16th century quadrangular palace. It was remodelled by the Earl of Sutherland (made hereditary keeper in 1557) and the five storey NW tower was probably then added. It contains bedchambers opening off private rooms at the west end of large halls on the second and third storeys of the main block. The tower has gunloops and the top storey lies partly within the roof, there being a parapet with three angle-roundels. The building was allowed to decay in the 18th century and the east and west ranges of the the original quadrangle then demolished. The remaining parts were restored by the Countess of Sutherland in 1810-14 to serve as a gaol, and a school was added on old foundations at the SW. The building was altered in 1859-60 to make a residence for the Sheriff of Sutherland. Additions were made in 1925 and further restoration was carried out in the 1970s when the building became an hotel and a SE wing was added.

Bishop's Palace, Dornoch

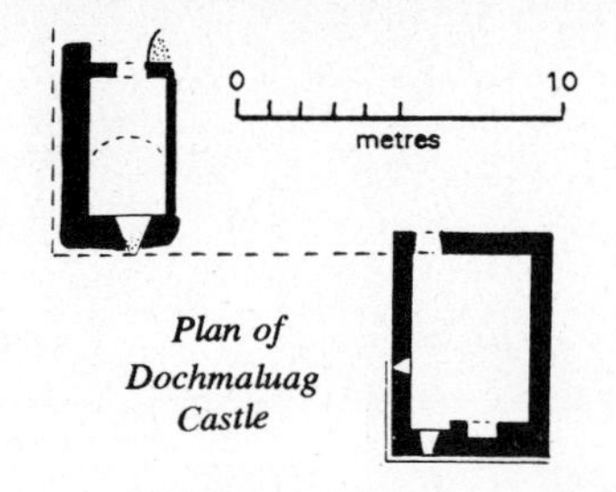

Plan of Dochmaluag Castle

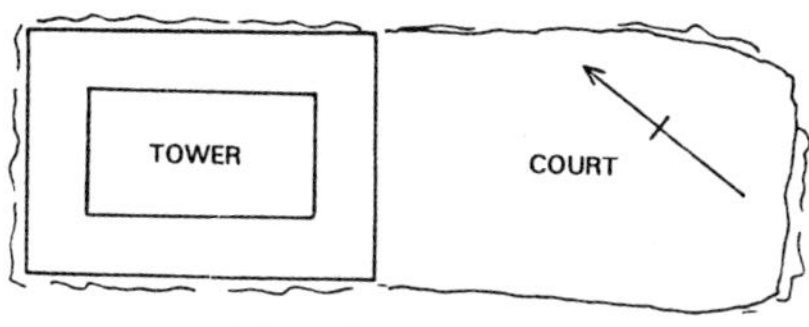

Plan of Dirlot Castle

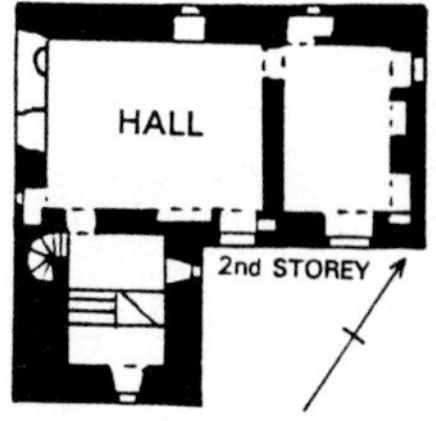

Plans of Dounreay Castle

DOUNREAY NC 983669

Dounreay is best known for its atomic power station, through the precinct of which lies the only access to the ruined castle. It was built about 20 years after William Sinclair of Dunbeath acquired the estate from Adam, Bishop of Orkney, in the 1560s. William later incurred the wrath of his kinsman, the Earl of Caithness, and is said to have been besieged in the castle by the Earl's brother. It was later held by Lord Forbes but in 1624 was sold to Sir Donald MacKay. The castle was occupied by a Cromwellian garrison in 1651 and in 1726 was described as "one of the Earl of Caithness's lodgeings". It remained occupied, if only by fishermen, until 1861. The castle has a wing 5.2m wide containing the entrance and a scale-and-platt staircase projecting 4.2m from the south side of a main block measuring 11.3m by 6.4m which contained three storeys and an attic. The stair rises up over a tiny prison or strongroom to the hall, above which a narrow spiral stair in the thick west wall of the wing gives access to the third storey. From the entrance lobby a vaulted passage gives access to three low unvaulted cellars. Below the western cellar is an extra room with an inserted wooden-lintelled opening to the outside. The hall has a private living room divided off at the far end, and the third storey had one bedroom in the wing and two in the main block with a straight stair to the attic between them.

Dounreay Castle

Dunbeath Castle

Dounreay Castle

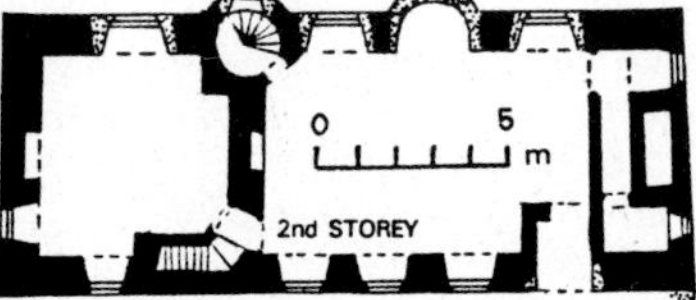

Plan of Dunbeath Castle

DUNBEATH ND 158282

Parts of the massively walled basement of a rectangular four storey block on the neck of a coastal promontory may go back to the time of the first mention of a castle here in 1428, or (more likely) the 1530s. Admiral Sir George Crichton held Dunbeath in 1452, have succeeded to it from his mother. In 1507 Dunbeath was resigned to the Crown by Malcolm Colquhoun and regranted by James IV to Alexander Innes. In 1529, Alexander Sinclair of Stamister, a younger son of William, 2nd Earl of Caithness, was confirmed in possession, having married the heiress Elizabeth Innes. His son William was so harassed by his kinsman, the Earl of Caithness, that he resigned his estates to his grandson in 1590 and retired to Moray. The grandson, supposedly facile, resigned the barony of Dunbeath to his brother-in-law Lord Forbes. The Sinclairs recovered the property c1624 when Alexander, Master of Forbes sold it to John Sinclair of Geanies, 2nd son of George Sinclair of Mey. John is thought to have built the existing upper storeys of the building in the 1630s. After a siege of several days in 1650 Lady Sinclair was obliged to surrender the castle to a small Royalist force led by the Marquis of Montrose as he advanced down the Caithness coast from Orkney. After he was defeated at Carbisdale the garrison he installed to patrol and hold the Ord of Caithness surrendered to General Leslie after a few day's siege when the water supply failed.

The castle is approached by a straight, tree-lined avenue through private grounds. The facade has a central entrance flanked by loops with bottom roundels, over which project round turrets crowned by square caphouses reached by narrow stairs in subsidiary turrets. Bartizans with conical roofs contain closets off both the third and fourth storeys. There are tiers of windows between these turrets, the uppermost being dormers with fancy pediments. The facade is thus symmetrical, but it had a different appearance a century ago, and the entrance, the left hand central turret, and all the windows of the two lowest levels are in their present form not ancient. The entrance does, however, replace one in the same position with a heraldic stone above it. It led into a lobby with a vaulted kitchen on the left and a pair of cellars to the right, one of which has a service stair to the hall above. The one original central turret contains a stair leading to the third storey bedrooms and has behind it a cross-wall dividing the hall from a private room to the right. Whatever ancient buildings there may have been in the former court behind are now replaced by a large modern extension. A yett from Dunbeath has gone to the Museum of Antiquities at Edinburgh.

Dunbeath Castle

Dunrobin Castle

DUN CREICH NH 652882

Footings of a tower said to have been built by Paul MacTire in the 13th century lie within the ramparts of an older fort on a rocky hill jutting out on the north side of Dornoch Firth. The tower measured about 10m by 9.5m over walls about 2m thick.

DUNROBIN NC 850008 OP

Dunrobin lies above the Moray Firth NW of Golspie. From the 12th century it belonged to the Freskins of Duffus. They became Earls of Sutherland after Norse influence in this area waned in the mid 13th century. The Earldom passed by marriage to a branch of the Gordons of Huntly in 1514. Another marriage brought it in the late 18th century to an English family, the Leveson Gowers, later raised to be Dukes of Sutherland. The existing castle has grown up around a small tower house and has been occupied by the family ever since. The tower measures about 8m by 7m externally and has four vaulted storeys. It probably dates from c1520 but parts of it may go back to the time of William, 3rd Earl (died 1327), or William, 5th Earl (died c1371). A round stair turret at one corner dates from the time of John, 13th Earl (1594-1615) and has window pediments bearing his initials with those of his wife Agnes. Either John or his successor, another John (Earl from 1615 to 1679) added a mansion with ranges within a small court, the outer walls of which could be partly 16th century. Further extensions were built for the Countess Elizabeth in 1785 and in 1835 Sir Charles Barry was commissioned to built substantial facades extending the buildings to the north and east. The castle was damaged by fire in 1915 but was repaired after World War I by Sir Robert Lorimer. Everything seen by visitors as they approach down the avenue from the A9 coast road is basically Barry's work, which has entirely hidden the original tower house. Even the 17th century mansion with its high whitewashed walls with slender corner turrets with conical spires only comes into view as one passes round the west side down towards the gardens below the south side of the castle.

EMBO NH 809923

The original house (eventually destroyed by fire) was built by a fourth son of James Gordon of Drummoy after he acquired Embo in the late 16th century. Robert Home Gordon's house of c1785 contains a reset stone in the kitchen dated 1657 with arms of Sir Robert Gordon and Jean Leslie. Another stone recorded in the steading was dated 1627 with initials of John Gordon and Margaret Leslie. John had a long feud with the Greys of Skelbo over a boundary dispute. He was made a baronet in 1631.

Fairburn Tower

Fairburn Tower

FAIRBURN NH 469523

Murdoch MacKenzie built this tower on a ridge between the valleys of the rivers Orrin and Conon. Built under the terms of a charter of 1542, it is lofty in proportion to its small size, being 20m high to the chimney tops, yet only 8m square over walls 1.5m thick in the vaulted basement. That room is reached only by a service stair from above and has three double splayed gunloops in each side, two of which are blocked by a stair turret 3.5m square added against the south side. This turret contains a new entrance on the outer face at ground level. The original entrance at second storey level has a draw-bar slot and now looks into the stair-well. A spiral stair in the SE corner originally connected the second, third, and fourth storey rooms, each of which had a fireplace, a latrine, a locker, and a window in each wall. The fifth storey is probably an addition of the same period as the stair turret as it has no other means of access. It has a fireplace and two closets in round bartizans with shot-holes on the SW and NE corners, but was poorly lighted. There was a garret room over the top of the stair.

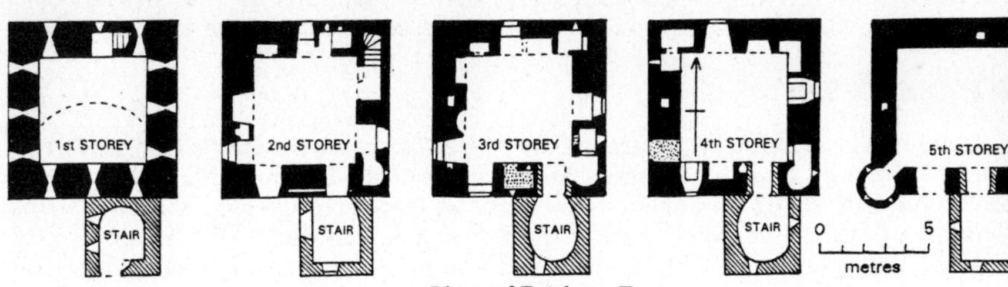

Plans of Fairburn Tower

FORSE ND 224338 F

Forse was held by Reginald Cheyne in the early 14th century and the very primitive tower may be of his time or somewhat earlier. It was held by the Keiths in the latter half of the 14th century and then passed by marriage c1400 to Kenneth Sutherland. Forse was granted by James V to William Keith, Earl Marischall in 1538, but the castle, if not the lands, appears to have remained in Sutherland hands. It lies on a steep sided coastal promontory with the narrow neck cut by a ditch. The tower commands the approach and measures 10m by 7.5m over walls up to 2m thick. The NW wall still over 7m high is featureless apart from three internal offsets. The upper and lower of these carried floors. The middle offset perhaps carried arched ceiling trusses. The cellar had only a narrow ventilation shaft facing SE and was reached by a trap-door from above until an entrance was broken through the SE wall later. Above it was the original entrance, with slots for a draw bar. It led into a dark room lighted by a loop in the SE wall and a slot through to what seems to have been a guard room over a courtyard gate beside the NE wall. There was no fireplace and no staircase survives, although it is likely that one was provided in the collapsed western corner. Unfortunately most of the SE wall also fell down in 1994 destroying most of the features. On the west side of the court behind the tower are remains of a 15th or 16th century block containing a hall and a chamber (at the south end) over unvaulted cellars slightly below courtyard level. On the east side of the court are slight traces of a smaller and probably later building which is more crudely constructed.

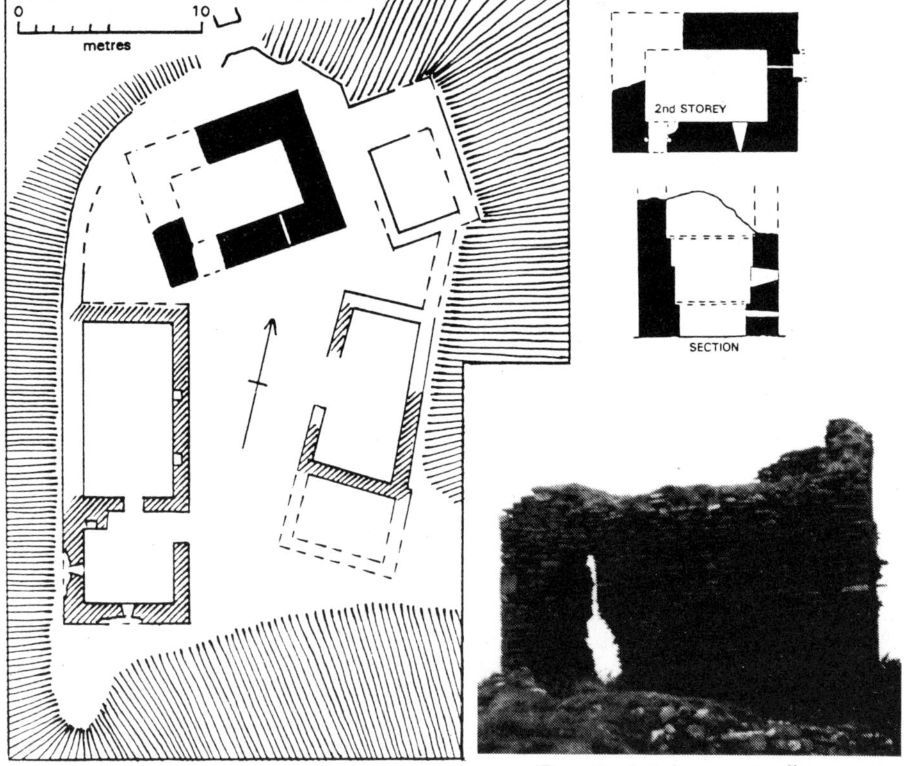

Plans of Forse Castle

Forse Castle before recent collapse

FOULIS NG 589641

Foulis overlooks Cromarty Firth to the SW of Evanton and has been the home of the Munro family since the 12th century. A 14th century charter refers to Robert Munro as being of the Tower of Strath Skiath, possibly then a wooden building on a motte. In 1632 the Munros were reported to be able to raise a thousand armed men and in 1634 their chief was made a baronet. Many of them served in the army of Gustavus Adolphus of Sweden and formed a substantial part of his officer corps. They were staunchly Protestant and Hanovarian, their seat at Foulis being plundered by the Jacobites in 1746. In 1750 the house, then being remodelled, was gutted by fire and Henry, 7th Baronet, then laid out the present E-plan mansion. The east wing incorporates parts of a tower house probably of 15th or 16th century date.

FYRISH NG 614679

The present long and low mansion of 1672 on the side of Cnoc Fyrish, NW of Evanton, stands on the site of a castle of the Munros.

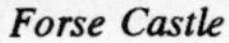

Forse Castle

Girnigoe Castle

Girnigoe Castle

GIRNIGOE ND 379549 F

William Sinclair was made Earl of Caithness by James II in 1455. He was also 3rd Earl of Orkney until obliged to surrender that Earldom to James III in 1470. Girnigoe was the chief seat of the earldom of Caithness and from it the county was governed. The 4th Earl, George, suspected his heir John of an assassination plot and had him kept prisoner at Girnigoe from 1571 until he died in 1578. John's son George, succeeded as 5th Earl in 1582 and lived until 1642. He remodelled the castle and built a complete new domestic suite in an outer court which is sometimes confusingly referred to under the separate name of Castle Sinclair. His great-grandson George, the weak-willed 6th Earl, willed his estates to Campbell of Glenorchy in lieu of debts. George Sinclair of Kiess claimed Girnigoe as the rightful heir and forcibly occupied the castle in 1679. He was subsequently forfeited for rebellion and both Girnigoe and Kiess were then allowed to decay, being described as ruins in 1700 by Reverend John Brand. He mentions a window lintel in the outer court as being dated 1607.

Old sketch of Girnigoe Castle

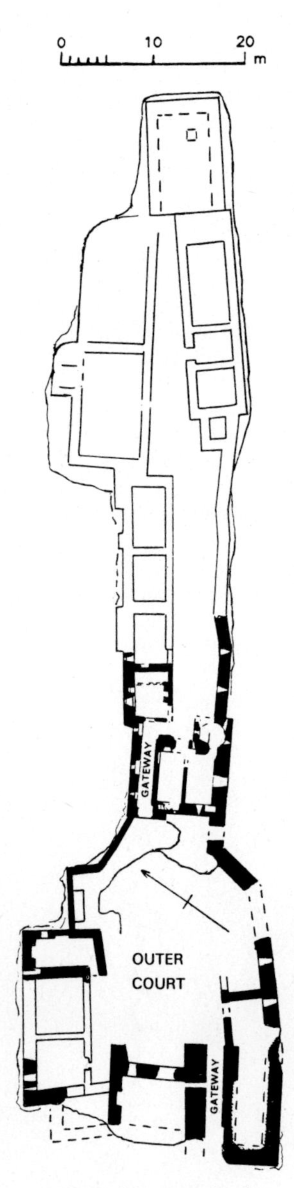

Plans of Girnigoe Castle

The inner court of the castle lies on a long vertical sided peninsular with a sea-inlet or goe on the south side. This court could only be approached by a drawbridge over a chasm descending to sea-level and then via a passage through the north end of a tower house occupying the whole width of the promontory (currently there is access via an opened out loophole in the tower house basement). Over the entrance, and also over a doorway to the beach in a short length of walling closing of the south side of the chasm are recesses for former amorial panels. This section of walling is coeval with the tower and had a sloping roof over it rather than a wall-walk and parapet. The tower is 10.9m long by 8m wide. On the east side towards the inner court it has a stair wing on the south and a larger wing on the north. The stair wing makes the building look bigger when seen from the south than it really is and is shown by a joint in the lowest courses (with quoins of a former corner) to be an afterthought. At the level of the entrance passage the rest of main block contains two rooms vaulted axially with a thin non-weight-bearing wall between them. The northern room has a straight stair down to cellars below the court. Above is a hall which had a fine oriel window, now destroyed, in the upper part of a shallow projection pierced below by the gateway. A passage in the NE corner leads to a private room set over a kitchen at courtyard level in the north wing. From the passage a doorway led to a wooden gallery projected on corbels along the north side of both the main block and wing. There was another state room over the hall, and there were two bedrooms in the north wing connected to the private room by a spiral stair in the wing east wall.

Although a late 15th century date is sometimes claimed for this tower, and there must have been a gatehouse of some type here from the time the castle was first built, the provision of panel spaces and the two gunports on the east side at courtyard level, the fairly thin walling, the lack of any parapets or turrets, and the presence of an oriel window paralleled in the north of Scotland only by those of c1606-10 at Kirkwall, all suggest a date as late as c1590-1600 for the present building on the site.

The NW wing is continued by footings of a range containing three rooms and extending to what may be the remains of an older hall-block. The eastern tip of the promontory (which is over 60m long but never more than 24m wide) is a platform at a lower level. It contains an opening to a flight of steps to a water gate with a pointed head on the north side. On the south side of the court, facing level ground across the inlet from which the site could be bombarded, was a curtain wall 1.6m thick of which a 12m long portion with two loops stands high. The loops are arched over in a very unusual way. At the east end of the south side lie footings of another range.

Old sketch of Girnigoe Castle

The outer court is wider and more oval in shape. It is protected on the west and south sides by a wide rock-cut ditch. Parts of the outer court buildings stand as high fragments but little detail remains. The 1.6m thick wall on the south side has loops similar to that of the inner court. This wall and the lowest two storeys of the tower containing the outer gateway passage, and perhaps also the room immediately north of the passage, may be 15th century. The passage was closed by a portcullis operated from the middle of a vaulted room above. Two upper storeys were added or rebuilt in the 17th century and have corbelling for oriel windows in a square turret projecting diagonally from the NE corner. On the north side of the court are remains of a 17th century block with a cross-wing at the east end. The main block seems to lie over blocked cellars no longer accessible. There was also a 17th century range on the south side of the court. In the SE corner of the court lies an oven.

HALBERRY ND 302377

This site is a larger but less defensible version of that at Girnigoe with a long narrow goe or sea inlet isolating, from higher ground on the mainland, a promontory 160m long by 50m with a tilt towards the sea. Across the neck is a ditch 10m wide and 2m deep which presumably once had an inner wall or bank and stockade. Close behind the ditch are the grass-covered footings of a tower house about 13.5m long by 8.3m wide which was probably in existence by the mid 15th century when George, Crowner or chief of Clan Gunn had a residence here.

HELMSDALE ND 027151

A tourist information office now stands on the site of a castle on a knoll overlooking the sea to the west of the town and the river. The original building was erected in 1488 by the 7th Countess of Sutherland, probably as a dower house, although the Earls later used it as a hunting lodge. In 1567 the castle was the scene of the poisoning of John, 11th Earl of Sutherland, and his wife Helen by his aunt Isobel Sinclair. She did it at the instigation of her kinsman George, 4th Earl of Caithness (see page 97) with the object that her own son should inherit the Earldom of Sutherland. Her son, however, was accidentally poisoned along with the others whilst the rightful heir escaped and succeeded to the Earldom. The ruin which survived until the 1960s seems to have been a later building erected on the same site in 1616 by Sir Robert Gordon of Navidale, a younger son of one of the Earls. It had a square wing embracing one corner of a thinly walled main block 9.6m long by 7.6m wide. One of the re-entrant angles contained a square turret containing the entrance and a spiral staircase.

INVERSHIN NH 573964

Slight traces of earthworks and former stone buildings lie on a heavily overgrown site on an eminence above the River Oykell just below the confluence of the River Shin.

KEISS ND 357616

On a 20m high vertically sided headland at the north end of Sinclairs' Bay is an unusually small Z-plan castle built by the Earl of Caithness c1600. It has thinly walled round towers 3.5m in diameter at diagonally opposite corners of a four storey main block 8m by 7.2m. The towers increase the accommodation and picturesqueness of the building and make it fit tightly onto the cramped site. Both face to seaward so neither fulfils the one real military need of providing flanking fire along the landward west wall. The flattened west face of the SW tower contained an entrance (now vanished) at the foot of a spiral stair rising up to the third storey. Above the former entrance is a recess for a long lost heraldic shield. The bullet marks around the window above are a reminder of the events of 1679 when George Sinclair attempted to make good his claim to the earldom of Caithness by force, and after occupying the seat of the earldom at Girnigoe, was forcibly ejected both from that castle and his own seat at Keiss. From this level a turret stair on the west side led up and two rooms are squeezed over the main stair. The other tower has a dome-vaulted cellar and three bedrooms linked by a narrow turret stair on the south side. The topmost room in the main block had dormer windows and closets in bartizans on the NW and SE corners. The Reverend John Brand describes Keiss as a ruin in 1700 but an account of 1726 refers to it as "in repair and at the side of it a convenient house lately built". This house has now gone and the tower has been ruined by a fall of the cliff which has taken with it the NW corner and much of the adjacent walls.

Keiss Castle

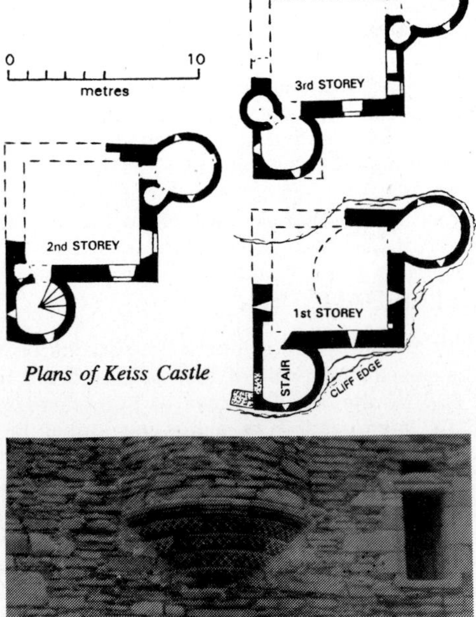

Plans of Keiss Castle

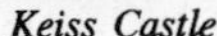

Keiss: corbelling detail

KILCOY NH 576512

Kilcoy was built by Alexander MacKenzie, 4th son of the 11th Baron of Kintail, after he aquired the property in 1618. Along with other MacKenzie castles at Kinkell and Redcastle it controlled the landward approach to the Black Isle. In 1890 the building was restored from ruin, extended and re-occupied. It became neglected again but has since been restored and is now well cared for. The four storey main block is 16.2m long by 8m wide and has a round stair turret 4.8m in diameter at the SE corner, a round tower 6.6m in diameter at the NW corner, and bartizans with conical roofs on the other two corners. The original entrance lay at the east end of the south wall and opened onto a passage connecting two cellars and a kitchen with the main stair. The kitchen has a fireplace in the east end wall with an oven in the NE corner and has a slot drain and water inlet on the north side, whilst the adjacent cellar has a service stair. From the furthest cellar there is access to a hexagonal cellar in the round tower. There are three gunports in the lobby at the foot of the main stair and another opens off the service stair. The hall has a fireplace with a splendid mantlepiece dated 1679 with shields and initials commemorating the marriages of Alexander MacKenzie with Jean Fraser (widow of Sir James Stewart of Kilcoy) in 1611, Colin MacKenzie with Lilias Sutherland in 1640, and Alexander MacKenzie with Mary MacKenzie in 1664. On either side are mermaids playing harps and at one side a hound and on the other a hare. Beyond a crosswall which helps to accommodate a stair to the bedrooms in the wall thickness is a withdrawing room, with a bedroom beyond in the round tower. Another stair to upper rooms in the main block and three smaller rooms in the square upper part of the stair turret is contained in a turret corbelled out over the entrance. The topmost room over the main stair has quatrefoil shaped loopholes.

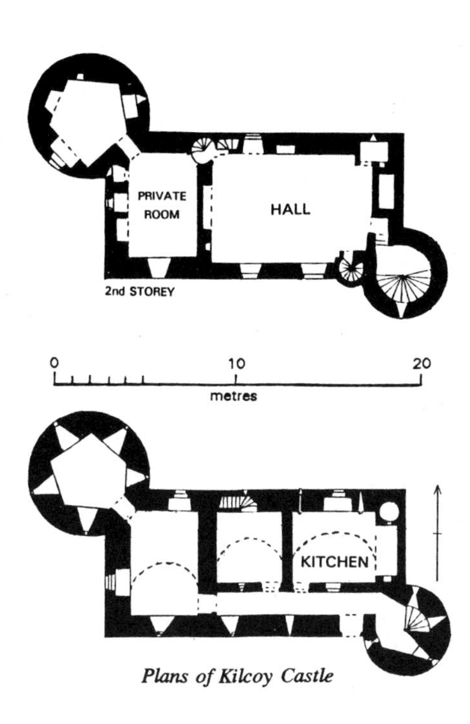

Plans of Kilcoy Castle

Kilcoy Castle

Kinkell Castle

Kilcoy Castle

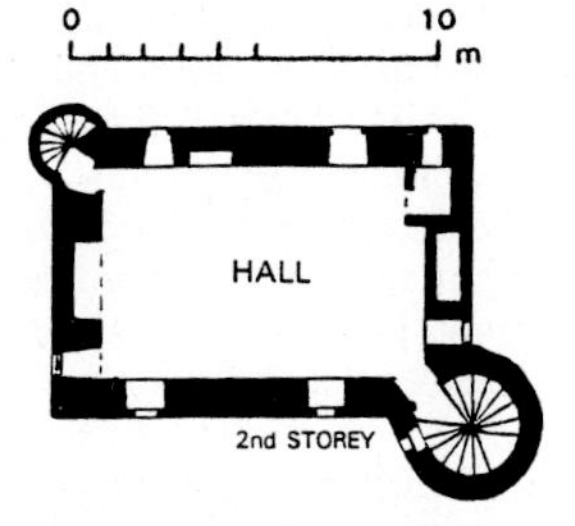

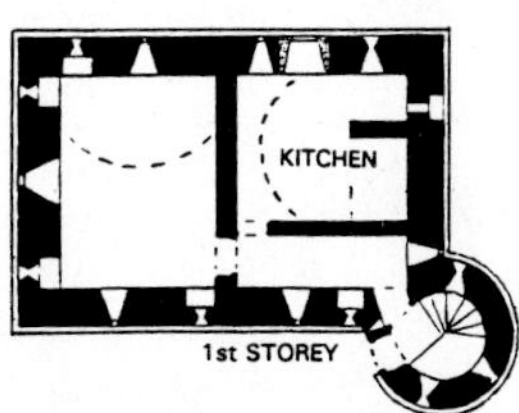

Plans of Kinkell Castle

KINKELL NH 554543

Kinkell was the seat of the MacKenzies of Gairloch. The recess for a heraldic stone above the entrance is empty but the hall fireplace is dated 1594, a likely period for the construction of the building. In later years the building became a farmhouse but it was derelict when purchased by the sculptor Gerald Laing in the late 1960s. It has since been restored to its original appearance and a late 17th century wing demolished. Externally the only non-original features are a large window filled with an iron grille in the kitchen (still used as such) and three dormer windows lighting the attic. Internally the subdivisions of the two upper levels have been altered from the original to comply with modern requirements for bathrooms and bedrooms. The main body measures 11.5m by 7.7m above an external offset marking the top of a low plinth, an unusual feature in buildings of this type. A turret 3.9m in diameter at one corner contains the entrance and a staircase with three gunports at its foot. Other gunports appear in the kitchen and cellar and the passage linking them to the stair. Some of these gunports have redented (stepped) outer splays to reflect incoming bullets. The kitchen has a fireplace and a water inlet in an end wall. The main stair serves all four storeys and there is a secondary stair leading up from the hall in a round turret corbelled out from the corner diagonally opposite from the main stair.

KNOCKKINNAN ND 181315

Foundations of this building lie on high ground commanding the A9 coast road between Dunbeath and Janetstown. The castle is said to have been begun and left unfinished at the beginning of the 16th century. The nature of the remains (which have been in about the same state since at least 1726) is in general accordance with this. The site is a pear-shaped rock platform 60m long by 30m wide with vertical sides 1.5m to 2m high which are partly natural and partly quarried for materials. A ramp for access was left on the west side. There was a rectangular building containing three rooms at ground level at the south end of the site and there are indications of a square building in the NW corner. Probably a breastwork around the perimeter of the platform was intended but nothing remains of it. In the middle, marked by a prominent concrete shelter, are buried foundations of a tower about 14m long by 8m wide which seems to have had a thick NE end wall presumably containing the entrance, staircase, and several mural chambers. Beyond it are remains of range with a latrine projection at the east corner. SW of the tower is what appears to be a length of curtain wall and there are signs of another range on the west, with a cistern to the south of it.

0 10 20
metres
TOWER
CLIFF EDGE

Plan of Knockkinnan Castle

Knockkinnan Castle

Knockkinnan Castle

Latheron Castle

LATHERON ND 199334

Set on a cliff above the Latheron Burn, and mostly hidden from the A9 coast road by the garage of an adjoining house, is an ivy-clad section of walling about 2m thick remaining from a tower probably built by the Gunns in the 15th century and still complete in the 1720s. The building was round cornered and lacked any dressed stone. Part of it fell down c1910. The lower part of another wall rising from the bank of the burn before it tumbles over a waterfall adjoins the north end of the fragment.

LITTLE TARREL NH 911819

An L-plan building in a steading 1km south of Portmahomack was restored as a house in 1981-4. It remained in use as a farm store until the whole of the east end wall of the main block 12m long by 6.5m wide collapsed. An inscription on a window sill has a defaced date in the 1550s and initials of Alexander Ross and his wife. However the existing building is probably a generation or two later. On the south side a wing 4.7m wide projects 4.9m and contains a private room over a kitchen with a fireplace in the south end wall. The main block has a doorway in the re-entrant angle leading to a passage connecting a vaulted cellar with two gunports at the west end with the kitchen and another space that once formed two other vaulted cellars. No stair survived, but there may have been one of wood squeezed into the wide east end of the passage. The main block upper storey was also divided into two with a passage between the eastern room and that in the wing. At a later date an external stair, now removed, led up to an inserted entrance into the upper passage. The only upper level opening in the north wall is a gunport in the NW corner.

LOCH BRORA NC 856060

The island of Eilean Nan Faoileag in Loch Brora was a hunting seat of the Earls of Sutherland. On its east side is a retaining wall 1.5m high and 10m long with traces of possible steps at the north end. A depression towards the south may indicate a well.

Little Tarrel

Plans of Little Tarrel

Little Tarrel

LOCH KINELLAN NH 472576

William, 4th Earl of Ross entertained Robert Bruce on the crannog in the loch after they settled their differences. Until they transferred to Fairburn in 1507, the MacKenzie chiefs used the island when they were managing the Earldom of Ross for James IV. In 1494 Kenneth MacKenzie's widow was kidnapped from the island by a party of Munros who were pursued, defeated and mostly killed near Castle Leod.

LOCHSLIN NH 849806

This castle stood on top of a gentle eminence overlooking Loch Eye north of Fearn. It was almost complete in 1900 but all that now remains is the base of one corner of the SW corner of the main block of a tower which had a wing engaging the SE corner. Until it fell in 1953 the remaining corner stood to the full height with a bartizan at the top. There was another bartizan on the SE corner of the five-storey wing. A kitchen lay in the basement. Lochslin was held by the Vass family from the 15th century and the castle must have been new when they were forfeited as rebels in 1603 and the lands given to the Munros. By 1623 it had passed to Rory MacKenzie of Castle Leod.

MESTAG ND 340764

Low retaining walls of a small court or tower lie in a now inaccessible position on a high stack on the north side of the SW end of the Island of Stroma in Pentland Firth.

NEWMORE NH 680719

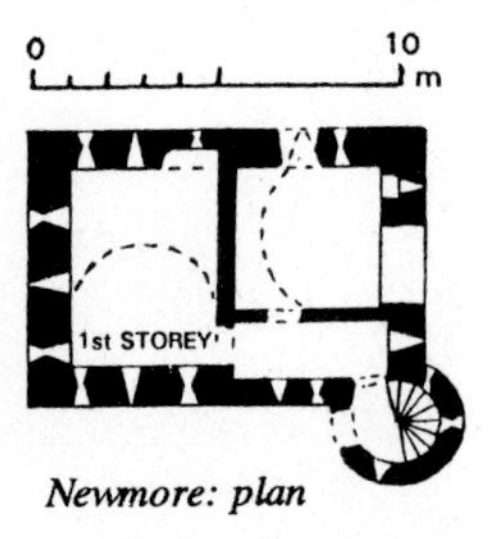

Newmore: plan

In the garden of a house lies the lowest storey of a tower of c1600 probably built by the MacKenzies, although the Munros held the eastate earlier. It has a round stair turret 3.5m in diameter at the east corner of a main block 11m long by 7.4m wide over walls 1m thick. A passage runs from the stair past a probable kitchen to a cellar at the far end. All the compartments have lighting slits and double splayed gunloops.

OLD WICK ND 369488 HS F

This tower on a long narrow peninsular 2km south of Wick may have been built by Harold Maddadson, Earl of Caithness, in the 1160s. Alternatively it was erected by the Cheynes, one of whom was Lord Chamberlain of Scotland in 1267. Reginald, last of the Cheynes here, held a third of Caithness and was a man of some influence. Nicholas Sutherland obtained Wick by marrying one his daughters, and in the 15th century the estate passed to the Oliphants. In 1526 it was sold to Laurence, Lord Oliphant. The Oliphants and Sutherlands had continual difficulties with their belligerent neighbours, the Sinclairs. In 1569 it was reported to the Privy Council that after a brawl in the burgh of Wick, John Sinclair, Master of Caithness, besieged Lord Oliphant in the castle of Old Wick for eight days until he was obliged to surrender through lack of food and water. The Sinclairs later took over the castle but it was probably a ruin by 1679 when it passed along with the Earldom of Caithness to Lord Glenorchy, who sold the castle to Sir William Dunbar of Hempriggs.

The tower measures 11.2m by 9.1m over walls averaging 2m thick at ground level but diminishing by internal offsets to carry the floors of three upper storeys. All the rooms were dark and low and the only surviving features are a loop in the basement south wall and another in the west wall at third storey level. The entrance and any latrines, stairs, and further loops must have been in the destroyed parts of the south and east walls. Stairs still existed when Cordiner were here in the 1770s. It seems unlikely that such a comfortless building would have continued to function other than as a purely military post after the end of the 15th century but there are footings of ranges of domestic buildings on either side of a court 17m wide extending for 70m behind it. One of the flanking sea-inlets is large enough to provide a harbour for a small ship or galley, access to the sea here being possible from outside the castle.

The castle of Old Wick

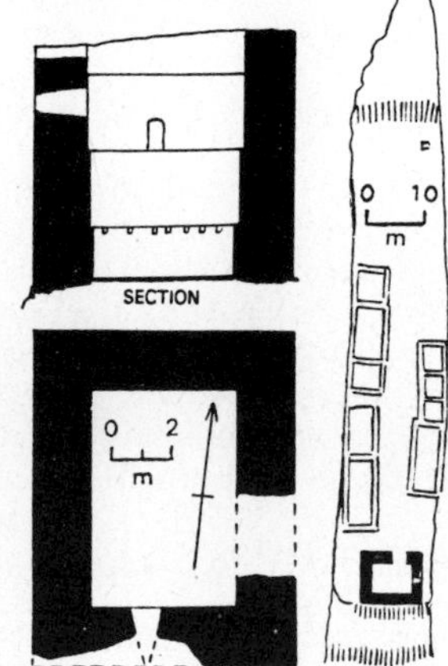

Old Wick: plans

Newmore Castle

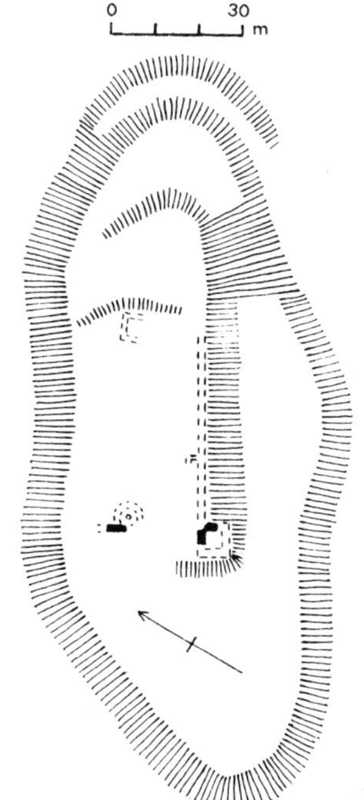

Plan of Ormond Castle

ORMOND NH 696536

Remains of this once important but little known castle lie hidden in a plantation on a spur of a hill south of Castleton Farm on the east side of the Black Isle. It was probably founded c1200 by King William the Lion. Walls probably of 13th century date enclosed a court about 45m long by 26m wide on the highest part of the site. Footings remain of a wall about 1.7m thick on the south side, together with traces of a building on the east, and the north and east sides of the lower part of a tower about 7.5m square projecting from the SW corner (this part was revealed by clearance in 1883). There is also a fragment of the west wall with evidence of a tower or other structure enclosing a well on the inner side of it. Robert Bruce gave Ormond to Sir Andrew Moray, later Regent for the young David II. Sir Andrew died in the castle c1338. It later passed to the Douglases, a young brother of the 8th Earl of Douglas being created Earl of Ormond in the 1440s. The castle was annexed by the Crown after the defeat of the Black Douglases by James II in 1455. James III in 1481 gave his second son James the titles of Duke of Ross, Marquis of Ormond, and Earl of Edradour, the last referring to an old name for the Black Isle. In 1503 this Prince resigned these lands in exchange for the Abbacy of Dunfermline. Nothing is known of the subsequent history of the castle although the discovery of several cannon balls in the adjacent field suggests that it may have been attacked at some time during the 16th or 17th centuries.

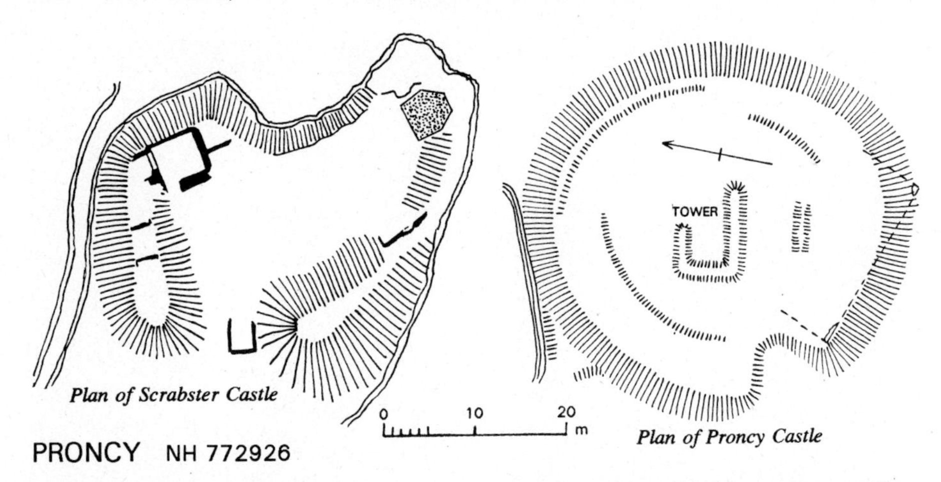

Plan of Scrabster Castle

Plan of Proncy Castle

PRONCY NH 772926

In the middle of a circular platform or ringwork 3m high and 34m across, with a modern pool beside it to the NW, are earth-covered footings of a tower about 9m long by 6.6m wide over walls 1.5m thick. To the south are bases of two corners of an outbuilding 19.3m long probably dating from after 1525, when Proncy was given to William Sutherland by Adam Gordon, Earl of Sutherland. The ringwork may go back to when lands here were given c1200 by Hugh Freskin to Gilbert de Moravia. The tower may be as early as the 13th century but is first recorded in 1562.

REDCASTLE NH 584495

Redcastle lies on the site of the earth and timber fortress of Edradour (Eddradovir) built by King William the Lion in 1179, although nothing is recognisable of that date. The castle was held by Sir John Bisset in 1230 and by Sir Andrew de Bosco in 1278. It later became part of the Earldom of Ormond created for one of the Douglases along with the secondary title of Lord Edradour. Redcastle reverted to the Crown in 1455 after this noble rebelled, was defeated, and went into exile. From 1570 until 1790 the castle was held by the MacKenzies and they gradually created a large L-plan mansion out of part of the earlier court. They changed the name to Redcastle on account of the colour of the sandstone walls. The building, now owned by Lord Burton, was left in a bad state after being used by troops in World War II and is now a ruin.

The site is roughly triangular with wooded slopes descending to a stream on the west and towards the Beauly Firth on the south, but with level ground on the east. From that side most of the features appear to be of the time of Roderick MacKenzie, whose initials appear on it, together with the date 1641. However, the masonry 2.2m thick surviving in the east and north walls up as far as the cellar vaults may be the remains of a 13th century courtyard about 23m wide. The western part of the building has walls 1.9m thick above a plinth which suggests that this part was once a tower house 8.6m wide and at least 13.4m long. As reconstructed later the part east of the supposed tower house contained a hall and chamber over three large vaulted cellars. Above were bedrooms and an attic with dormer windows. At the NE corner is a turret, and at the SE corner is a polygonal stair turret with a square caphouse. The stair allowed direct access to the private room from the court. The tower was altered to provide a pair of rooms on each of four storeys and has round bartizans on the southern corners and a square bartizan on the NW corner. The angle between this now irregularly shaped block and the main body has a square stair tower rising high above the rest of the building as a lookout platform.

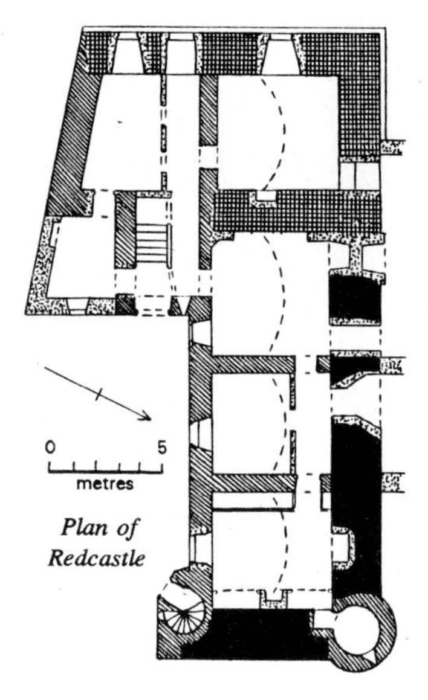

Plan of Redcastle

Redcastle

SCRABSTER ND 107691 F

Not far NW of Thurso is the site of a castle of the Bishops of Caithness first recorded in 1328. In 1455 Bishop William granted it to his brother Gilbert Mudy and this was confirmed by James III in 1478, although it was later returned to the Bishops. The castle was seized by the Earl of Caithness c1544, when the Bishop was banished and Alexander Gordon, son of the Earl of Sutherland, was made temporary Bishop, In 1557 Bishop Robert made John, Earl of Sutherland, its hereditary keeper and it was then described as being "situated among the wild and uncivilised Scots, and in a wintry region". By 1726 it was completely ruinous. The site recalls that of the episcopal castle at St Andrews, having low cliffs to the sea on two sides, the mouth of a burn on a third, and a ditch (now greatly decreased in width due to landfilling) on the landward side. A World War II concrete pill box lies on the base of a polygonal tower at the north end of a court about 30m long by 20m wide. There are remains of walls among the mounds covering other remains on the east and SW parts of the site. A kitchen fireplace is said to lie buried in the latter.

Scrabster Castle

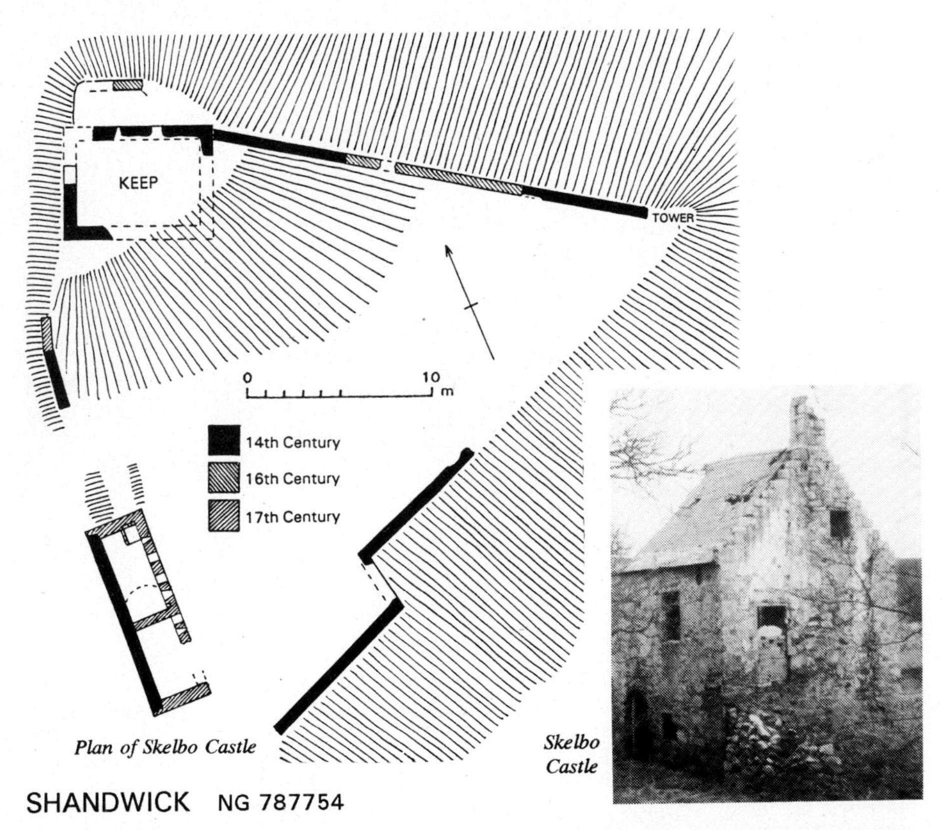

Plan of Skelbo Castle

Skelbo Castle

SHANDWICK NG 787754

To the north of the present mansion of 1936 of the Ross family is the derelict older mansion, mostly 18th and 19th century, but with 16th or 17th century work at the back including a semi-circular stair-turret with a shot-hole.

SKELBO NH 792952

On an eminence overlooking the site of a former ferry across the mouth of Loch Fleet is a fragmentary wall 1.2m thick around a triangular court with the longest side measuring about 80m. The wall may be 14th century and is best preserved on the north where its middle section has been rebuilt later. There are indications of a round tower at the east corner, possibly a relic of an early 16th century twin-towered gatehouse like that at Urquhart. Between these two positions is a 17th century block 21m long by 6.8m wide containing what was divided by wooden partitions into a hall and two chambers over a pair of vaulted rooms probably used for storing and preparing food. The SE corner and roof of the block collapsed a few years ago, since when scaffolding has held the remains of the upper level together. At the NW corner the ground rises to a mound, possibly natural, which bears fragments of a keep which seems to have been a smaller version of that built in the late 14th century at Duffus in Moray. It measured 16.5m by 11.8m over walls 1.4m thick and probably contained a hall and chamber side-by-side on the upper storey with storage space and servants' quarters below. The SE corner and most of the adjacent walls have fallen, and so has the NW corner. On the north side of the keep are slight remains of a later wing.

Hugh Feskin gave Skelbo c1211 to Gilbert de Moravia, later Bishop of Caithness. Gilbert's brother Richard was residing at Skelbo at the the time of his death in a battle against the Norsemen at Embo the 1240s. English and Scottish commissioners met at Skelbo in 1290 to greet the Maid of Norway as the Queen of Scots and whilst there were told of her death at Kirkwall. Thomas Kynnard obtained Skelbo c1440 by marrying Egidia, heiress of Walter Moray. In 1494 The Earl of Sutherland was ordered by the Lords of Council to pay 1,800 merks compensation after he captured the castle and removed from it two of John of Moray's children. In 1529 John Kynnard sold Skelbo to William Sutherland of Duffus. A feud later arose between the Sutherlands and the Gordons of Embo over a dispute over the boundary dividing the estates of Coul and Skelbo. After an affray in 1621 in which the heir to Embo was wounded, his kinsmen besieged Skelbo Castle. Alexander Sutherland was created Lord Duffus in 1651. The castle was occupied by Jacobites under the Earl of Cromartie in 1746. It was still occupied in 1769 but probably decayed after 1787 when it was disposed of to the Countess of Sutherland.

SKIBO NH 735891

A castle here is first mentioned in 1275 when Archibald, Bishop of Caithness, and the Earl of Sutherland disputed its ownership. It was captured in 1544 by the MacKays of Strathnaver and retaken by James Cullen. In 1565 Bishop Robert Stewart assigned the castle to John Grey. The Marquis of Montrose was brought here a prisoner after being betrayed at Ardvreck. Robert Grey was subsequently fined by the authorities after an incident in which his wife Jean Seton hit the officer guarding Montrose with a leg of mutton. After a later Robert Grey died in 1776 Skibo passed to Sir Patrick Dowall and it went in 1786 to George Demster of Dunnichen. The house was rebuilt about that time but the present building was erected for Andrew Carnegie in 1899-1903. It contains a datestone of 1663 and contemporary arms (probably later copies).

Skelbo Castle

TARBAT NH 770736

In an estate by the Bay of Nigg is an Adam-style building of 1787 on the site of a late 15th century castle built by Andrew Munro, and destroyed in 1745. The Ross family of Balnagown were very annoyed by the construction of this castle (which was originally called Milntown) just 1.5km SE of their seat and Munro had to borrow a garrison from the Earl of Sutherland to guard the place and allow the masons to work in peace. His son, who succeeded in 1501, in turn terrorised his neighbours. Additions were made c1660 by the then owner, Sir George MacKenzie, 1st Earl of Cromartie.

THURSO ND 127689

On the NE side of the town is a castellated ruin of 1875 lying on the site of a mansion with conical roofed turrets erected in 1660 by George, 6th Earl of Caithness. A still earlier building probably occupied the site. Here lived Sir John Sinclair (1754-1835), compiler of the Old Statistical Account of Scotland. A castle at Thurso belonging to the Norse Earl of Caithness was attacked in 1196 by King William the Lion.

TULLOCH NH 547605

It was probably Duncan Bain, who was given a charter of lands here in 1541, who built a castle on top of a bank overlooking the north side of Dingwall. In 1760 the Davidsons obtained Tulloch by marrying the heiress Jean Bain, and they lived in the castle until the 20th century, when it became an academy. The building is consequently much altered with little appearance of antiquity. Facing the town is a small three storey tower house with a round stair turret, probably later, at one corner. The vaulted basement has a pair of narrow loops and a gunport with a stepped outer embrasure like those at Kinkell. The upper parts with large windows, battlements, and a cap over the stair have been remodelled. The building behind is partly 17th century, again much rebuilt, whilst the range continuing the main axis of the tower is of c1920.

Tulloch Castle

OTHER CASTLES IN CAITHNESS, SUTHERLAND, ROSS & CROMARTY

BALCONIE NH 632699 Angus Og MacDonald held this vanished castle in the 1480s.
BALNAKIEL NC 403687 Cellars may be relics of house of Bishops of Caithness.
CONTILLUCH NH 636705 Mansion of site of supposed 11th century stone castle.
CYDERHALL NH 758886 House on site of a Gordon castle. Estate was held by Hugh Siward in 13th century and then Bishops of Caithness until 1557.
FRESWICK ND 378672 High 18th century house adjoins ruined wing of c1660-1700.
GEANIES NH 894792 Dated 1742 with initials of Hugh MacLeod. An armoral stone of c1650 has initials of John Sinclair and Katherine Fraser.
GOLSPIE NC 836009 Farm called Golspie Tower marks site of former castle.
KINBEACHIE NH 634621 The last traces were removed in 1959. It was dated 1546.
MUIR OF ORD NH 528497 Worn motte by golf course south of town.
NOVAR NH 614679 Reset stone dated 1634 with initials of Robert Munro and his wife Helen upon John Munro's house of 1720, altered in c1770, 1897, and 1956.
ORD NH 514505 Present house of c1810. Date 1637 refers to older house built soon after John MacKenzie obtained a charter of lands here in that year.
TONGUE NC 592587 Single storey mansion with wings. It bears the MacKay arms and the dates 1678 and 1750. Probably nothing is earlier than those dates.
NO REMAINS: Abirscurs, Achnacloich, Arboll, Balloan, Clentredwale, Clyne, Corbet, Cratok, Cuttle, Dulrossie, Dunskeath, Durnies, Edderton, Haven, Innerbreakie, Kincardine, Mhic Cneancall, Ormellie, Ospidale, Sorline, Tain, Torrish.

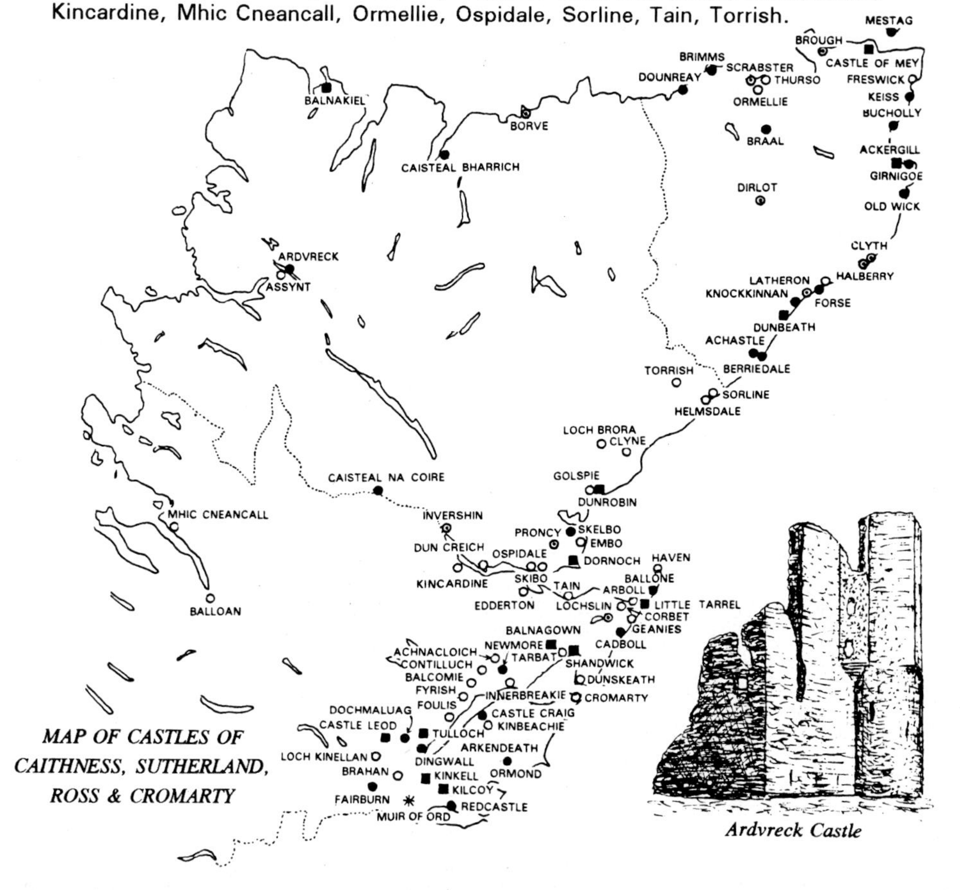

MAP OF CASTLES OF CAITHNESS, SUTHERLAND, ROSS & CROMARTY

Ardvreck Castle

INVERNESS AND NAIRN

ACHNACARRY NH 175878

The house of 1802 situated between the lochs of Arkaig and Lochy is the successor of a nearby castle of the Camerons of Lochiel which was destroyed by the Duke of Cumberland in 1746. The family returned from exile under an amnesty of 1784.

ALDOURIE NH 602372

In the early 17th century the Frasers built a castle consisting of a main block with a round tower at the SW corner. The main block has a parapet with angle rounds. It passed to the Mackintoshes in the 18th century. A west wing was added in 1839 and very considerable extensions on all sides were made in 1853-61.

BALBLAIR NH 873553

Most of this mansion which belonged to the Rose family is of the late 17th century and later. It now serves as an eventide home. In 1746 the officers of Cumberland's army lodged here but the Duke himself stayed in the nearby town of Nairn.

BEAUFORT NH 507431

This 19th and 20th century red sandstone mansion on the south side of the River Beauly lies on the site of an early castle of the Bissets later superseded by a stone castle of the Frasers of Lovat destroyed by Cumberland in 1746. Simon, 11th Lord Lovat, a noted Jacobite executed in 1747, was the last British peer to be beheaded.

BOATH NH 918356 NTS

The circular 17th century dovecot maintained by the Scottish National Trust lies in the middle of a ringwork with a diameter of about 40m. The housing estate on the ridge to the SW may be on the site of a bailey. This was the royal castle of Eren from which William The Lion issued the second of his two charters to Inverness in 1185. Soon afterwards it was betrayed by his constable Gillecolm of Maddertie to Donald MacWilliam and was probably destroyed soon afterwards.

Castle Roy

BUNCHREW NH 621459

Within the much altered and extended L-plan house is a fireplace dated 1621 on the lintel. The square stair turret with the outer angle chamfered off may be original but its balustrade is later and most features of the house are 18th and 19th century. Bunchrew belonged to Forbes of Culloden, but has now passed to the Frasers.

CASTLE ROY NJ 007219

The Comyn Lords of Badenoch are thought to have built this simple castle of enclosure in the early 13th century. A wall 1.8m thick surrounds a rhomboid court 23.8m long by 16.1m wide entered through a wide gateway on the NE with a pointed head of thin voussoirs. At the north corner, near the main gate, and beside a NW postern, is a rectangular turret containing two storeys of small rooms. The diagonally opposite southern corner is missing and another turret or tower, perhaps of later date, may have stood there. The only relics of lean-to wooden domestic buildings within are a pair of superimposed latrines at the west corner and one jamb of a nearby upper window.

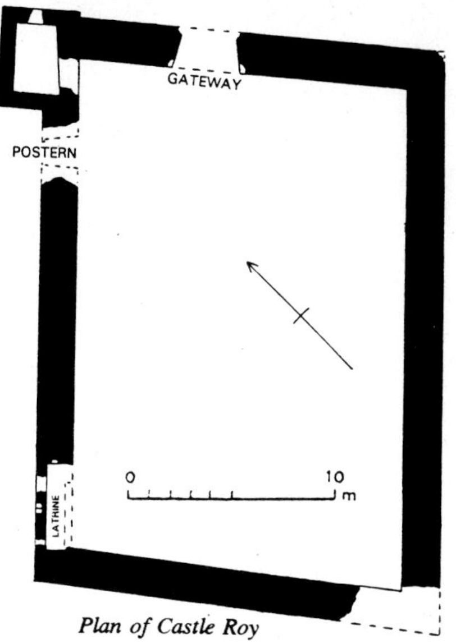

Plan of Castle Roy

Castle Roy

Castle Stuart

Plans of Castle Stuart

CASTLE STUART NH 741498 OP

Castle Stuart lies in the former lordship of Petty once held by the Mackintoshes but later, much to the clan's annoyance, lost to the Stuart Earls of Moray. This explains the incident in 1624 when the Mackintoshes went to "ane house which the Earl of Moray hath now of late built in Pettie called Castel Stuart, they drive away his servants from thence and doe possess themselves of all the Earl of Moray his rents and of his handsom residence". The house in question was restored in the 1980s after standing empty for a while, previous to which it was let to tenants. It has a four storey main block 19.3m long by 9.9m wide over walls up to 1.6m thick and has a pair of five storey towers about 7.2m square. The basic plan shape is symmetrical but there is no symmetry in the layout of the windows and doorways and in any case the SW tower has been heightened and given modern open battlements with a caphouse over the stair surmounted by an openwork crown spire. This stair is one of two corbelled out of the re-entrant angle between the main block end walls and the towers. On the northern corners there are two storey square bartizans corbelled out diagonally. The SE tower has three bartizans with conical roofs, and there are numerous top storey dormers, plus chimney stacks and gables giving the building an impressive skyline.

An inserted later entrance near the middle of the south front leads through to a passage connecting all the lowest rooms. Five double splayed gunloops open off this passage, and there are others in the towers giving a heavy concentration facing the approach. They seem to have been to impress visitors more than for defence as the main block has only one gunloop facing north. The main block contains a kitchen with a fireplace and oven in the west end wall, a wine cellar with a service stair next to it, and two other cellars. The eastern cellar, plus another in the base of the SE tower can now only be reached from outside by doorways broken through their east walls as the east end of the passage which served them has been blocked by a new stair inserted at this end. The SW tower contains a scale-and-platt staircase up to the hall from the original entrance doorway in its east wall. Beyond the hall is a private room from which is reached a bedroom in the SE tower. This layout is repeated on the third storey, except that there is also a bedroom in the SW tower. Many other bedrooms are contained in the main block top storey and the upper parts of the towers.

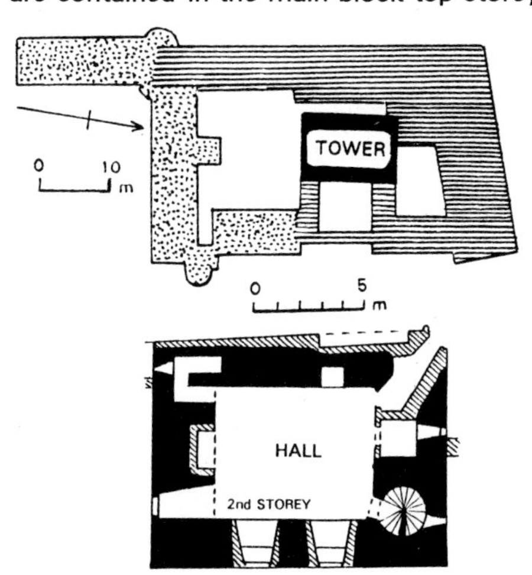

Plans of Cawdor Castle

Castle Stuart

Cawdor Castle

Cawdor Castle

CAWDOR NH 847499 OP

This famous castle lies above the east bank of the Cawdor Burn south of the River Nairn. It is often associated with Macbeth, who was Thane of Cawdor before being King of Scotland from 1040 to 1057, but in fact the castle is a much later building erected by descendants of his brother. The present laird is the 25th (and 6th Earl Cawdor) taking as the first Donald, Thane of Cawdor in 1295. Both the Thanedom and family name were then spelt Calder, which is how the name is pronounced. It is thought to have been William, 3rd Thane in this series, who built a tower on his lands here in the 1390s to supplement the castle of Nairn of which as Sheriff of the county he had custody. The stump of a hawthorn tree still rising from the floor of the vaulted cellar of the tower is explained by a legend that William was directed in a dream to let loose a donkey and built his castle where it stopped to lie down under a hawthorn tree with the promise that his line would prosper there.

The 6th Thane, Crown Chamberlain beyond the Spey under James II, was licensed to refortify the castle. He built the courtyard, fitting its gateway with a yett taken from Lochindorb Castle in Moray which was dismantled after its owner, the Douglas Earl of Moray was forfeited for rebellion in 1455. The oldest parts of the domestic buildings may have been built by John, 8th Thane, who died in 1498. His young heiress Muriel was kidnapped by the Campbells, taken off to distant Inverary Castle in Argyll, and at the age of 12 obliged to marry the Earl of Argyll's son Sir John Campbell. Their descendants still reside at Cawdor. John, 11th Thane, was tutor to his kinsman the young Earl of Argyll and was murdered by the jealous Campbell of Ardkinglass in 1591. The castle survived unharmed during the Covenant Wars as its owners took no part in them, the 13th Thane being insane and his son dying as a young student at Glasgow University in 1647. The next Thane, Sir Hugh, built much of the present apartments. The title of Thane, which survived here much longer than anywhere else in Scotland, was superseded by a modern peerage when John, 19th Thane, was created Lord Cawdor in 1796. His son John was created Earl Cawdor in 1827. However, from 1716 onwards the family lived in North Wales, where they had inherited vast estates, and they only returned to Cawdor in the mid 19th century.

The tower house measures 14m by 9.5m and has four storeys plus an attic within a parapet with angle rounds which is perhaps part of additional works carried out c1456-60. The rounds were given octagonal tops with conical roofs in the 17th century. There are 17th century box-machicolations on the south and west. An original machicolation protects a doorway at ground level from which a straight stair leads up to the hall. A spiral stair then rises in the NE corner and there are small rooms at the upper levels in the thick north end wall. In 1979 the equally thick south end wall was discovered to contain in its base a long-forgotten bottle-dungeon reached only from above. A window lies in the blocked original late 14th century doorway at hall level towards the south end of the east wall. The fourth storey is covered by a lofty pointed barrel vault, probably added in the 1450s.

The courtyard around the tower measured about 51m by 28 but much of it is now filled by ranges on all four sides. The three sides away from the burn were protected by a dry ditch which still survives on the east where it is crossed by a drawbridge. On the north is a postern with an original yett leading out from cellars below courtyard level. The north range has a hall with private rooms at either end and four almost square bedrooms on each of the third and fourth storeys. The range is mostly of c1600-10 but the top storey is of 1639-43. The kitchen in the NW corner dates from then, and probably also the scale-and-platt stair projecting into the court. There is a turret stair leading to a gabled caphouse projecting from the top of the north front, although this is modern, at least in its present form. The NW corner has a square bartizan on ornamental mouldings set well below the eaves of the roof. There are shot-holes in the bartizan and below the windows in the north range. The dormers dated 1674 with initials of Sir Hugh Campbell and Lady Henrietta Stewart were renewed in 1855. The 15th or 16th century "Lytill tower" in the NE corner was rebuilt in 1699. The west range has just two upper levels, the main drawing room being at courtyard level. A fireplace lintel in this room is dated 1511 referring to the marriage of Muriel Calder with Sir John Campbell. The actual carving is 17th century as the decoration includes a fox smoking a pipe, tobacco being unknown in Scotland in 1511. In the angle between the ranges is a square space containing a scale-and-platt staircase. At ground level this has an entrance above which is the date 1672 and the initials A.S.C. Walls pierced by arches connect the main tower to the outer east wall to create a small entrance court, an equally small north court, and a larger south court. The range on the east side of the south court is partly old but has dormers dated 1855. The south range dated 1702 has been modernised. A SW range beyond it is Victorian.

Cawdor Castle

Daviot Castle

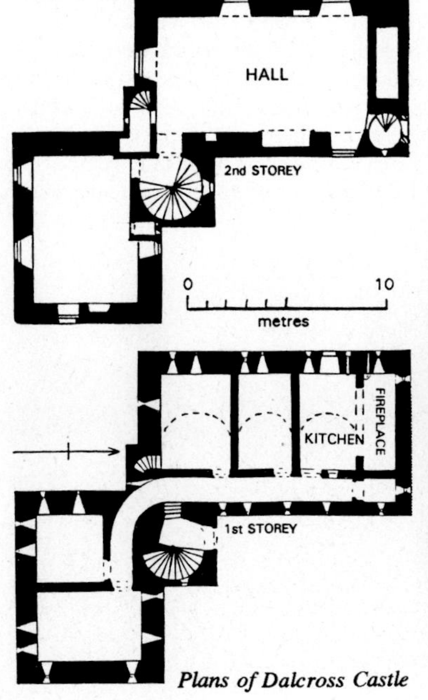

Plans of Dalcross Castle

Dalcross Castle

CLUNY NN 646943

A late 18th century Adam style house high above the River Spey lies on the site of a castle destroyed by Cumberland after Culloden because its owner Ewen, chief of the Macphersons, was a Jacobite. A reward of £1,000 was offered for help in his capture but he managed to remain in hiding on his estates for nine years before he escaped to France in 1755, only to die there the following year. The forfeited estates were eventually restored to his son but the Macphersons lost them again later.

CULLODEN NH 721465

Culloden was held by the Mackintoshes until they sold it to Duncan Forbes, M.P. and Provost of Inverness in 1626. The house then built was destroyed by Cumberland after his victory on the nearby moor in 1746, although the family managed to retain the estate until 1897. Parts of the cellars of the old house are incorporated in the large new mansion built by Arthur Forbes in 1772-83.

DALCROSS NH 779483

At the east end of Culloden Moor is a mansion built by the 8th Lord Lovat in 1620. It later passed to the Mackintoshes who added the lower north wing dated 1703 over its doorway. The arms of both families and the date 1720 appear on a panel over the entrance to the main house. Here in 1746 the Duke of Cumberland marshalled his troops prior to his defeat of the Jacobite army on the moor. The castle was ruined except for the extension, but was re-roofed in 1897-8 and is still occupied. The castle consists of a main block and a wing only touching each other by one corner. There are no obvious signs of one part being later than the other but it is quite likely that there was a gap of a few years between their building. In the main re-entrant angle is a square tower rising one stage higher than the rest and containing the entrance and main stair. A slight thickening of the main block south wall in the other re-entrant angle contains a service stair from the wine cellar to a lobby by the hall. From the entrance there is access to a long passage extending northwards past two cellars to a kitchen with a fireplace in the north end wall. In the other direction the passage extends round into the wing to connect with two more cellars there. The passage and all the lower rooms have double-splayed gunports. There are two storeys of bedrooms over the hall, the top level being partly in the roof and having closets bartizans with conical roofs. Many of the upper windows retain their original grilles.

DAVIOT NH 728407

Immediately east of the house built in 1821 by Alexander, 24th chief of Mackintosh, on a low ridge above the River Nairn is the site of a castle said to have been built by David, 3rd Earl of Crawford, in the early 15th century. The building is supposed to have been a courtyard castle with round corner towers. Its foundations may survive under vegetation and soil but the only recognisable part is the NE tower which is 7.5m in diameter over walls 1.7m thick standing 3m high above the sloping external ground. Only one fragment of the tower now rises above the courtyard level.

Dalcross Castle

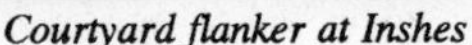

Courtyard flanker at Inshes

Erchless Castle

ERCHLESS NH 410408

The heart of the estate is almost enclosed by a loop of the River Beauly and the Erchless Burn, the castle being near the latter. Hugh, Lord Lovat, was licensed to build a castle here in 1529, but the present building was erected after Simon, Lord Lovat, gave Erchless to John Chisholm in 1606. His descendants lived in the area until 1838. A Williamite garrison was besieged here in 1689 by 500 Jacobites. Roderick Chisholm led his clan on the Jacobite side in 1715 and in 1746 the then chief's son and 30 of the clan died at Culloden, but somehow the castle survived this period intact. It is a white-harled L-plan of the early 17th century with the wing on one side set so as to also project slightly from an end wall of a main block containing the usual twin vaulted cellars, hall above, and two upper storeys. There are bartizans and dormer windows which have lost their pediments. The hall windows have been enlarged and the upper windows are mostly of 1787-93. The wing rises above the main block and, until its stair was later continued to the top, it contained three bedrooms over a main stair from the entrance to the hall. A stair turret over the main re-entrant angle served the upper rooms and there is another stair in a turret corbelled out at the furthest corner from the wing. The existing entrance in the wing outer wall is assumed to be later and that there was originally an entrance within the re-entrant angle, thus covered by the gunports. The oriel on the wing and the northern extensions are later additions.

HALHILL NH 763504

This castle, seat of the Mackintosh lordship of Petty, is thought to have stood near the level crossing on the Inverness to Nairn railway line 1.5km south of Inverness Airport. It was destroyed in 1513 but soon afterwards a new castle was built to replace it, either on the same site or where Castle Stuart now stands.

INSHES NH 695437

The present house, restored in the 1980s, is of 1767, that year and the name A. Robertson appearing on it. Remaining from a court attached to an older building on the site probably destroyed during the 1745 rebellion, is a turret 3.9m square containing two wide mouthed gunports in each side in the basement. An upper storey and an attic within the still-surviving gabled roof both have fireplaces but now lack floors. The second storey has gunports piercing the corners, an uncommon feature.

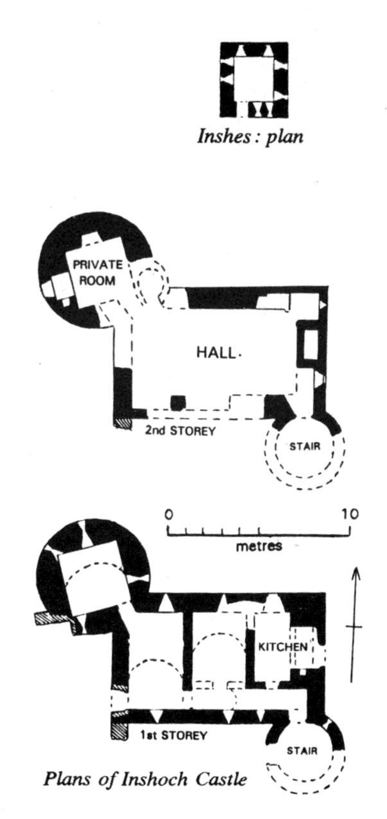

Inshes: plan

Plans of Inshoch Castle

Inshoch Castle

INSHOCH NH 936567

The Hays of Lochloy, cadets of the Earls of Erroll, held Inshoch from an early date, although the present castle was not built until c1580-1600. It was left to decay after the barony passed to the Brodies in 1695. A round tower 6.2m in diameter containing a private room and two upper bedrooms for the laird over a square cellar with four double splayed gunloops lies at the NW corner of a main block 11.6m long by 6.9m wide. The hall is very ruinous and not much remains of the two storeys of bedrooms above, whilst the two cellars and the unusually small kitchen with its fireplace in the east wall are somewhat choked with rubble. At hall level a small room was squeezed into the NE corner beside the kitchen fireplace flue and from it seems to have descended a service stair to the middle cellar. A wide spiral stair from a west facing entrance up as far at the third storey was contained in a round tower 4.4m in diameter, now mostly destroyed, on the SE corner. Only traces of corbelling remain of turret stairs rising from the third storey over the eastern re-entrant angle, and of another stair rising from the hall to the laird's suite. Claude Nattes' drawing of 1799 shows the stair tower as having an embattled top on a corbel table. Very little now remains of a 17th century wing to the NW containing a large new drawing room over a spacious kitchen with extra bedrooms on top. The arrangement of this wing was striking similar to that added in a similar position at neighbouring Brodie Castle.

INVERGARRY NM 315006

This spacious L-plan building dramatically positioned on a cliff above the NW side of Loch Oich was built by Donald MacDonald of Glengarry, who died in 1645, or his grandson Aeneas. It was referred to as new when burnt by General Monck in 1654. It was restored, and after the Revolution of 1688 Alasdair MacDonald fortified the castle for the exiled King James. The Williamite government had forces stationed at either end of the Great Glen but they respected the castle as a place of strength and not until early in 1692 was Glengarry obliged to surrender it. It was eventually returned to the family and was twice visited by Prince Charles Edward. In consequence the castle was blown up by the Duke of Cumberland in 1746, the outer part of the wing, and the adjacent corner of the main block being reduced to the ground.

The castle has a wing 8m wide projecting 7.4m from a main block 16.6m long by 9.7m wide. The wing contained a wide scale-and-platt stair leading from the entrance up to a lobby from which there was access to the hall and onto the foot of a narrower scale-and-platt upper stair in a turret in the re-entrant angle which, until it collapsed recently, rose high above the main building. This second stair served the third and fourth storeys and then a turret stair of which little remains served the fifth storey bedrooms in the main block and wing and two more in the square stair turret. The cellars below the hall were not vaulted and there is no sign of a kitchen fireplace. No bartizans survive but there is at the SE corner a round tower 4.6m in diameter which contained another stair giving the laird private access from his end of the hall (where there is a fireplace) to his suite of rooms above at this end.

Invergarry Castle

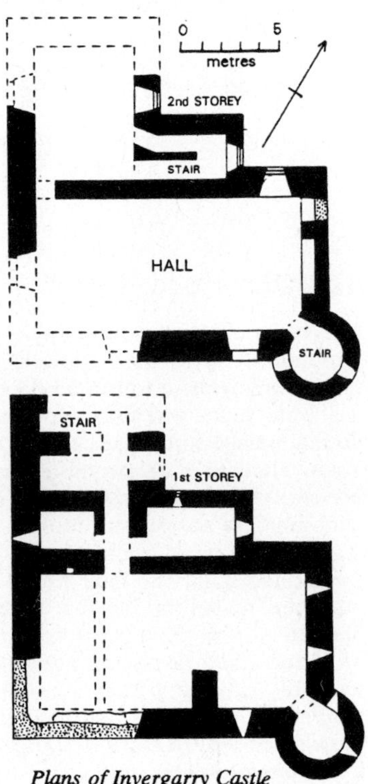

Plans of Invergarry Castle

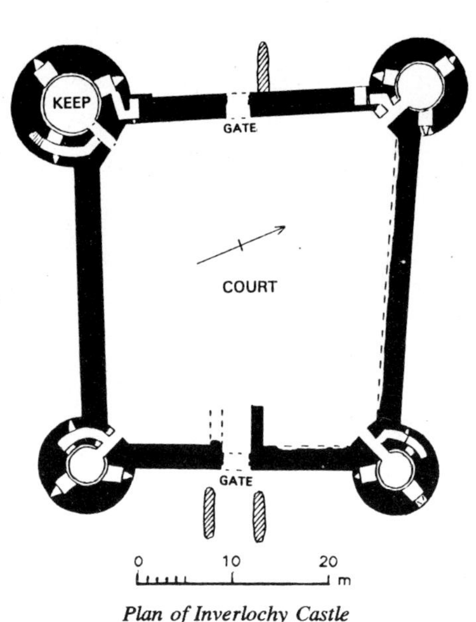

Plan of Inverlochy Castle

Inverlochy Castle

INVERLOCHY NN 120754 V

This ruin on level ground beside the River Lochy near Fort William is thought to have been built c1275-95 by the Comyn family. They were lords of Badenoch from c1200 until they were ousted by Robert Bruce in 1308-10. In 1431 the MacDonalds overwhelmed within sight of the castle a royal army led by the Earls of Mar and Caithness, the latter being killed. There was another battle at this strategic spot in 1645 when the Campbells were surprised and defeated by Montrose with his forces of Catholic Highlanders mainly composed of MacDonalds, Camerons and Appin Stewarts. However the only specific mention of the castle itself occurs in 1505 when it was garrisoned by Alexander Gordon, Earl of Huntly and Lord of Lochaber.

Walls built of rough boulders some 2.7m thick and 9m high to the ruined walkway on top enclose a court 33m long by 30m wide. At each corner is a boldly projecting round tower, three of them being from 9 to 10m in diameter, whilst that at the SW corner is 12.6m in diameter. Known as Comyn's Tower, this building was a keep serving as a residence for the lord and having a latrine opening out of its second storey, a feature not found on the other towers. This tower has an intake towards the court allowing circulation of the wall-walk to be uninterrupted here. Otherwise all four towers are similar, each having a very low unlit basement and two upper storeys lighted only by narrow slits and connected by mural stairs curving up within the outer wall thickness from one jamb of an entrance at ground level. There are gateways with portcullis slots in the east and west walls. The former was contained within some sort of gatehouse projecting entirely within the court. The battlements on the south wall and the restored loops in the keep date from Lord Abinger's attempt at repairs c1905. The north wall contains openings for an early 16th century range against it which has otherwise gone except for a lump of walling by the west gate. Other lumps of masonry outside the east gate are all that remains of a barbican of about the same period.

Inverlochy Castle

INVERNESS NH 666451

Inverness Castle was a royal stronghold established probably by David I. The name Auldcastle Road is thought to recall an older fortress perhaps of the time of Malcolm Canmore on higher ground further from the river, and long before that there was a fort further west on the hill of Craig Phadrick. The castellated building used as a Sheriff Court and County Police department now standing on the castle hill dates only from 1835. A well is the only survival of the ancient building. The original building on the site was of earth and wood and it is known when stone defences were first erected here. William the Lion fortified the town with a bank and ditch. The castle was dismantled by the Bruces c1308-10 and was not rebuilt until 1412 when Alexander, Earl of Mar, son of the Wolf of Badenoch, erected a new building in which he died in 1437. James I stayed in the castle in 1427 when putting the Highland chiefs in order and there summoned a parliament. In 1428 Alexander, Lord of the Isles, pillaged the town but failed to capture the castle, although it fell to his successor John in 1455.

James III was at the castle in 1464 when still a minor, and James IV came in 1499, when the Earl of Huntly was made its hereditary keeper. When Queen Mary and her brother the Earl of Moray came to Inverness in 1562 they were obliged to stay in a comparatively modest house only recently demolished to make way for a new building to house the Highlands and Islands Development Board. Their forces captured the castle from the Gordons and the keeper who had refused to admit them was hanged. In 1644 the castle was unsuccessfully besieged by Montrose, but in 1497 it fell briefly into the hands of a party of Royalists which included Sir Thomas Urquhart. When Cromwell came to Inverness in 1653 he found the castle damaged and outdated. He spent £80,000 on building a new fort called The Sconce to take 1,000 men on a new site by the river mouth. It lasted only until 1661, when Charles II declared it redundant and had it demolished. Just its clock tower now survives among oil storage tanks. After the expulsion of his brother James VII in 1688 the Government found itself needed another stronghold at Inverness so the castle was patched up. It was drastically remodelled by General Wade after the 1715 rebellion. It was renamed Fort George after the then King and was later superseded by the new Fort George at Ardersier after being captured and blown up by the Jacobites in 1746.

KILRAVOCK NH 814493

Kilravock, pronounced Kilrock, on the north bank of the Nairn, has been the home of the Rose family for at least 25 generations. The family either derive from the Celtic Earls of Ross or from the Norman family of de Roos, heraldic evidence making the latter most likely. Seventeen of the lairds here since Hugh de Rose acquired the lands c1280 have been called Hugh. Hereditary in the family from 1450 until 1777 was the office of Provost of Nairn, 45 of them having held this title. Construction of the tower house in the 1460s was authorised by the Earl of Ross, then all-powerful in this area. In c1482 James III's favourites sought unsuccessfully to have the tower destroyed, but it was damaged about this time after being captured by the Mackintoshes. Queen Mary was entertained at Kilravock in 1562 and in 1746 Prince Charles Edward was entertained at Kilravock whilst the Duke of Cumberland was occupying the Rose family's town house in Nairn, a common instance of a family backing both sides.

The tower measures 11.5m by 9.3m over walls 2.2m thick and contains a hall over a vaulted cellar, three upper storeys, and an attic within a parapet with angle-rounds. The hall has an unusual instance of a window over a fireplace, the flue being taken round to one side. The entrance is at this level and the doorway leading into the cellar from the court is a later insertion. From beside the entrance rises a spiral stair ending in a form of caphouse amounting to no more than a slight raising of the walls with a square open turret on top. In the 17th century a range 20m long by 8.3m wide was added, being joined to the tower by a square turret containing a new entrance and a scale-and-platt staircase serving four storeys in each part. The range has windows set in tiers and a slight square projection at the SW corner, plus a round stair turret connecting the three upper levels corbelled out of the middle of the south wall. In 1759-61 corridors and a central porch were added to the north side of this range and wings built northwards from the western end of the range and from the old tower, each ending in short lean-to wings facing each other to enclose a court. A stone with the year 1631 was reset on the west wing when the 17th century block was remodelled at the west end and a Venetian window inserted. SW of the 17th century range is a length of the original courtyard wall ending in a two storey tower which was given a pyramidal roof c1815. This building was probably the "mekell towr of Kilraowk" for which the Elgin smith George Robertson made a yett in 1569.

Kilravock Castle

Loch-an-Eilean Castle

Plans of Kilravock Castle

LETHEN NH 937518

A new house built by Alexander, second son of David, 13th laird of Brodie, after he acquired the estate in 1634 was burnt down in 1680 and replaced by a new house to the north. This building survives in a much altered state. To the east of it is a 17th century granary with crowstepped end gables and a small central gable on one side.

LOCH-AN-EILEAN NH 899079

This castle occupies an island (probably a crannog) off the eastern shore of a small loch in Rothiemurchus Forest. Alexander Stewart, the celebrated Wolf of Badenoch is said to have had a seat here, but present building was begun by Mackintoshes, and then passed in the 16th century to the Gordons. In c1680 it was reported that the castle "is useful to the countrey in times of trouble or wars; for the people put in their goods and children here, and it is easily defended, being environed with steep hills and crags on each side, except to the east". The castle was attacked by Jacobite forces after their defeat at Cromdale in 1690 but was successfully defended by the Gordon laird's wife Grizel Mor. It was last used in 1715 when Mackintosh of Balnespick and others were confined within it by Jacobites to prevent them joining the Hanovarian forces. In the late 19th century and in more recent times the ruin has been a breeding ground for ospreys and consequently few experts have ever been able to examine it.

In the NW corner is a late 15th century tower house now reduced to two storeys. A stair in the NE corner rises to what was a hall over a vaulted cellar. The hall has a fireplace in the south wall and large windows to the east and west. The line of the north wall is continued by a contemporary wall containing a gate. The curtain wall adjoining to the SW is later. It contains a doorway and traces of a range with a fireplace and latrine on the upper storey. This range was later replaced by a single storey building adjoining the tower south gable. On the south side of the small court is a early 16th century century block containing a hall over unvaulted offices. On the east side of the court are slight remains of a 17th century block against the curtain.

LOVAT NH 540461

This building on a slight eminence above the south side of the Beauly near its mouth has vanished without trace except for a few stones uncovered by a farmer. It was founded in 1230 by the Bissets and passed to the Frasers in the early 15th century, Hugh Fraser being made Lord Lovat in 1458. The castle was an important seat of the family until destroyed by Cumberland after his victory at Culloden in 1746.

Moniack

MONIACK NH 552436 A

This early 17th century L-plan building, now the home of a winery, has a rather odd appearance as a result of alterations of 1804-8. The two arms were then lowered and given hipped roofs and large new windows, whilst the stair turret in the re-entrant angle was embattled. This turret has a round outer angle corbelled out square higher up and contains the entrance with an empty niche for an heraldic panel over it. Part of the main building retains some old windows still having their original grilles. A range of 1813 joins the main block to a detached block built to the east c1760. The angle between these two parts is filled in with an addition of 1920.

MOY NH 775443

The most prominent feature now of the heavily wooded island 300m long by 80m wide in Loch Moy is an obelisk commemorating Sir Aeneas Mackintosh, who died in 1820. His forebears had on the island a castle and township affording them some measure of security against raids by the MacDonalds. Of the buildings only slight remains, including two ovens and a paved street, have been discovered.

MUCKRACK NH 986251

John Grant of Freuchie gave Muckrack to his second son Patrick in 1583 and the castle was built soon afterwards. Patrick was knighted by James VI and lived until 1626, being the ancestor of the Grants of Rothiemurchus. In 1978-85 the building was restored after lying in ruins for some time and a stone dated 1598 with the arms and initials of Patrick and his wife, plus the motto "In God Is Al My Trest" which had been removed to Rothiemurchus was replaced over the entrance at Muckrack. The tower house measures 8.5m by 7.9m and has a round turret 4m in diameter containing a stair linking the lowest three storeys. A rough arch is thrown across a segment of the stair under each step, an unusual arrangement. A conical-roofed stair turret carried on a squinch arch over the entrance then rises to the fourth storey of the main block and to two upper rooms in a square caphouse over the main stair. A bartizan has been reconstructed on the corner diagonally opposite the main stair. The tower stood on the east side of a small court of which the southern side was formed by a two storey block containing a hall and chambers. Except for the east end wall and a round stair turret at the SE corner this block was almost destroyed down to ground level.

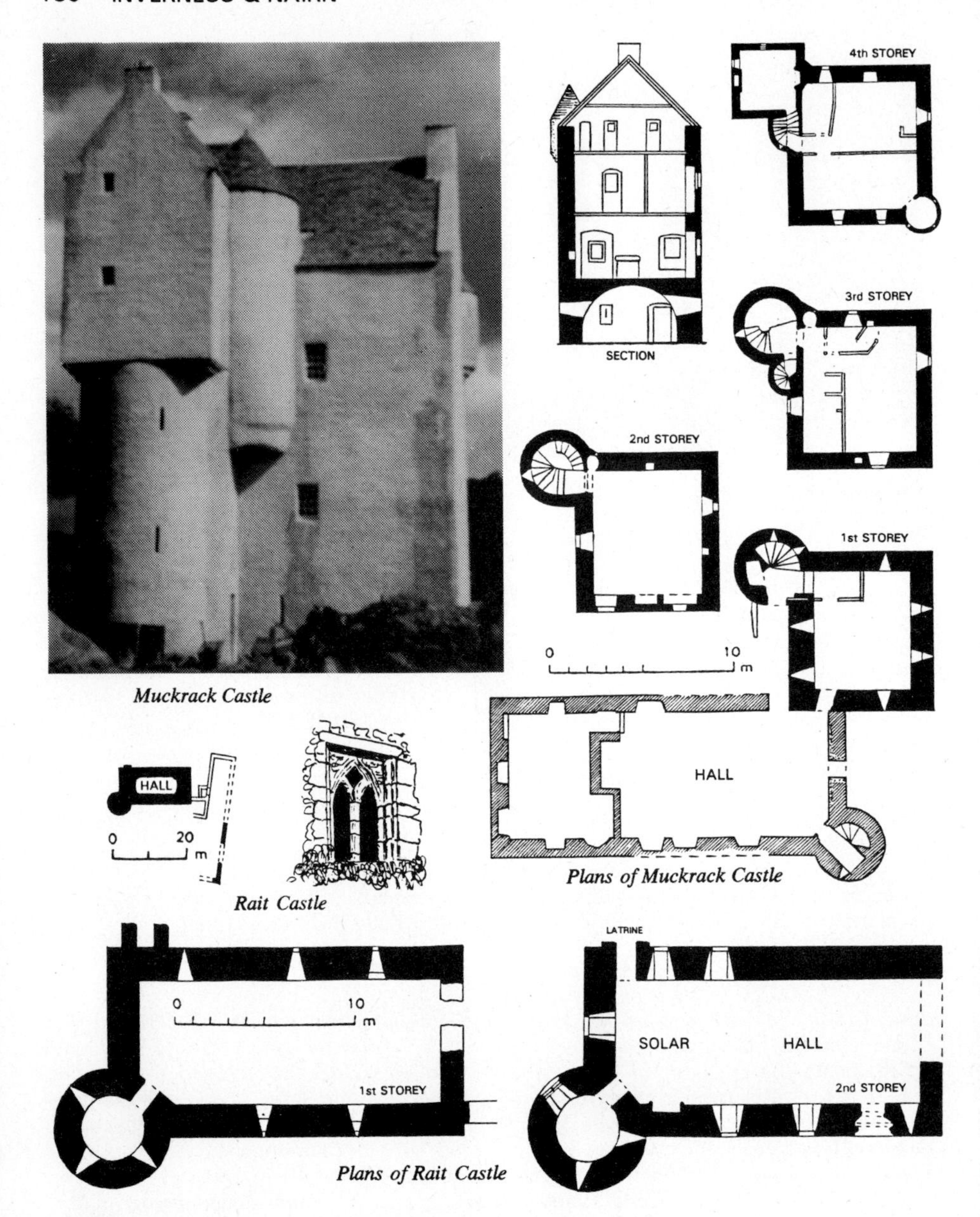

Muckrack Castle

Plans of Muckrack Castle

Rait Castle

Plans of Rait Castle

NAIRN NH 885565

The earth and timber castle built by William The Lion stood between the river and the present High Street, the site now being called the Constabulary Garden. This name derives from office of constable of the castle held by the Thanes of Cawdor, hereditary Sheriffs of Nairn until 1747. A late 19th century house in the garden has served as a dower house and office of the Campbells of Cawdor.

RAIT NH 894525 V

In 1238 there was a Thanedom of Rait then held by the Mackintoshes. By the late 13th century they had been replaced by the de Rait family, probably cadets of the Comyn Earls of Buchan. In 1290 Sir Gervaise and Sir Andrew de Rait strongly supported Edward I of England. In 1404 the last of them is said to have fled the district after killing Andrew, 4th Thane of Cawdor. Rait then passed to the new Thane of Cawdor, although in 1442 it seems to have reverted to the Mackintoshes. In the 16th century there were disputes over possession of Rait between the Campbells of Cawdor, who had purchased the estate, and the Ogilvies and Mackintoshes. The castle is recorded in 1590 on the accession of John Campbell as 12th Thane of Cawdor, but may have been abandoned soon afterwards, not being shown on Gordon of Straloch's map of c1650.

Rait is an unaltered and nearly complete example of a hall-house of the turn of the 13th and 14th centuries. Its features and position at the foot of a slope suggest a function more domestic than military. It has a main block 19.7m long by 10.2m wide over walls 1.8m thick, except that the NE wall, now much ruined, was only 1.2m thick. On the south corner is a round tower 6.4m in diameter containing a dome vaulted upper room with two loops and a west facing window with seats in the embrasure, the room below having just three narrow loops. The main block basement was unvaulted and has three rectangular windows on the NW and two on the SE. It is likely that at least part of it was used as living space rather than just all storage. The hall above has towards the north end of the SE wall a remarkable elaborately moulded pointed-headed entrance which must have been reached by timber steps. At the other end is a fireplace in the SE wall, and a latrine in the NW wall and there are in all five windows with seats in the embrasures and which had two lights with Y-tracery like the solitary example surviving complete in the round tower. These are rare in Scottish castles and suggest English influence (the Rait brothers are known to have gone to England). Probably two of these windows, and the fireplace and latrine, served a solar partitioned off at the SW end, with the tower room serving as a bed-chamber, whilst the other three windows lighted the hall proper which can only have been heated by a fire in the centre if the floor with a louvre in the roof. To the NE are scanty remains of a barn-like range of late date 35m long by 7.4m wide.

Rait Castle

Rait Castle

RUTHVEN NN 764997 HS

Overlooking the River Spey SE of Kingussie is a large mound rising 15m to a flat summit 80m long by 34m wide. Cross-beams discovered in the 18th century show that the summit is at least partly artificial although the core is likely to be natural. The Comyn Lords of Badenoch had a castle here in the 13th century and a fallen fragment of walling at the mound base may be a relic of a thick former curtain wall around the summit. In 1451 the lordship of Badenoch was granted to the Earl of Huntly. However in 1452 the castle at Ruthven which was its chief seat was captured and destroyed by the Earl of Ross. It was rebuilt in time for a visit by James II in 1459. Cameron of Lochiel and MacDonald of Keppoch were imprisoned in the castle in 1546 prior to being taken to Elgin for execution. In the early 17th century the castle was twice damaged by accidental fires and was rebuilt by the Earl of Huntly. His work lasted only until 1689 when the castle was burnt by the Jacobites.

In 1718 what remained of the castle was cleared away and replaced by a barracks to accommodate troops to control the Highlanders. A wall just 0.6m thick pierced by loopholes for musketry surrounds a court 24m square. Two diagonally opposite corners have angular flankers of two storeys which had gabled roofs. There are gates to the east and west, the latter giving access to a detached stable block added in 1728. Wall-walks on these side were formed over open-backed storage spaces. In the middle of each of the north and south sides are three storey barrack blocks each having a single room on each side of a wide central staircase on each floor.

In 1745 Sergeant Molloy and just twelve men made a gallant defence of the barracks against the attacks of 200 Jacobite Highlanders led by Dr Archibald Cameron and John O'Sullivan. The stables were burned but the garrison held out and were left in peace until 1746 when Gordon of Glenbuchat led 300 Jacobites in another attack. After a brave defence for three days the garrison surrendered on honourable terms and were allowed to march away. The Jacobites assembled at Ruthven after the defeat at Culloden but instead of carrying on the campaign they dispersed on the instructions of Prince Charles Edward after burning the barracks to prevent their further use.

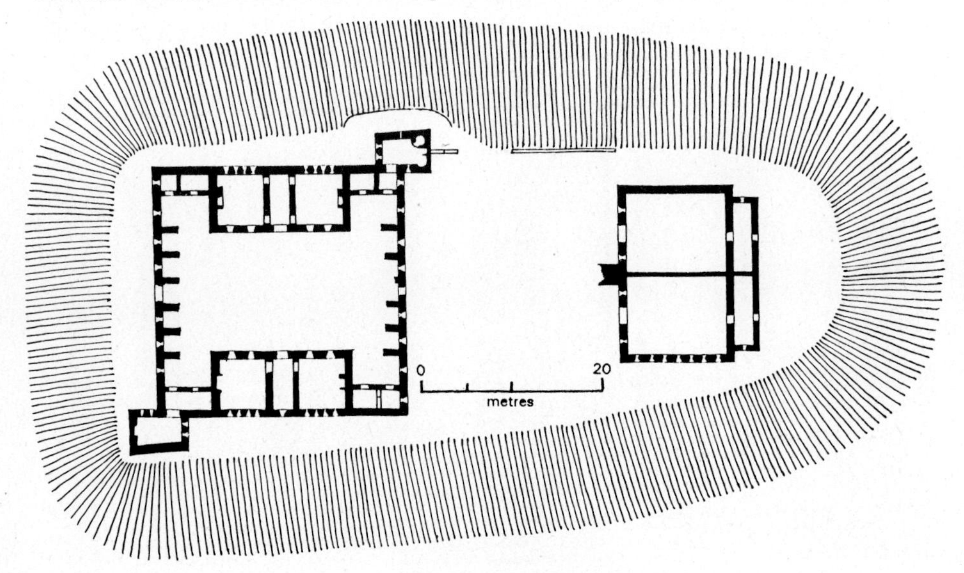

Plan of Ruthven Barracks

TIORAM NN 133786 F

This ruin has a delightful and very isolated location on a rock on one of several small tidal islands at the entrance to the inner section of Loch Moidart. A 13th century curtain wall 2m thick and 9m high surrounds a pentagonal court about 22m across. with a lower northern half and an upper south half. Built against the east wall is a 14th century tower 10m long by 7.5m wide containing a hall and three upper storeys over a vaulted cellar. The hall has a latrine in the north wall and a staircase in the NW corner. The box machicolations over the entrances to the tower and the courtyard, the topmost storey of the tower and the square bartizan on its NW corner, plus the rooms south of the tower are probably coeval with the south range of c1600 which has a square staircase turret facing the court. The west end of this range is carried up as a four storey tower with round bartizans on fine mouldings at the three outer corners. There is a service stair in the SW corner. Robert Bruce gave the lordship of Garmoran including the lands of Moidart, Arisaig, Morar, and Knoydart to Roderick MacDonald. His heiress Aimie married John, first Lord of The Isles, but became estranged from him and retired to her castle at Tioram c1350. Her son Ronald was the ancestor of the MacDonalds of Clanranald who lived at Tioram until 1715. The then chief had it burnt, correctly guessing that he would never return from the Jacobite campaign of that year.

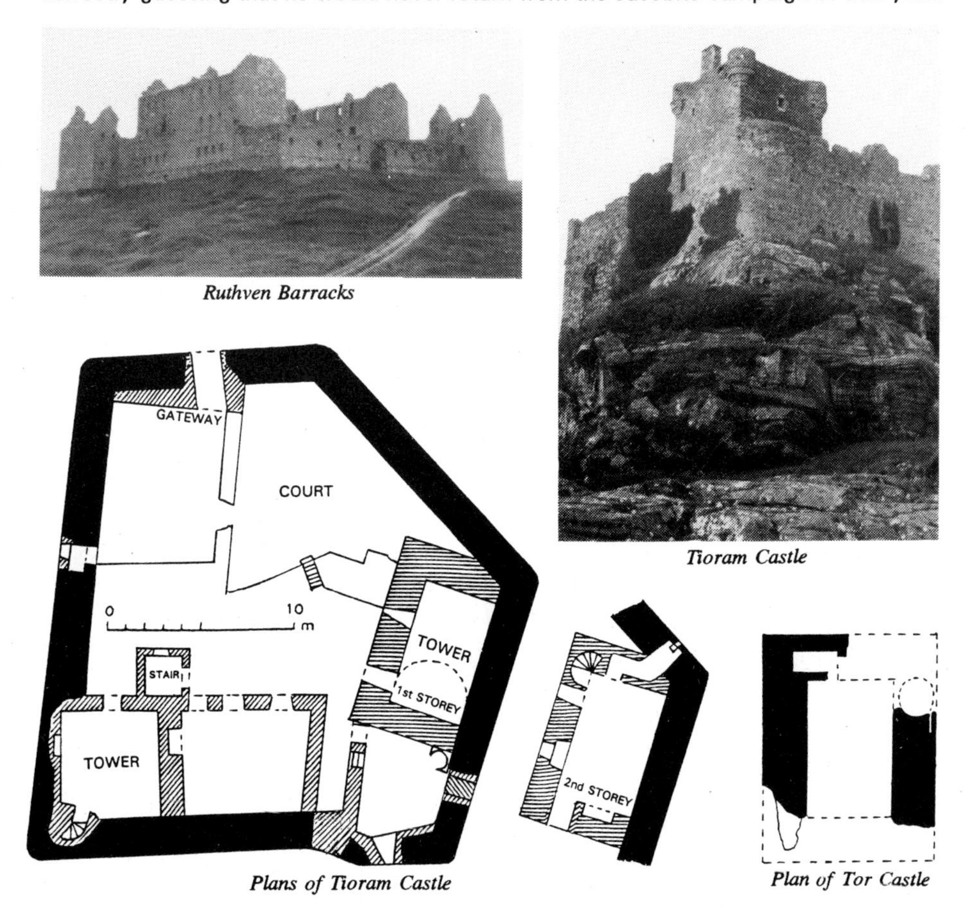

Ruthven Barracks

Tioram Castle

Plans of Tioram Castle

Plan of Tor Castle

Tor Castle

Urquhart Castle

Urquhart Castle

TOR NN 133786

Although there are no remains of early buildings, there is evidence that the Mackintoshes occupied this strong site on the end of a bluff above the north side of the River Lochy until c1308, when Angus Mackintosh and his wife Eva removed themselves to Badenoch. Tor was then granted by the Lord of The Isles to the Camerons, despite still being claimed by the Mackintoshes, thus precipitating a lasting feud between the two clans. In c1380 The Lord of The Isles granted Tor to his youngest son Alasdair Carrach, who lived there until 1440. It was presumably he who built the tower house. Alasdair was the ancestor of the Keppoch MacDonalds who were forfeited along with the Lord of The Isles by James IV in the late 15th century. In 1505 Lochaber and Tor Castle were granted to the Earl of Huntly who in turn gave them to the Camerons. Ewen, 13th chief of the Camerons, refortified the castle as a much needed stronghold against the Keppoch MacDonalds who had managed to retain most of their lands by force. The Cameron chiefs continued to reside at Tor until Sir Ewen, 17th chief, built himself a new house at Achnacarry on land obtained in a treaty with the Mackintoshes. However, Ewen's youngest son Ludovick continued to live at Tor in the early 18th century. Defaced portions of the side walls 2.4m thick and 4.5m high remain of a tower 9.6m wide and about 12m long. The northern corner contained a chamber, perhaps a prison, at ground level. There are traces of a spiral stair in the SE wall close to the east corner with a doorway drawbar slot at its foot. The tower lies in the west corner of a D-shaped court about 30m across each way with traces of a dry ditch to landward. There are foundations of walls 1m thick on the NW side.

URQUHART NH 531286 HS

The land route down the Great Glen was of importance from the earliest times and the small pieces of vitrified masonry found on the highest part of the rock beside Loch Ness suggests there was a stronghold here as early as the Iron Age. Alan Durward became lord of Urquhart c1230 and he probably built the wall around the citadel on the highest part of the site, although it is possible that William the Lion had a timber fortress on the site. The upper and lower baileys were walled in by the Comyns in the late 13th century, and the domestic buildings in the lower bailey were begun then or soon after. Urquhart was among a number of important castles occupied by the English after Edward I deposed John Baliol. A letter from its commander, Fitzwarine, describes how insecure the English hold on the castle was when the English army was not in the area. The castle withstood an attack by Sir Andrew Moray but not long afterwards it is recorded as being held for the Scots by Sir Alexander de Forbes. Edward came north again in 1303 and had Urquhart recaptured after a long siege. It was taken by the Bruces c1308 and in 1313 was granted to Sir Thomas Randolph, who was made Earl of Moray. Under Sir Robert Lauder a garrison at Urquhart successfully held out against the forces of Edward III and Edward Balliol.

In 1346 the barony and castle of Urquhart reverted to the Crown but they must have been granted away again for in 1398 the Scottish parliament decreed that such a strong and strategically placed castle should be held by the King until peace was restored to the troubled land. The Crown held onto the castle and maintained and improved it as a bastion against the depredations of the Lords of The Isles. It just managed to hold out against an attack after James I was murdered in 1437, but it was captured by the Lord of The Isles during the Douglas rebellion of 1452. The Lord of The Isles was confirmed in possession of Urquhart in 1456 but was later forced to surrender his eastern conquests, Urquhart being handed over to the Earl of Huntly. The barony was wasted by the fighting, there being no rents from Glen Urquhart in 1479.

Urquhart Castle

Even the powerful Gordons could not control the MacDonalds and in 1509 James IV gave the castle and lordship to John Grant of Freuchie on condition that he "repair or built at the castle a tower, with an outwork or rampart of stone and lime, for protecting the lands and the people from the inroads of thieves and malefactors; to construct within the castle a hall, chamber, and a kitchen, with all the requisite offices, such as a pantry, bakehouse, brewhouse, oxhouse, kiln, cot, dovegrove, and orchard, with the necessary wooden fences". The Grants eventually implemented this but the work was interrupted by further invasions by the MacDonalds. In the chaos following the King's defeat and death at Flodden Sir Donald MacDonald of Lochalsh captured the castle and occupied it for three years, devastating the estate, and there was a repeat performance of this in 1545. Plunder removed on the latter occasion comprised twelve feather beds with bolsters, blankets and sheets, five pots, a basin, two brew cauldrons, six spades, several barrels of oats, gunpowder and firearms, and coinage worth £300. Hector Boece in 1527 refers to the castle as having "reinous wallis" although his information may have been out of date.

By the early 17th century the castle was standing strong and stately with much comfortable accommodation but in 1644 Lady Urquhart was raided by a force of Covenanters who plundered everything of value but left her in possession. Cromwell placed a patrol frigate on Loch Ness so his forces probably occupied Urquhart throughout the 1650s, although no record of this survives. The castle was repaired in 1676 and in 1689 was successfully held by Captain James Grant against a blockade by 600 Jacobites. After 1691 the castle ceased to be used as a strongpoint and was probably dismantled to prevent it being occupied by Jacobites as in 1695 the Scottish Parliament voted substantial compensation to the Grant laird. Local inhabitants were prosecuted for removing materials from the ruin in 1708, and a report of February 1715 evidently refers to the natural collapse of the missing corner of the tower house in a gale. The remains continued to decay and be robbed for materials until 1912 when the Trustees of the Seafield estate handed it over to the State for preservation.

Urquhart Castle

Urquhart Castle

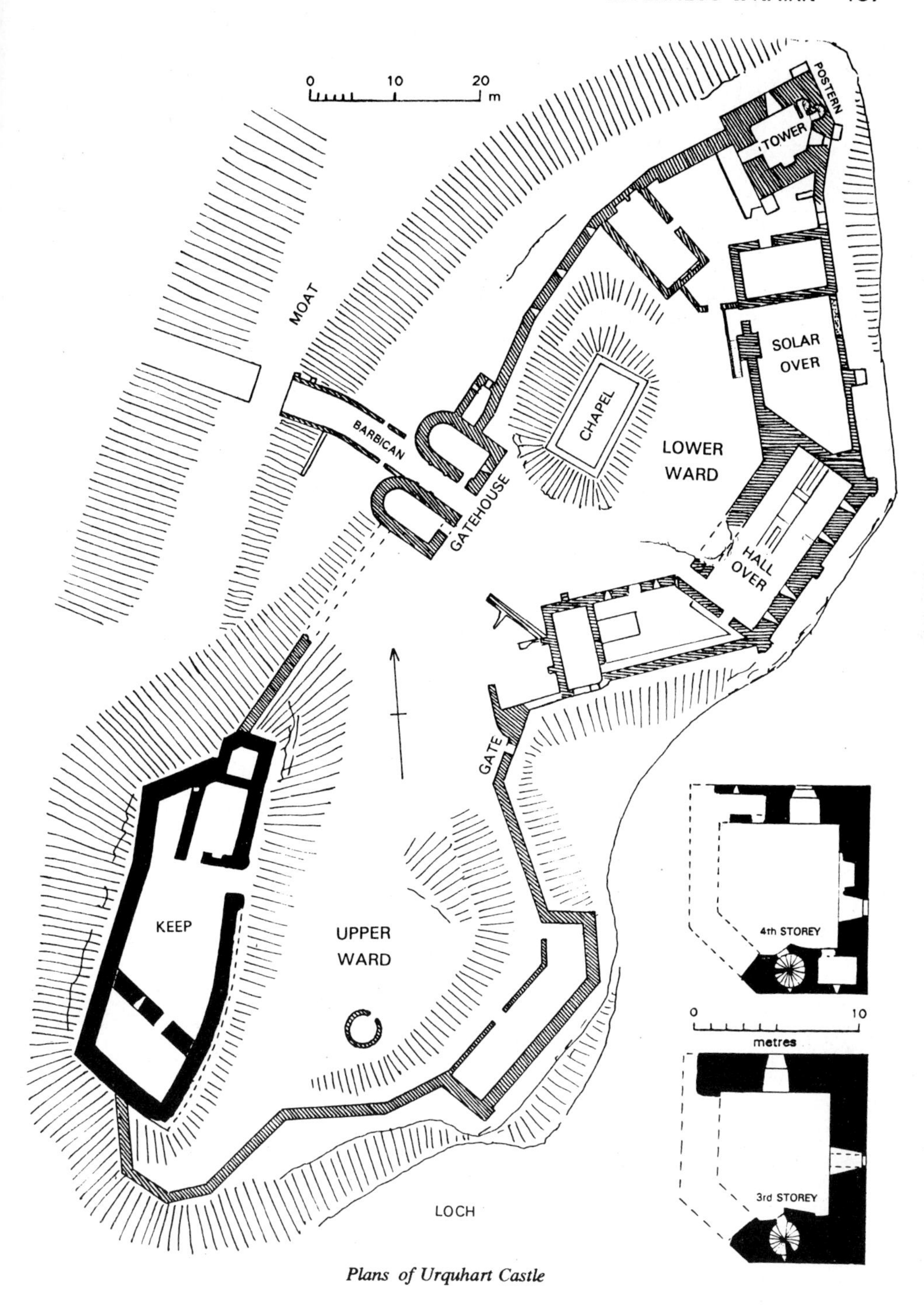

Plans of Urquhart Castle

The buildings are very ruined and architectural details of note only survive on the tower house, making dating of the other parts rather a matter of guesswork. Much of the interest of the castle stems from its superb site and unusually large size by Scottish standards. The Durward citadel has a wall about 2m above a battered plinth surrounding an area 37m long by 11m wide. The north end has a tower roughly 6m square projecting beyond a building flanking the gateway on the east side. At the south end was a two storey hall block up to 12m long by 6.6m wide internally. The main enclosure is roughly hourglass shaped with a length of over 150m. There are referred to as the upper and lower (or nether) baileys but there is no evidence that either was ever intended to be independently defensible of the other, although a domestic building of some sort seems to have divided them. Most of the wall of the upper bailey is destroyed to its base. It appears to be entirely 16th century work. One higher part contains a water gate towards the loch and there is a tall fragment of a long building facing the loch which is thought to have contained workshops for a smith and other craftsmen. Near the latter is the base of a round dovecot.

The lower bailey has remains of a very large suite of domestic buildings dating at least in part from the turn of the 13th and 14th centuries. In the centre was a massively walled block containing a hall about 21m long by 8m wide over cellars below courtyard level with small lintelled windows towards the loch. SW of the hall was a spacious kitchen and service area, whilst to the north is an apartment block nearly 10m wide inside, which was presumably divided by partitions into several chambers. The thin wall towards the loch may be a 17th century rebuild. In the middle of the landward side of the castle is a gatehouse with elongated D-shaped towers on either side of a vaulted passage closed by a portcullis and probably two pairs of doors. The lodges for porters and guards on either side also have vaults, and the rooms above them were also vaukted. Although on a plan commonly used in late 13th century castles and town defences in Wales, and possibly on foundations of that period, the present building is clearly 16th century work imitating royal gatehouses at Falkland and Stirling. The wide dry ditch in front was crossed by a drawbridge and then thin walls formed a barbican constricting the approach.

Urquhart Castle

From the gatehouse a fairly well preserved curtain wall containing a few loops extends in four straight sections to a tower measuring 12.3m by 10.9m at the northern end of the lower bailey. The late 14th century vaulted basement below courtyard level has a postern towards the loch. The upper storeys containing a hall at courtyard level and two storeys of bedrooms above were rebuilt in the 16th century, whilst the parapet and rectangular gabled top turrets may be part of the work done under a contract with the mason James Moray in 1623. The hall was entered by a timber bridge across a dry ditch from a small cobbled close delineated by the chamber block and another building west of it. The walls are here 2.4m thick. From this level one staircase led down to the cellar and another up to the bedrooms and battlements. The internal walls have remains of plaster. The top storey was vaulted and had two closets in the walls. There was an attic within the parapet and the turrets each contained a chamber equipped with a fireplace, latrine and a window with a gunloop below. These turrets are carried on corbels and are connected by a parapet upon a corbel course. Over the entrance was a machicolated platform carried on four great corbels and there was a similar arrangement to defend the postern. In the middle of the lower bailey are foundations of what is likely to have been a chapel.

OTHER STRONGHOLDS IN INVERNESS AND NAIRN

CANTRAYDOUNE NH 788460 Pudding-shaped mound 6m high on open ground.
CROMAL MOUNT NH 782556 Overgrown mound on ridge above village of Ardersier.
LOCH EIL The Cameron chiefs (titled Locheil) had their seat from c1335 until at least 1607 on island of Eilean N Craoibhe (Tree Island), opposite Corpach.
LOCH LAGGAN NN 498875 Slight remains of a MacPherson castle on an island.
LOCH LOCHY Crannog (now sunk) built by Mackintoshes in 1580 against MacDonalds
NESS NH 654420 Damaged mound 3m high above stream west of Inverness.
ROYBRIDGE NH 270808 Quadrangular mound with rampart around edge of summit 44m long by 25m wide. Small outwork and ditch to east.
SHION NH 917498 Worn down mound bearing last traces of a house or tower on top.
SOUTH KINRARA NH 874073 Motte & bailey discovered from the air in 1990.

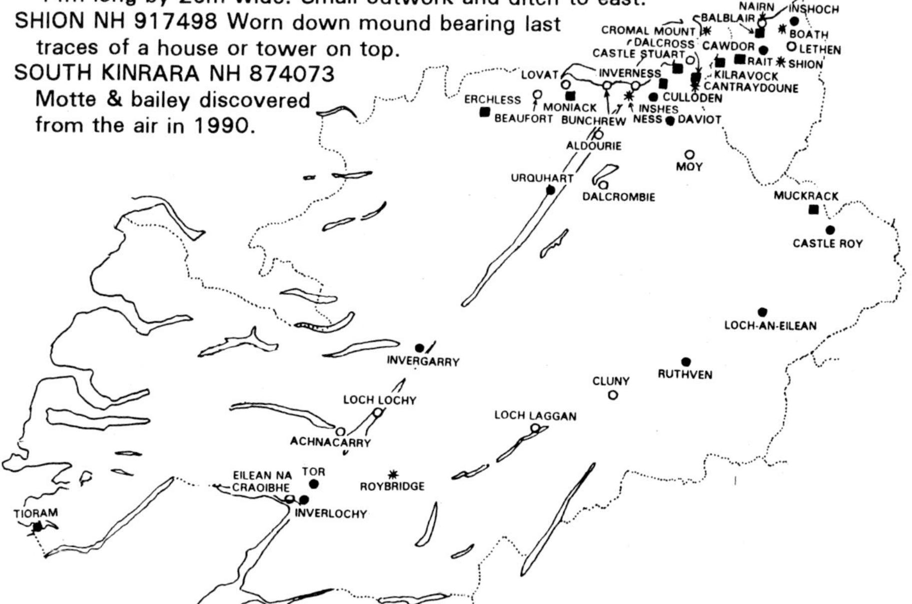

MAP OF CASTLES OF INVERNESS AND NAIRN

ORKNEY

BIRSAY HY 248279 HS

This ruined palace was begun by Robert Stewart, Earl of Orkney, an illegitimate brother of Queen Mary. He and his son Patrick, who completed the structure, ruled Orkney and Shetland like monarchs, oppressing the poor islanders to pay for their extravagances. Earl Patrick, a noted builder, was attainted for treason and executed by James VI in 1614. The charges were partly based upon the rather poor Latin of a former inscription over the gate at Birsay, intended to mean that Robert Stewart was a son of King James V, but (because the nominative Rex was used instead of the genitive) translatable as meaning that Robert himself claimed to be King of Scotland! The palace had a south range 6m wide and east and west ranges 5.7m wide around a court 19m wide by 30m long with a well in the middle. Five dormer pediment finials were found in the well in 1929. Over a blocked entrance on the west are the initials of Earl Robert and a window dated 1574. Two rooms north of the gate survive intact but otherwise not much remains of the ranges. These rooms have gunports facing both the court and the exterior. The southern corners have towers 6.2m square with double-splayed gunports in their vaulted basements. A third tower at the NE corner is smaller but has an extra (third) storey. The south range contained a gallery on the upper storey. Earl Patrick added a range 9.2m wide in place of what was probably just a screen wall on the north side. It had a kitchen at the east end, next to a staircase wing, probably two cellars in the middle, and a passage beside them leading to a large room, perhaps an office, at the west end. Robert Menteith in 1633 described rooms at Birsay with painted ceilings depicting Noah's Flood and Christ Riding to Jerusalem.

CAIRSTON HY 273096

Walls up to 1.4m thick built of beach boulders set in clay surround a court roughly 18m square entered through a gateway on the north side. A tiny round turret with one gunport projects from the NW corner within which are remains of a range which extended along the whole west side and included a straight staircase going across the width of the building about a third of the way down from the north end. It seems that there were buildings on the east side of the court also, and excavations in 1927 showed that the vanished SE corner had had a turret 4.6m in diameter added to it. The turrets and west range were probably built by William Gordon, who was given Cairston by Earl Robert in 1587. The rest may be contemporary, or could be somewhat older.

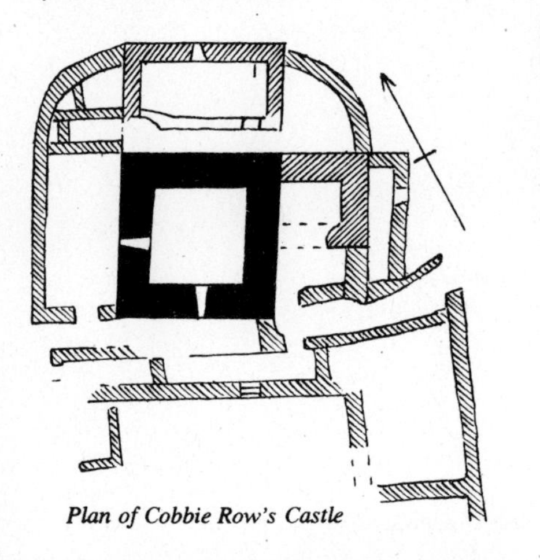

Plan of Cobbie Row's Castle

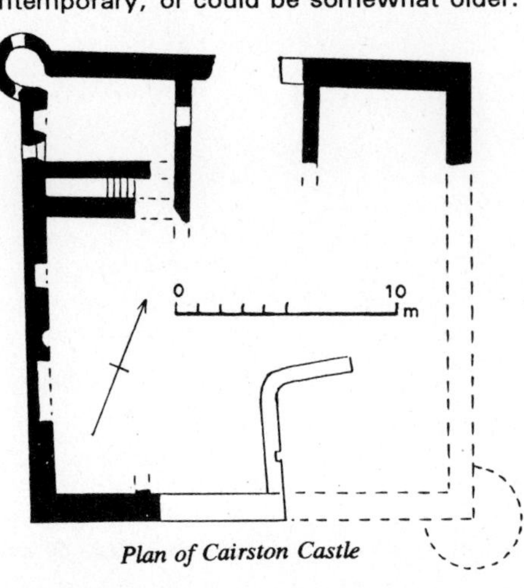

Plan of Cairston Castle

Birsay Palace

Cobbie Row's Castle

CARRICK HY 567384

On the NW side of a court lies a range 15.7m long by 6.1m wide of two storeys and an attic. The roll-moulded courtyard gateway has on its keystone the date 1633, and must have been built by John Stewart, a younger son of Earl Robert (see Birsay), created Earl of Carrick in 1628. There is also the date 1662 with initials of Arthur Buchanan and Marjory Buxton. A document of 1628 refers to a now-vanished tower.

COBBIE ROW'S HY 442264 HS F

The name of this castle on a ridge in the middle of the island of Wyre is thought to be a corruption of that of the Norseman Kolbein Hruga who married a local heiress and is recorded in the Orkneying Saga of c1150 as having recently built a stone castle here. It is likely that this refers to the tower 7.9m square over walls 1.7m thick of which the lowest storey survives. It is built of slabs in a hard lime mortar and has loops facing SW and NW but no stair or entrance, so it can only have been reached by a trap-door from the main living room above. At a later period a more thinly walled wing the same width as the tower and projecting 5m was added to the NE side, whilst the smaller but more massive wing projecting from the northern end of the SE wall may have been associated with the access arrangements to the entrance. Further thinly walled extensions and enclosure walls were added later. The remains are closely surrounded by double rampart and ditch system of modest dimensions which has been swept away on the south side. In 1230 Hanef, an officer of the Norwegian Crown, was unsuccessfully besieged in the castle after the murder of John, Earl of Orkney.

The Bishop's Palace at Kirkwall

GERNANESS HY 301119

There are very slight traces of buildings on the west side of a peninsular now lying just half a metre above the raised level of Loch Stenness north of Nether Biggin farm. The remains were excavated in the 1920s and in the Proceeding of the Society of Antiquaries of Scotland for 1926 were described as being a Norse-built castle probably of c1130. The remains, even then very defaced, were interpreted as a D-shaped tower keep about 9m in diameter projecting east from a partly paved oval court about 18m by 14m containing a triangular bath-house on the south side and an hour-glass shaped hall with a central fireplace on the north. The rectangular room in the base of the keep was thought to have been a kitchen and was reached from the hall (at which level would have been the entrance) by a spiral stair in the east corner. Three walls of the keep were up to 2.5m thick but the west wall facing the court was just 0.7m thick.

KIRKWALL HY 450110 HS

In the Bishop's Palace are the lower parts of an early hall-block 27m long by 8m wide. Either this building or the now-vanished castle of the early Earls of Orkney would have been the scene of the death in 1263 of Haakon IV, King of Norway, following his defeat at Largs by Alexander II of Scotland, and the death in 1290 of Haakon's seven year old grand-daughter Margaret whilst she was being brought from the Norwegian court to be crowned as Queen of Scotland. The walls were thickened internally to carry vaults and rebuilt above basement level to make a splendid new palace of three storeys and an attic for Bishop Reid (1541-58). His private apartments lay in the 8.4m diameter round tower at the NW corner. It contained three square rooms between the vaulted basement and the corbelled parapet, plus two more rooms in a square caphouse within the wall-walk. The three storey southern extension with oriels on either side and the three heavy buttresses on the west side of the main block probably date from the time of Patrick, Earl of Orkney who took over the building in the 1590s.

Earl Patrick also built another palace at Kirkwall just 60m to east of the other. A street now divides the two, which are thought to have once been linked by a court. This second palace is dated 1607 over an entrance with complex mouldings lying in the longer of two wings projecting westwards from a main block 27m long by 8.5m long. This block contains at ground level four cellars linked by a passage to the kitchen at the end of the SW wing and to a scale-and-platt staircase beside the entrance in the same wing. Above the cellars is a splendid hall with two large bay windows to the east, a oriel window and a big fireplace on the west, another fireplace on the north, and a triple window facing south. Beyond the north end of the hall is an audience chamber with an east bay window and a west facing oriel. From this room is reached a private room in the NW wing with closets in round bartizans on the west corners and a staircase rising up in the SE corner. The SW wing contains another private room between the main staircase and the kitchen fireplace flue and has a third storey above, also with round bartizans on the west corners. The whole double-palace complex was captured from the forces of the rebellious Earl Patrick in 1614 and given back to the Bishops. They occupied the complex until the death of Bishop Mackenzie in 1688.

Tankerness House, a much altered and extended mansion with ranges around a central court, lies near the palaces. It is dated 1574 & 1722 with initials of Gilbert Fulzie and Elizabeth Kinnard and Robert Baikie and Margaret Sinclair.

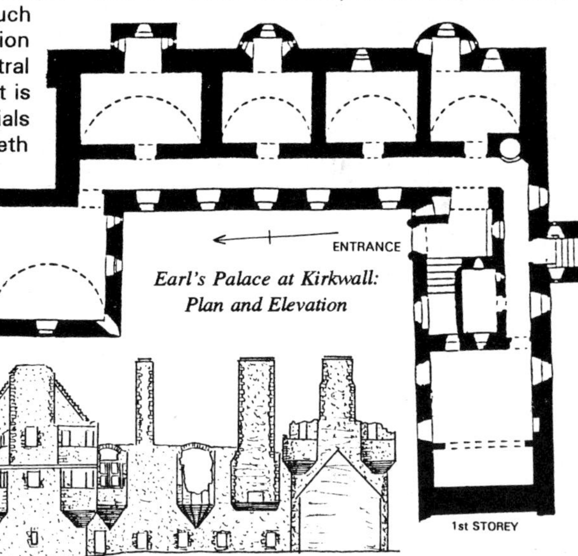

Earl's Palace at Kirkwall: Plan and Elevation

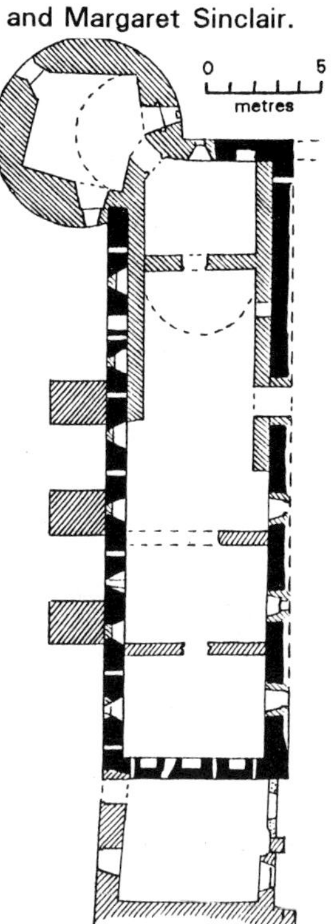

Bishop's Palace: plan

Hall Fireplace, Earl's Palace at Kirkwall

LANGSKAILL HY 434220

The present house is a block 20m long by 6.8m wide of one storey and an attic. It bears the date 1676 on a skew-put and the entrance on the west side has a monogram of the initials of Sir William Craigie of Gairsay and his wife Margaret Honeyman. Sir William was descended from the Craig family of Craighall, near Edinburgh. The block seems to have originally had a central staircase across its width. Two other doorways on either side of that with the monogram have now been converted into windows. Connecting this range with another 11.5m to the west, of which only the south wall and part of the west wall survive, is a screen wall 1.2m thick with pairs of oval gunloops flanking a central gateway over which is a worn heraldic panel and another monogram of Sir William and his wife. There are further gunloops in a parapet protecting a wall-walk on the screen wall which can only have been reached by a long-removed upper storey to the east range south end. There are only traces of a wing which projected westwards from the west range.

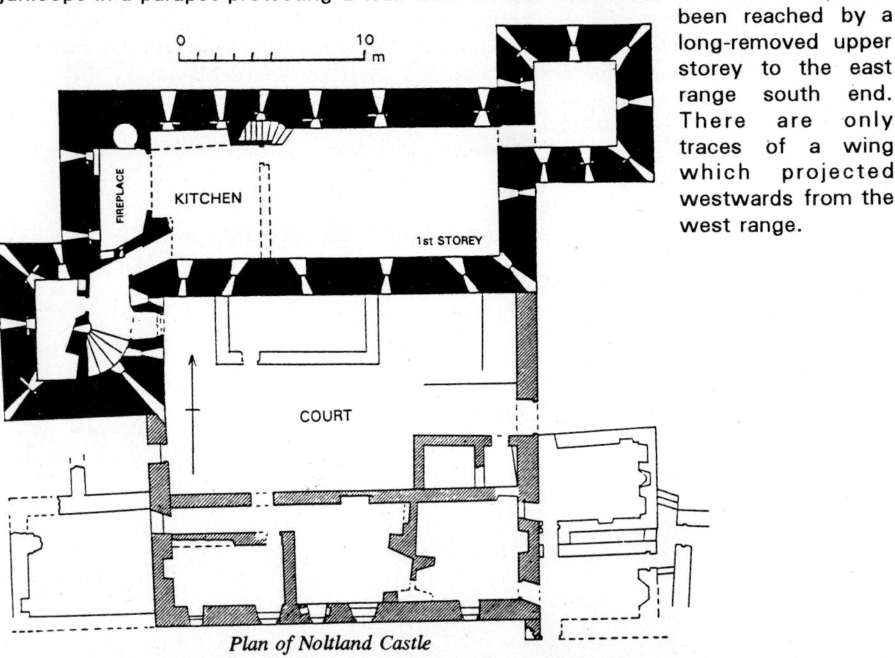

Plan of Noltland Castle

Noltland Castle

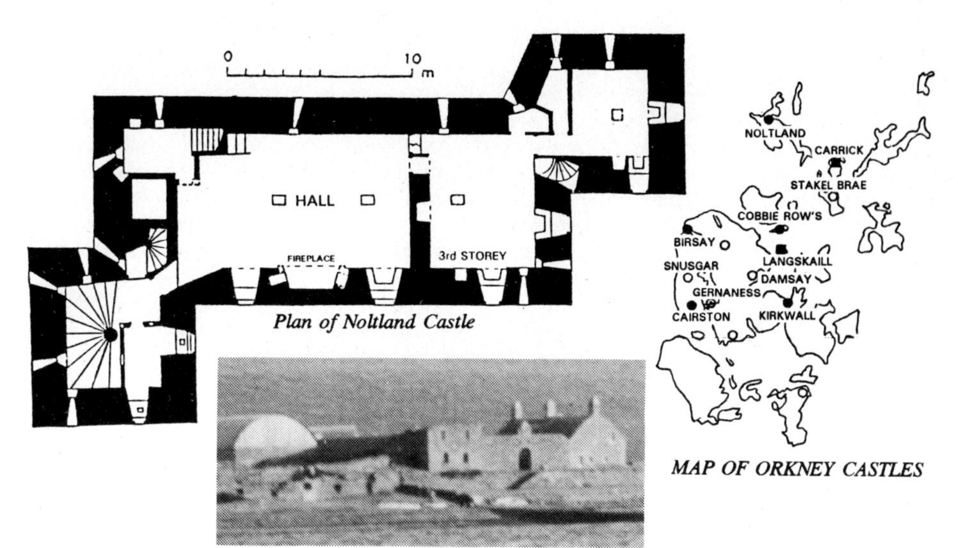

Plan of Noltland Castle

Langskaill

MAP OF ORKNEY CASTLES

NOLTLAND HY 430487 HS

This building on the island of Westray was built c1568-75 as a refuge by Gilbert Balfour, brother-in-law of Bishop Adam, and a participant in the murders of Cardinal Beaton in 1546 and Lord Darnley in 1567, who expected to be arrested at any time. The result of this sense of insecurity is one of the most military-minded buildings of its period in Scotland. It has a main block 25.6m long by 10.7m wide over walls up to 2m thick which are bristling with splayed gunports. All round flanking fire is achieved by the provision of two wings about 8m square on the NE and SW corners. One contains bedrooms over a cellar, the other contains a wide spiral stair with an anti-room at the top. The main block lowest storey contains a kitchen and two cellars above which were dark rooms used either as stores or barracks with a series of three hatches in their vaults. Above the vaults are a hall and chamber. The hall was a dark room having just two windows set either side of a fireplace on the south side. In the NW corner is a servery at the head of a long service stair from the nearest cellar. Above the private chamber and the adjacent wing the walls stand to their original height with one more storey of bedrooms and wall-walks with the stumps of corbelled parapets. It has been claimed that remainder of the building, now broken off at hall ceiling height, never stood any higher but it seems unlikely that this part would have remained unfinished whilst outbuildings were being added. South of the main block is a court 10m wide by 19m long with an east gateway. South of the court is a two storey range with a bartizan on in the SW corner. Earl Patrick was punished by the Court of Session for besieging and capturing the castle in 1592. When Jerome Dennison gave Noltland in dower to his wife Helen Trail in 1761 four rooms and the gardens remained in use but the site was probably abandoned soon afterwards.

OTHER CASTLES IN ORKNEY

Damsay HY 390139 Vanished Norse-built castle in existence by 1136.
Snusgar (position uncertain) Gone, but remains visible in 1795 and late 19th century.
Stackel Brae HY 564288 Mound with some remains of drystone and mortared walling on site of castle of the pirate John Gow. Fragments of old glass found on site.

SHETLAND

JARLSHOF HU 398096 HS

Jarlshof is one of the most interesting ancient sites in Scotland and is of great antiquity. Here, however, we are concerned only with the ruined house probably built in the 1590s by William Bruce of Symbister, and later extended by Patrick, Earl of Orkney. The house is a purely domestic building originally having two ranges of slightly different dates facing each other across an open space that became a closed court entered only at the NE corner when east and west ranges were added later. The east range has an added oven at the south end. The west range was subdivided later when it became a burial place. The south range is the most stoutly built and contained two room on each of two storeys. The lower rooms each have doorways with draw-bar slots facing the court. Those above, now very ruined, were reached by a forestair from the court. The north range is the oldest and had smaller rooms at either end of a central ground level hall with a fireplace in a breast on the north side.

LOCH STROM HU 629012

On a tiny island called Castle Holm in Loch Strom are remains of a small tower probably dating from the 16th century. It measures 6.4m by 5.5m over walls from 1.1m to 1.5m thick which are mostly reduced to footings except for a 3m high fragment of the NW corner. There was once a causeway to the shore 30m away.

MUNESS HP 629012 HS

Laurence Bruce transferred to this remote spot on the most northerly of the Shetland Islands under the protection of his half brother, Robert Earl of Orkney, after killing a man during an affray in his native Perthshire. His castle, dated 1598, has a main block 22m long by 7.5m wide and north and south corner towers 4.6m and 5.3m in diameter respectively with gunloops in their basements. The entrance on the SW side gives onto a passage connecting three cellars and a kitchen at the NW end. The kitchen fireplace adjoins an internal crosswall and has an oven in a block of masonry projecting into the adjoining cellar. From the passage rises a scale-and-platt staircase which projects into the internal spaces either side of a cross-wall. Also squeezed in beside this cross-wall is a service stair from the cellar at the SE end. The second storey has a central hall and private rooms of differing sizes at each end. From the laird's room at the NW end rises another stair in the NE sidewall to his bedroom above. The third storey containing numerous bedrooms was partly dismantled in the 19th century to provide material for a surrounding boundary wall. At that level there were round bartizans on the east and west corners. Both the upper storeys have windows with shot-holes in the embrasures.

Jarlshof

Loch Strom Castle

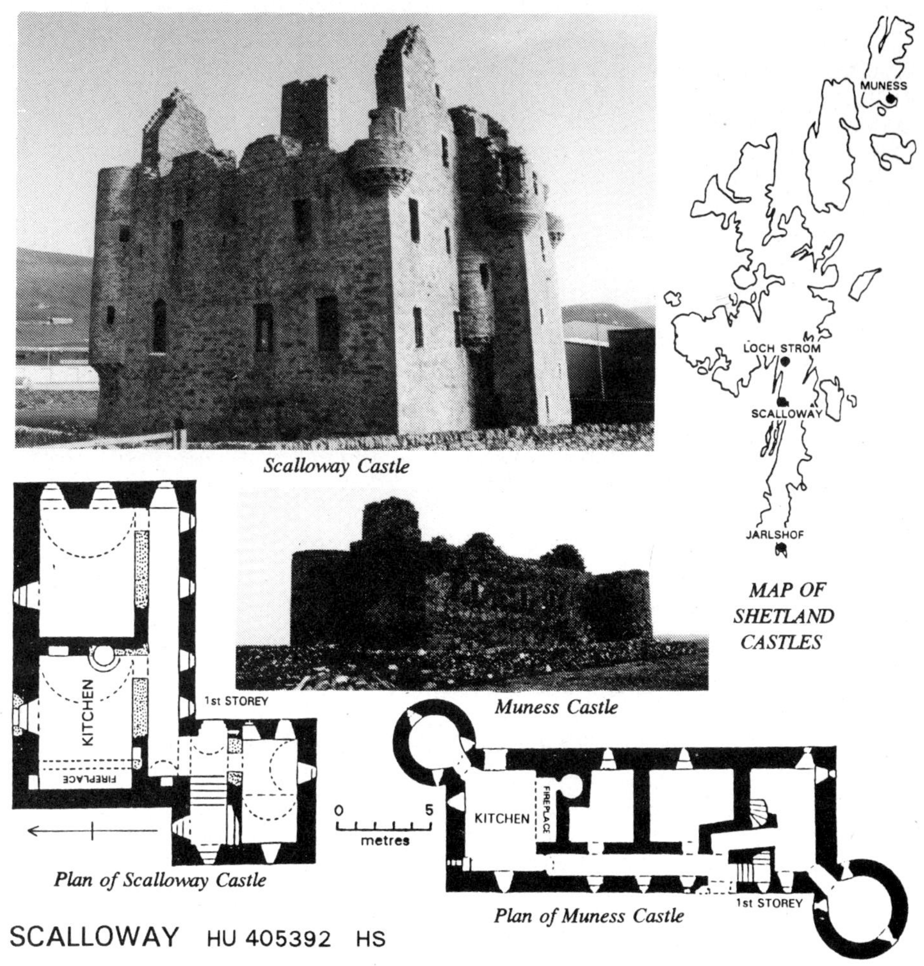

Scalloway Castle

MAP OF SHETLAND CASTLES

Muness Castle

Plan of Scalloway Castle

Plan of Muness Castle

SCALLOWAY HU 405392 HS

Patrick, Earl of Orkney, built this fine tower on a peninsular between the East Voe and the harbour c1600. It was only used until the 1680s and has been a ruin ever since. It consists of a main block 17.5m long by 10.1m wide containing a splendid hall over a cellar and a kitchen, plus two storeys of bedrooms and an attic. The kitchen contains a well and has a wide fireplace in the west wall. The SW of the main block corner is engaged by a wing containing a scale-and-platt staircase from the entrance up to the hall. The hall is a magnificent apartment with no less than nine windows, fireplaces on the south and east, and a recess for a dresser on the north. The west end of the room may have been screened off as a service area. Access up from the hall is by a stair turret corbelled out in the western re-entrant angle and by another stair in a round turret at the NE corner. The SW turret stair rises only to the third storey and another stair over the over re-entrant angle then continues. At the summit the other corners have round bartizans with shot-holes. There are further shot-holes below many of the upper windows, which have signs of their former grilles. The fourth storey of the main block was divided into three bedrooms. Little remains of the armorial panels around the entrance but it seems that the Royal Arms were included along them.

THE WESTERN ISLES, SKYE AND WESTER ROSS

BORVE NF 774506 F

The three storey tower of uncertain date measures 18m by 11m over walls from 1.5m to 2.7m thick standing up to 9m high with evidence of three unvaulted storeys. There is evidence that the walls were thickened either during initial construction or later. The massive south wall contains an entrance with a window to the west of it.

BROCHEL NG 584463

This ruin is impressively perched on a precipitous crag high above the eastern shore just below the northern tip of the isle of Raasay. The tiny triangular turret with a corbelled parapet stood to the west of an earlier tower house, the last fragment of which has been destroyed since being drawn in 1819 by William Daniel. The tower was probably built c1510 by Calum MacGillichaluim, the first of the MacLeod lairds of Raasay and was occupied until the death of Mighty John (Ian Garbh) MacLeod in the late 17th century. A slight shelf below the south side summit is occupied by irregularly shaped rooms east and west of a tiny court reached by steps up from a gateway commanded by a round fronted platform east of the main tower. The western room was a kitchen and has a chamber above. The larger eastern building, although more ruined, retains sections of its parapet projected out on a corbel table.

CAISTEAL BHEAGRAM NF 761371

The island 80m in diameter near the shore of Loch-an-Eilean, near Howmore, has remains of low perimeter wall. There are ruins of a harled tower standing 3.6m high with evidence of two storeys, the upper room having an entrance on the east, two small square windows on the north, and another window to the west. The tower measures just 3.8m by 3m within walls from 1.2m to 1.5m thick. It was presumably the home of Ronald Alanson, mentioned in 1505 and 1508 as of "Yland Bafrim".

Borve Castle

Caisteal Camus

CAISTEAL CAMUS NG 672087 F

A fort called Dun Thoravaig is said to have occupied this rock on the east side of Sleat. A ditch runs across the neck of a headland roughly 45m square. The very ruined SE range about 21m long by 10m wide over walls at least 1.7m thick is probably best interpreted as a 13th century hall house containing a hall and chamber over a pair of lower rooms. The shute near the north end of the SE side marks the side of a latrine probably serving the private room. The southern section of this wall stands in a defaced condition two storeys high. It was presumably in this building that William, 4th chief of the MacLeods, died in 1402. He left a young son, during whose minority the MacDonalds took over much of Skye, capturing the MacLeod seats of Caisteal Camus and Dunscaith. Caisteal Camus was recaptured by the forces of James I during his struggle with the Lord of The Isles. It is next mentioned in 1513 when Alasdair Crotach MacLeod unsuccessfully besieged the castle in the interest of Sir Donald MacDonald of Lochalsh during his attempt to claim the Lordship of the Isles. However the MacDonalds did obtain possession of the castle eventually. In 1596 and 1614 Donald Gorm of Sleat was confirmed in possession of his lands with the proviso that the "Castle of Camus shall always be open to the King and his men". The thinly walled range 15m long by 7.7m wide on the SW side of the site and partly lying over where the missing southern half of the NW wall of the older building would have been is a house possibly of this period. There are indications that this building lay within a court 16m wide extending 18m NW from the older block. By 1689 this new building was already ruined and it was robbed of materials for building the nearby house of Knock from which the castle takes its alternative name.

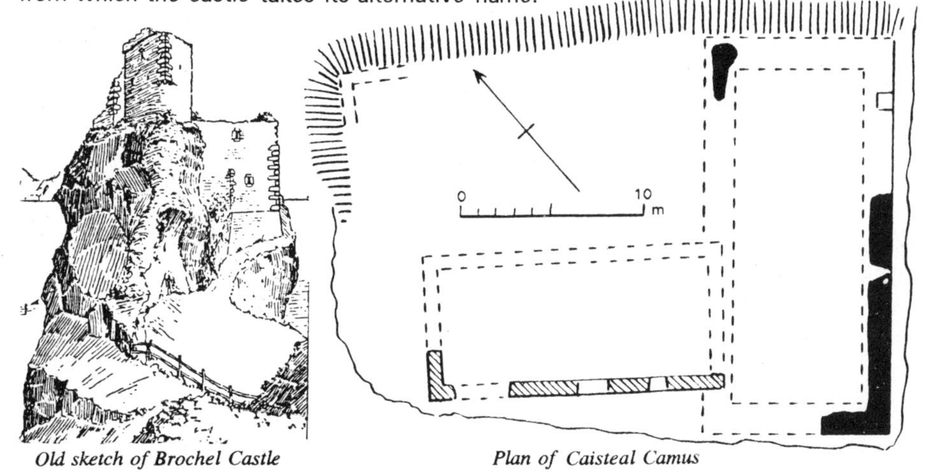

Old sketch of Brochel Castle

Plan of Caisteal Camus

CAISTEAL MAOL NG 758264 F

A path leads round the shore from Kyleakin to a ruined tower perched on a rock overlooking the ferry across to Kyle of Lochalsh. The tower measures 14.5m by 10.3m over walls 2.5m thick except for the more vulnerable south wall which is 2.7m thick above a plinth extending down the side of the rock. The hall has one fairly complete window embrasure with traces of seats in the south wall, and a portion of one jamb of another opposite in the north wall. Part of an window embrasure of an upper room also remains. It is assumed that there was a dark basement, now choked with rubble, below it. The entrance and staircase were probably in the west wall. The castle was built c1490-1500 by the MacKinnons and was originally called Dunakin. Here in 1513 various chiefs met and agreed to support Sir Donald MacDonald in his claim as Lord of the Isles. By the early 17th century the tower was abandoned in favour of a new house at Kilmarie, close to the original family seat at Dun Ringill. The NE corner fell during a gale as recently as 1989 and considerable repairs have just been carried out.

CAISTEAL UISDEAN NG 381583

In a remote position far from a public road on a shelf by the west coast of Trotternish lies a building 15.2m long by 9.9m over walls now 5m high and 2.3m thick at the level of the unvaulted basement, but somewhat thinner above because of an internal offset to carry the hall floor. The basement has a loop in each of the long north and south walls but no other features. It can only have been reached by a trap-door from the hall. The hall was entered by a doorway in the west wall from which steps led up towards the SW corner. Each of the other walls contains the remains of a window embrasure and there is a fireplace in the north wall. The castle is allegedly named after Hugh, son of Archibald the Clerk, a notorious late 16th century plotter who was eventually starved to death at Duntulm by order of his uncle Donald Gorm of Sleat. Hugh may have owned the building and perhaps remodelled the missing upper parts, but the original construction of such a primitive and massive building is far more likely to have been the work of Hugh MacDonald, Lord of Sleat, who died in 1498.

Caisteal Uisdean

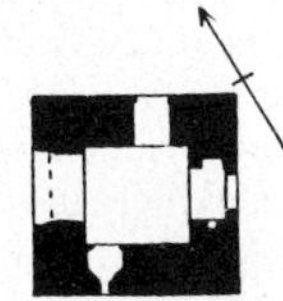

Castle Sinclair

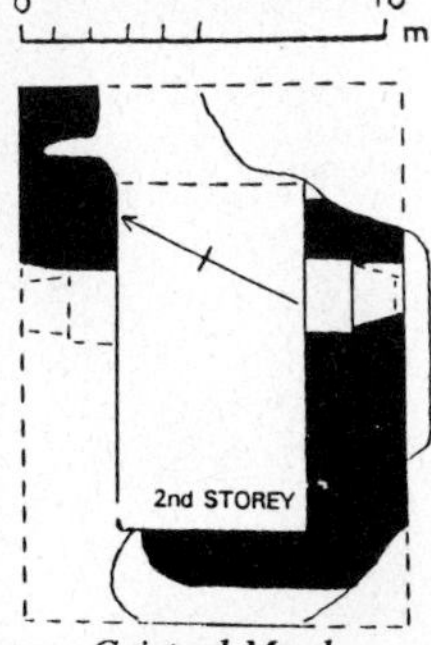

Caisteal Maol

Castle Calvey

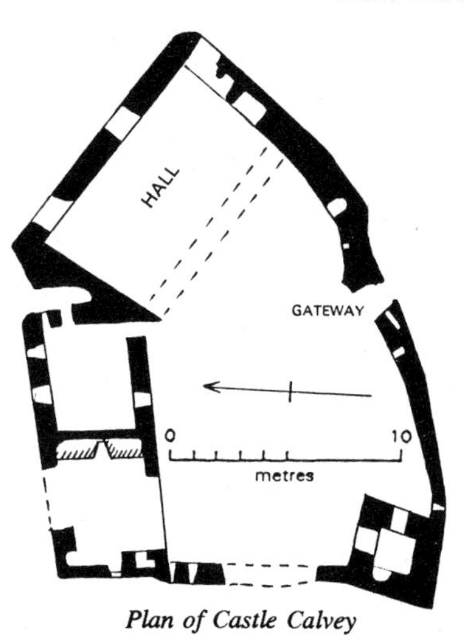

Plan of Castle Calvey

Caisteal Maol

CASTLE CALVEY NF 817182

The summit of a rocky tidal island linked by a causeway to Calvey Island is occupied by an irregularly shaped court 15m by 21m with walls up to 1.5m thick. A well lies 9m in front of the entrance, which has a draw-bar slot on the SE side. Within the SW corner is a tower 3.8m square, and there were ranges of two storeys, now choked with debris, on the north and NE sides. Between them is what appears to be a postern.

CASTLE SINCLAIR NL 648996

At the SW corner of a small island in Loch Tangusdale on Barra lies the ruin of a small late medieval tower known either as Castle Sinclair or Dun Mhic Leoid. It measures 5.4m by 5.5m over walls 1.4m thick. The only feature of the basement is a loop facing SW. The storey above has a doorway to the NE, a narrow loop to the SW, and breaches where there were wider window embrasures in the other two walls. Possibly one of these was a fireplace instead. Nothing remains of an assumed third storey.

COROGHON NG 288055

A small two storey forework probably of 17th century date lies at the top of a steep path forming the only access to the summit of a vertical sided 24m high stack of agglomerate to the NE of Canna Pier.

DUN BAN NF 844608

A ruinous wall 2m thick surrounds a court roughly 16m square occupying the whole of an island 195m from the south shore of Loch Caravat. A thin crosswall divided off the whole of the western part as a poorly lit single storey living space 5.7m wide. On the east is a gateway in a recess large enough to take a medium-sized boat set between two angular bastions. The remains are probably of 15th or 16th century date.

DUN RINGILL NG 562171

This Iron Age fort contains the remains of two late medieval buildings both measuring about 4.5m by 2.4m internally. The 4.6m thick landward facing defences were repaired to protect these buildings, but there is a 15m wide gap in the defences towards the sea on the east. Dun Ringill is said to have been the seat of the MacKinnons until they abandoned it in favour of Caisteal Maol in the late 15th century. It may be the their castle of Fingon mentioned in an Act of Council of 1360.

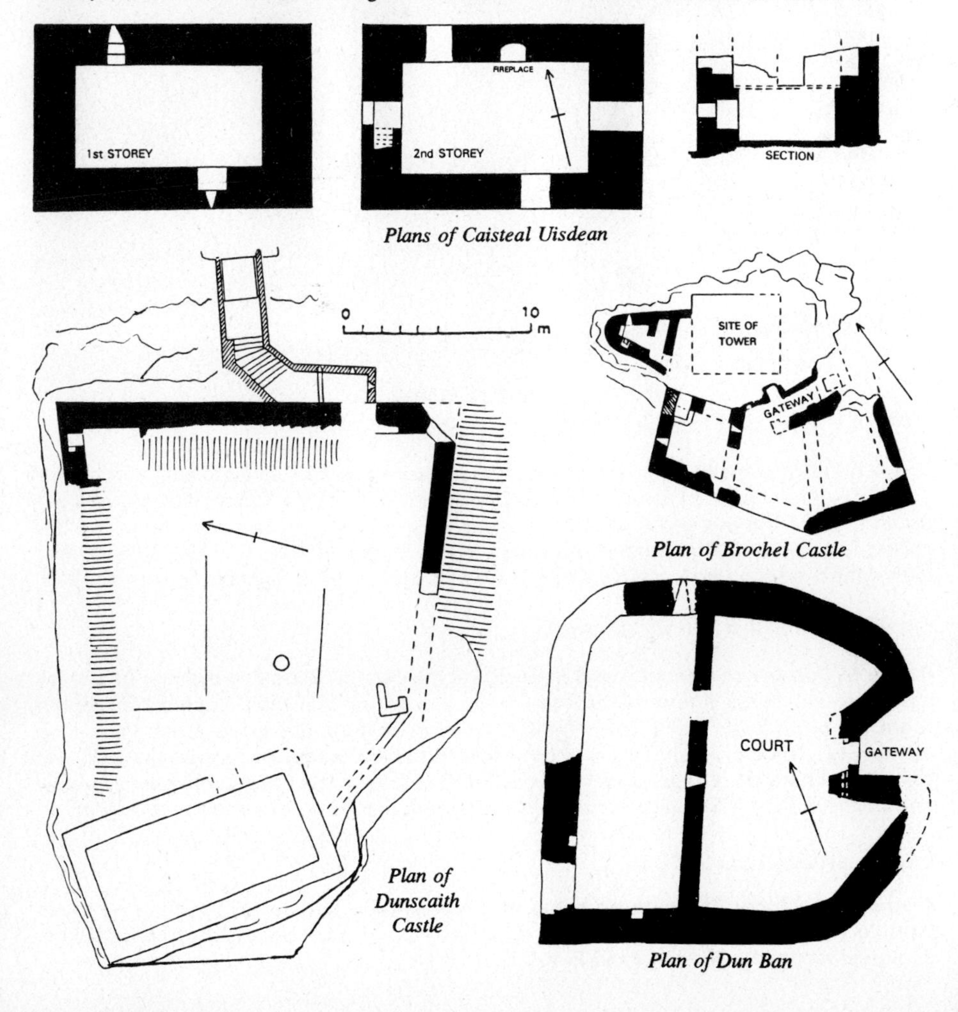

Plans of Caisteal Uisdean

Plan of Brochel Castle

Plan of Dunscaith Castle

Plan of Dun Ban

Dunscaith Castle

DUNSCAITH NG 595121

There has probably been a fortress of some kind from an early date on the summit of this rock of the north side of Sleat. By the late 13th century there was probably a crudely built wall around a court up to 27m long by 19m wide. The 22m long straight east wall 1.6m thick and a shorter and thinner straight length of walling on the south side probably represent a 16th century remodelling. An L-shaped 17th century approach ramp flanked by parapets with musket loops led from a drawbridge over a ditch to landward up to a gateway near the south end of the east wall. In the NE corner are remains of a chamber, perhaps the lowest stage of a small tower, and on the north side of the court are foundations of what may have been a tower house about 12m by 8m. The foundations of a building 14m long by 7.4m wide on the west side of the court are of late, perhaps 17th century, date. A well lies in the court.

In the 14th century the MacAskills were keepers of Dunscaith for the Earls of Ross. Godfrey MacDonald may have occupied the castle in the 1390s and the MacDonalds certainly took the castle from the MacLeods in the early 15th century, holding it until James I's forces occupied it in 1431. Hugh, brother of John, 10th Lord of the Isles was granted much of Sleat in 1469, and presumably used Dunscaith as his residence. The castle is first mentioned in a document of 1505 when Hugh's son John made it over to Ranald Alansoun. John's half brother Donald Galloch occupied Dunscaith but was murdered there by another brother, Gillespic, who was pardoned for this deed in 1508. In 1515 there is a record of remission being granted "to Laughlan Maclean of Dowart and Alistair Macleod of Dunvegan for assisting in the treasonable segeing and taking of the Kingis castillis and hovs of Carnebog (Cairnburgh) and Dunskaith)". In the early 17th century the MacDonalds of Sleat transferred to Duntulm in pursuance of a claim to Trotternish and Dunscaith was allowed to gradually decay.

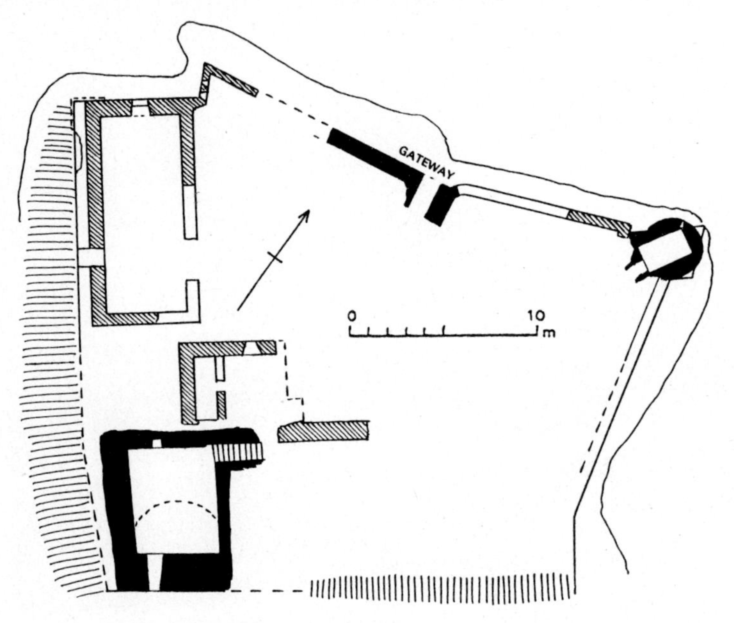

Plan of Duntulm Castle

Duntulm Castle

DUNTULM NG 410743 F

Duntulm lies on a 30m high basalt promontory near the north end of Trotternish. The castle seems to have existed by the 15th century, if not as early as the 13th, but is first mentioned in 1540 when James V anchored his fleet in the harbour below the castle, then held by the MacDonald chief of Sleat, Donald Gormson. The King received the submission of the local chiefs and was impressed by Duntulm's strength and commodiousness. In 1498 this part of Trotternish had been given to Torquil MacLeod of Lewis following the forfeiture of the Lord of the Isles but in the 1520s the MacDonalds had recovered the area by force. A "Description of the Isles" written c1577-95 suggests that Duntulm was then abandoned and that the chief had returned to Dunscaith in Sleat. A new contest later arose between the MacDonalds and MacLeods over possession of Trotternish. In 1618 James VI had a new charter issued to Sir Donald Gorm Og, 9th chief of Sleat, requiring him to make financial compensation to Sir Rory MacLeod for his claims to lands in Trotternish and binding Sir Donald to "Mak his residence and dwelling at Duntillum, and, yf he has not a sufficient comelie house ansuerable to his estate alreddy their that he sall with all convenient diligence prepair materiallis and cause build ane civile and comelie house, and if his house be decayit that he sall repair and mend the same". Some of the later chiefs resided elsewhere, and the estate was confiscated after the 1715 rebellion and not returned until 1726, but Duntulm remained occupied until the 1730s. It was then dismantled to provide materials for a new MacDonald residence at Monkstadt.

Walls up to 2m thick enclosed a court with maximum dimensions of 28m by 23m. A block about 9m wide and 26m long closed off the vulnerable SE side of the court. Of this range there remains just one vaulted cellar at the the southern end which may be a relic of a tower later extended. Of the early 16th century was the parapet on a corbel table with bartizans on moulded corbelling, part of which remained standing until c1910. The eastern part of the range may have been built in the 1620s, when a square wing was added on the NW, with probably a turret stair in the angle between them. A high fragment of this wing fell down just a few years ago. On the west side of the court a 17th century block 12m long by 6m wide over walls 0.8m thick overlies part of the older and thicker outer wall. The NW side has a gate overlooking the cliff edge in the middle and there are footings of a 17th century angular turret built upon the base of a round turret containing a rectangular vaulted room at the north corner.

Dunvegan Castle

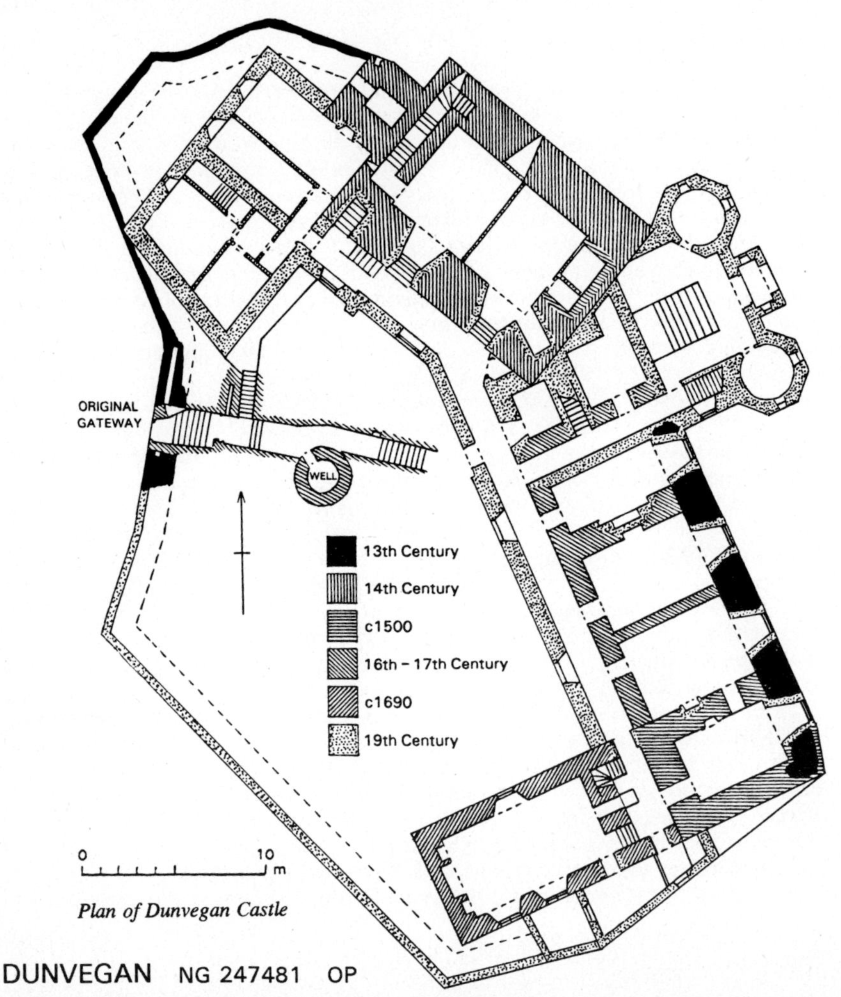

Plan of Dunvegan Castle

DUNVEGAN NG 247481 OP

In spite of what was done to it during the 19th century, Dunvegan Castle is a building of great interest with its social history and its complex architectural development both well recorded. It has been the seat of the MacLeods since their ancestor Leod built a castle here c1270. His castle had a pear shaped court about 53m by 28m enclosed by a polygonal wall about 2m thick and probably about 5m high from the court to the wall-walk. Of it there remain slight traces here and there below the existing buildings together with a west gateway facing the sea which was the only entrance until 1748. A narrower gate was set within the original wide opening in the late 16th or early 17th century. From this gateway a long series of steps rise up past a well to the court. In the late 14th century Malcolm, 3rd chief, added a four storey tower house on the NE side of the court. It measures 14.8m by 11m over walls averaging 2.4m thick. A wing projecting from the NW end wall (which contains the stairs) contains a prison with a pit below. In c1500 Alistair Crotach added the four storey Fairy Tower in the SE corner of the court. Between it and the tower house lay the medieval hall, possibly of wood, and now replaced by a range dating from the early 17th century.

In 1684-90 Ian Breac erected a range on the south side of the court, west of the Fairy Tower. This block was heightened by one storey in 1810-15, given a shallowly projecting wing on the south side in 1840-50, and repaired in 1940 after a fire. Balancing it at the north end, next to the tower house, and somewhat south of the original northern corner of the court, is The General's Wing, built in 1790-1 as a three storeyed barrack block to house part of the 2nd Battalion Black Watch which the then chief was raising from among his tenants. The existing entrance hall with its twin octagonal turrets dates from 1810-15 and was the work of John Norman, 24th chief. His successor Norman, 25th chief, transformed the whole castle, adding a fourth storey to the main east range, and giving it corridors on the west side, thus pulling the previously scattered accommodation together as an integrated unit. Work also then executed included the addition of the present battlements and ornamental tourelles. The whole building is now harled, giving it a slightly drab appearance. The present low parapet on the western side of the court dates from this era, the original curtain having been dismantled to improve the seaward view from the main rooms. A sketch of the castle seen from the north previous to the execution of these works survives showing the tower with a flat roof and battlements as now and with its wing covered with an unusual ogival shaped roof in place of the two extra storeys and flat roof it has now. The General's Wing then had a plain gabled roof with chimneys at either end.

Dunvegan Castle

Eilean Donan Castle

Eilean Donan Castle

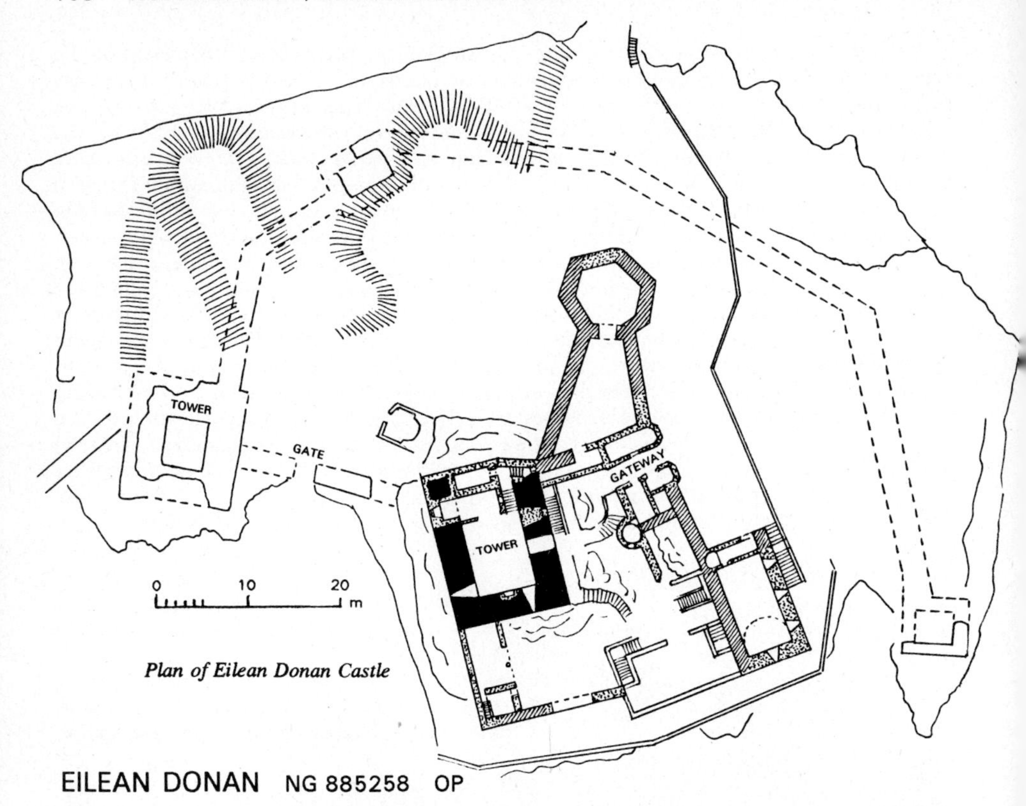

Plan of Eilean Donan Castle

EILEAN DONAN NG 885258 OP

Eilean Donan is one of the best known but least understood castles in Scotland, pictures of it having adorned many a calendar. In the 1920s fragments of vitrified material from a small Iron Age fort perched on the highest part of the island were visible. The island is named after a 6th century Irish saint, Bishop Donan, to whom an early chapel here was dedicated. It was probably Alexander II who built a stone castle on the island. By the late 13th century the castle was held by Kenneth MacKenzie who defeated a force led by his overlord William, 3rd Earl of Ross, to recover the castle. By the end of the 13th century Eilean Donan was one of the largest stone castles in Scotland, with walls mostly about 2m thick enclosing a roughly D-shaped court 80m long. On the south and NW slight traces of towers about 6.5m by 8.5m can still be seen and there are more obvious remains of the base of a big NW tower 13.6m by 12.6m over walls 4.3m thick. A gateway faced the sea to the south of the tower.

The present castle has a small square court on the highest part of the rock which projects beyond the west side of the court just described. This court could represent a modest original enclosure to which the D-shaped court was later added, but it may not have been walled off as a self contained court until after Murdo MacKenzie obtained a charter from David II in 1362 confirming his title to the barony of Kintail. This is the probable period of the tower house 17m long by 12.8m wide filling the northern corner of this court. The MacKenzies later transferred to Easter Ross leaving the MacRaes to guard Eilean Donan. In the 1420s the castle was occupied by the forces of Euphemia, Countess of Ross, but they were ejected in a surprise attack by Duncan MacAuley, the Constable of the castle, who had been absent trying to free Alexander MacKenzie from imprisonment in Dingwall Castle.

In 1497 Eilean Donan fell into the hands of the rebellious Hector Roy MacKenzie, and in 1504 the castle was occupied by the Earl of Huntly in the interest of James IV. After laying waste the MacKenzie lands of Torridon and Kinlochewe in 1539, Donald Gorm attacked Eilean Donan, which was manned by just three men, one of whom was killed by an arrow. One of the survivors mortally wounded Donald Gorm with his last arrow. From 1618 until he was expelled in 1651, a Reverend Farquhar served as both Vicar of Kintail and Constable of the castle, being host there to occasional visits by the Earl of Seaforth and his large retinue, when neighbouring chiefs would call to pay their respects. A Cromwellian garrison in the castle in the 1650s made such unreasonable demands on the locals for fuel that a foraging party was set upon and several killed. A Hanovarian garrison was ejected in 1716 and a dance was held on the roof prior to the Jacobite defeat at Sheriffmuir. In 1719 a party of Spaniards occupied the castle with stores for an abortive Jacobite rebellion until two warships arrived to batter them into submission. A magazine in the castle was blown up by a party sent ashore under Captain Herdman of the "Enterprise" and the building thus reduced to a wreck. It thus remained until rebuilt between 1912 and 1932 by Lieutenant Colonel MacRae-Gilstrap.

From a survey made by Lewis Petit in 1714 and drawings made in the late 19th century by MacGibbon and Ross some idea of the pre-restoration appearance of the castle can be obtained. The existing gate lies below a building on the south side occupied for many years as the Manse. The machicolations and portcullis are modern. At one time there was an east facing entrance. On that side are wing walls connecting a 16th century hexagonal bastion to the rest. The bastion served as a barbican and had a timber bridge over a cistern in which were found parts of a yett. The tower house and the L-plan building in the SW corner of the court are shown as roofless on the Petit drawings, although the bartizans still had conical roofs. The tower house SE corner (which contains the staircases) is chamfered off to fit it better on the rocky site. An adjacent round turret, apparently modern, flanks both the upper and lower entrances connected by steps climbing the rock face. The basement was once divided into a cellar and a kitchen (probably a 16th century arrangement rather than a 14th century one) but now forms one room. The west jamb of the upper entrance into the SE corner of the hall is original and so are two of the three narrow loops, but the two larger windows and the fireplace, plus all the features of the third storey and the attic are modern. The wing of the L-plan building has not been rebuilt above the vaulted lowest rooms now containing toilets, whilst the main block now contains a gift shop.

Eilean Donan Castle

Kisimul Castle

EILEAN GRUIDIDH
NG 952692

On an island on the west side of Loch Maree are very slight traces of a former castle of the MacLeods.

KISIMUL NL 665979

This castle occupying an offshore island at Castlebay on Barra was the seat of the Macneills for many generations. It was abandoned after the 1745 rebellion and gutted by fire in 1795. In 1937 the 45th chief, the American architect Robert Lister Macneil, repurchased Barra, which had passed out of the family in the 1820s, and between 1956 and his death in 1970 the ruined castle was restored. In his book about the castle and its restoration Macneill claims that the curtain wall up to 4.5m thick around the court 33m long by up to 18m wide is 11th century and that the tower house on the south side is a 12th century addition. Other writers have also claimed an ancient date for this castle, but it does not appear in Fordoun's late 14th century list of strongholds in the Western Isles, and there are no documentary references to it before the 16th century. The castle has similarities with Breachacha and Dunollie, both mid 15th century, and it was probably built some time after 1427, when Gillean Macneil was confirmed in possession of Barra by Alexander, 3rd Lord of the Isles. Barra was given to Sir Roderick MacKenzie of Kintail after the Macneils were forfeited for piracy in 1621 but the Macneils managed to remain in possession of Kisimul. In 1675 an attempt by officials to serve a writ against them was greeted by stones thrown from the walls and "foure scoir shott of hagbutts, guns and pistols".

Kisimul Castle

The tower house measures 9.6m by 8.4m above the battered plinth. Steps beside the north wall lead up to the curtain wall-walk over the gateway in a re-entrant angle between the curtain and tower. This gateway is 16th century and the blocked original entrance, which was closed by a portcullis, lies on the east. From the wall-walk the main entrance to the tower some 5.4m above the court was reached. The entrance leads into a hall from which straight flights of steps lead up the chief's apartment and down to a barrack-room which is lofty enough for there to have been a sleeping loft extending over half the floor space. A trapdoor in the barrack-room wooden floor gave access to a low cellar with a heavily barred door to the court. The chief's room has a window in each side, several recesses, and a latrine in the SW corner. From one of the window embrasures a straight stair leads to the battlements. As a result of 16th century remodelling (when the box machicolations over the tower and court entrances were added) both the tower and curtain wall have very high parapets requiring wooden walkways suspended behind them. Latrines for sentries lie at the tower SW corner and the curtain wall NW corner. Within the tower parapet is a thinly walled attic room.

A two storey kitchen range of c1500 adjoins the west side of the tower. Against the NW side of the court is a hall 12.8m long by 6m wide. Much restored in 1958-60, the hall appears to be late 15th century. In the 17th century a two storey extension was built at the west end and an upper floor inserted. Both the hall and extension have latrines in round projections from the curtain wall. Another range restored as a chapel (which it may have originally been) lies on the NE. Between the two ranges is a small tower formed by adding a curved wall against the obtuse angle of the curtain here. The lowest storey of the tower was a pit-prison. The upper level has a latrine. Between the chapel and gateway are foundations of a range known as the Gokman's House. The 16th century Tanist (heir's) House in the west corner of the court and the part of the curtain it adjoins were almost entirely rebuilt in 1956-7. On the rocks south of the tower house is a fragment of the house for the crew of the laird's galley.

KILMALUAG NG 546366

The MacLeods of Raasay once had a three storey tower standing in what is now the garden behind Raasay House. It was built in the early 16th century as a secondary residence but eventually proved more conveniently located than the original main seat at Brochel. It was demolished after a new house was built nearby c1750.

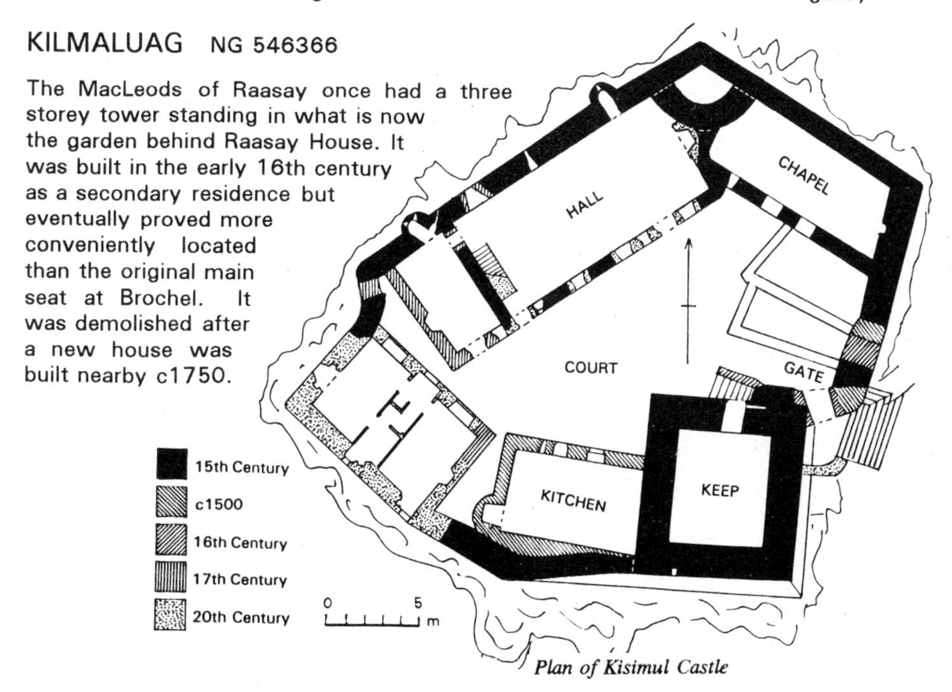

Plan of Kisimul Castle

STORNOWAY NB 422326

The pier now lies on the site of the castle of the MacLeods of Lewis in Anchor Bay which was removed in 1852. It was captured by the Earl of Huntly in 1506 and in 1554 it resisted a battering by the Earl of Argyll. In the early 17th century it fell to Rory MacKenzie of Castle Leod and in the 1650s was used by the Earl of Seaforth as a centre of resistance to Cromwell until it was captured in 1656 by Colonel Cobbett.

STROME NG 862354 NTS F

This remotely sited castle lies on a rock by the northern pier of the former ferry across Loch Carron. On the east, facing the approach, is a mound of debris marking the site of a tower about 13m long by 10m wide. More survives of walls 1.2m thick around a court 10.7m wide extending 22m to the west. There are remains of doorways and windows opening onto the tip of the promontory and the steep slopes on either side. The tower probably existed by 1472 when Strome was given to Allan Cameron of Locheil. In 1539 James V gave the castle to the MacDonalds of Glengarry. They had a long struggle with the MacKenzies which eventually resulted in the latter besieging and capturing Strome Castle in 1602, and the tower was then blown up.

WEAVERS NF 788072

Eilean Leathan, one of the Stack Islands, has an hour-glass shaped summit divided by a deep cleft. The southern part has remains of a hoisting place overlooking the cleft, up which access was obtained. In the middle of this part lie the remains of a small tower with rooms measuring 3.6m by 2.9m within walls up to 1.3m thick, now mostly only 1.2m high, although a fragment of one corner survives to a height of 4.5m

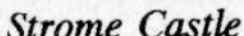

Strome Castle

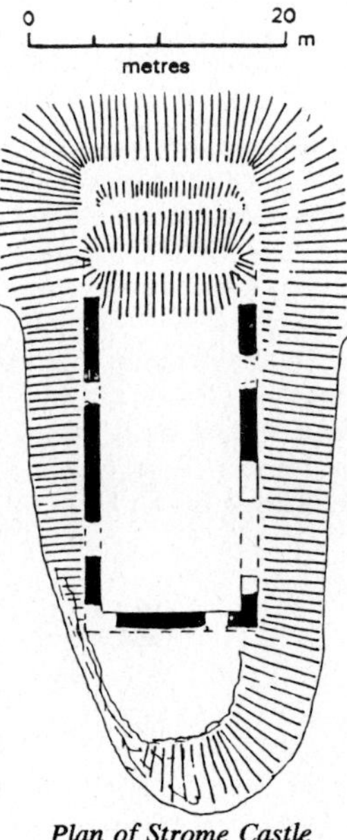

Plan of Strome Castle

Strome Castle

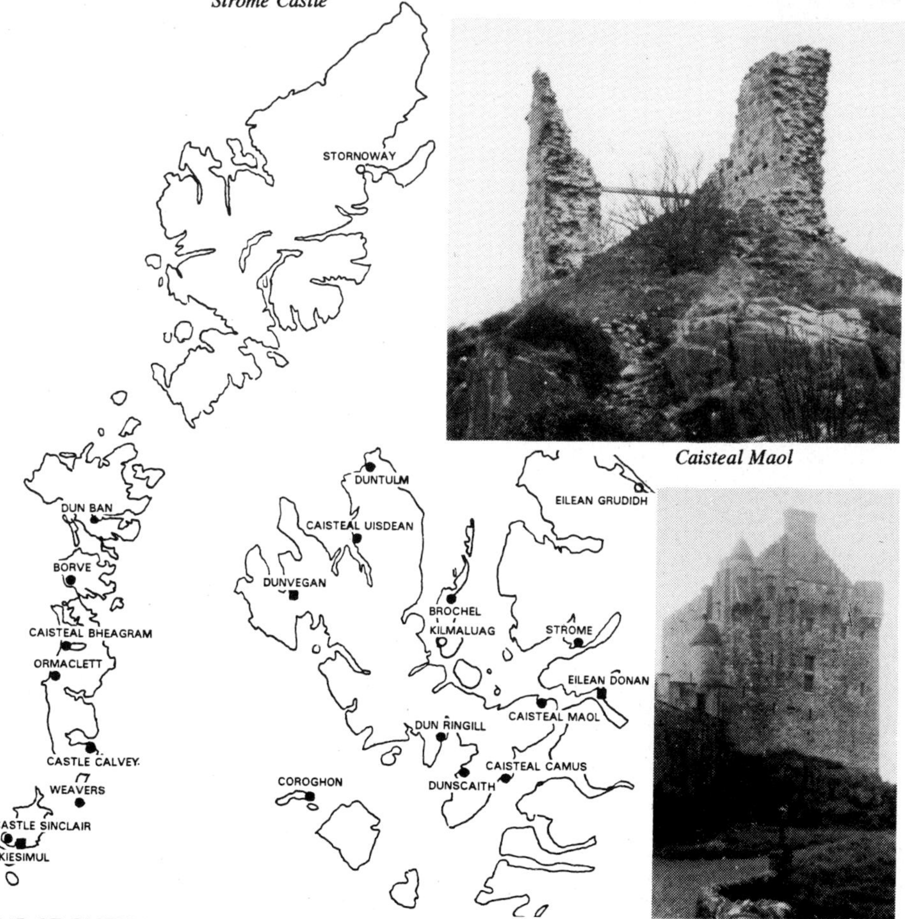

Caisteal Maol

MAP OF CASTLES OF THE WESTERN ISLES, SKYE AND WESTER ROSS

Eilean Donan Castle

INDEX